Paul Simon

A LIFE

Marc Eliot

WILEY
John Wiley & Sons, Inc.

Published by John Wiley & Sons, Inc., Hoboken, New Jersey
Published simultaneously in Canada

Design by Forty-Five Degree Design LLC

For general information about our other products and services, please contact our
Customer Care Department within the United States at (800) 762–2974, outside
the United States at (317) 572–3993 or fax (317) 572–4002.

Wiley also publishes its books in a variety of electronic formats. Some content that
appears in print may not be available in electronic books. For more information
about Wiley products, visit our web site at www.wiley.com.

Library of Congress Cataloging-in-Publication Data:

Eliot, Marc, date.
    Paul Simon : a life / by Marc Eliot.
        p. cm.
    Includes bibliographical references and index.
    ISBN 978-0-470-43363-8 (hardback); ISBN 978-0-470-90085-7 (ebk);
    ISBN 978-0-470-90086-4 (ebk); ISBN 978-0-470-90087-1 (ebk)
    1. Simon, Paul, 1941–   2. Rock musicians–United States–Biography.   I. Title.
    ML420.S563E45 2010
    782.42164092–dc22
    [B]

                                                                      2010030992

Printed in the United States of America

10 9 8 7 6 5 4 3 2 1

CONTENTS

PART FOUR

Going to Graceland

PART FIVE

Making Plans for the Past with Simon and Garfunkel and Joe

Introduction

F OR TWO NIGHTS IN THE DEAD OF THE WINTER OF 2009, SIXTY-seven-year-old native New Yorker Paul Simon, one of the iconic folk-rock singer-songwriters of the boomer generation, took the stage of Manhattan's venerable 2,800-seat Beacon Theatre on the Upper West Side to deliver a dazzling musical retrospective—the music of his life that had become the soundtrack to the lives of his audience. He appeared with the nine-piece backup band of distinguished musicians with whom he had recorded and toured for the better part of the past decade and a half. At the conclusion of the first night's encore, nearly three hours into the show, Art Garfunkel emerged from behind one of the stage's black curtain wings and was greeted with a mushrooming roar of approval. While Paul played acoustic backup and sang bottom harmony, Artie offered an

1

especially soulful rendition of "The Sound of Silence." He delivered it in his familiar signature style, his hands in his jeans back pockets, his body bent slightly forward as if he were about to kiss the microphone. When he reached for the song's impossibly high climactic notes, he got as close as he could, compensating at the top by going lower, then bowed his head once and held it downward as the audience rose to an enthusiastic and extended standing ovation—for the song, for the night, for the fifty-something years of wonderful music.

So there they stood, the diminutive, T-shirted Paul and the tall, sweatshirted Artie, together again on a stage, smiling and nodding in appreciation, looking pretty much as they did at the height of their popularity in the sixties. Except for the inevitable wear and tear of age—Artie's face and middle sagging a little here, a little there; Paul's once dark brown head of hair a wispy colorless fringe—they looked pretty much the way they did when they first appeared on the sixties folkie scene after their brief but skyrocketing late-fifties doo-wop stint as Tom & Jerry, a couple of cartoon characters—not Tom & Jerry the friendly cat and mouse, but Bud Fisher's starker Mutt and Jeff, minus the mirth and the jauntiness.

Thirty-four years earlier, at the height of American Beatlemania and the singular reign of rock's then royal prince, and Paul's idol and nemesis, Bob Dylan, Simon & Garfunkel broke back into the musical mainstream with their angst-for-the-memories adolescent anthem "The Sound of Silence," which began with one of the most memorable opening lines of the decade—"Hello darkness my old friend . . ."—no doubt lyrically influenced by Dylan's picaresque release earlier that year of "Chimes of Freedom." Four tumultuous years, five classic (and classically thematic) albums, and fourteen hit singles later—at a time when singles drove the music business—Simon & Garfunkel, who put out an average of five high-charting singles a year, had ensured their place in the pantheon of sixties popular music icons.

Yet, for all the accolades, Paul felt increasingly like the accompanying guitarist for Artie's stunning solo performances during which, especially in the early days of their folk period, Paul would look down at the neck of his guitar while Artie stood and sang with shoulders slightly hunched, elbows bent, body arched sideways. Although the duo's creative core, he perceived himself the underappreciated half of the act, the Stan Laurel straight-man genius who devised all the skits to bring out the performing brilliance of the Oliver Hardy star of their show. So when the creative limitations of singing with a partner became intolerable to him, Paul broke up the act and took the solo route with the release of "Kodachrome," which set the stage for a series of solo songs and albums that brought him his own special brand of recognition, a star that, no doubt, shone bright, but never as hot as the nova that was Simon & Garfunkel.

By the mid-seventies, when Paul's solo career appeared to have played itself out, and with nowhere left to turn, he made a huge leap forward by taking a strong step backward and opting for another go-around with Art, with whom from then on he reteamed on a more or less regular basis while each continued to release solo albums. This retro phase lasted until 1986, when Paul, in the midst of a deep and unshakable depression brought on by a solo career decline and marital woes, was turned around by some strikingly original music he had heard on a homemade cassette tape a friend had given him. This led him on a journey to South Africa to track down the musicians who had created these songs. When he returned to the States he made *Graceland*, an album that jolted rock 'n' roll out of the narcissistic complacency of the seventies and catapulted him back into the limelight.

After releasing a follow-up to *Graceland* (*The Rhythm of the Saints*, at least as good), he once more reunited with Artie, whose own career had no *Graceland* to rescue him from his own commercial decline. Whatever Paul's reasons—generosity of spirit; an intensified sense of nostalgia following the death of his father; a more basic (and more complicated) yearning to recapture the glory of his fading youth; or perhaps something colder, a business savvy that told him the sum of Simon & Garfunkel was always going to be bigger than its individual Paul and Artie parts—he kept the duo together, even as they continued to behave like a divorced couple who, despite their hostilities, simply could not stay away from each other. Thus, for the next half century, even as their lives went in radically different directions, they followed the industry trend for nostalgic reunions, continually putting the blue-jeaned uniform of their partnership back on and singing to packed houses around the world filled with soft-around-the-middle audiences for whom songs like "The Sound of Silence," "The Boxer," and most especially "Bridge over Troubled Water" brought back sweet memories of their own lost youth.

Even after the colossal failure of his 1998 Broadway show, *The Capeman*, and his bruised self-withdrawal from the public view, Paul couldn't stay away from performing or from Artie. Yet again he orchestrated a massive comeback for Simon & Garfunkel that resulted in some of the best live performances the two ever did, even as the sun (and the spotlight) slowly began to fade on them, on the century in which they thrived, and on the hearts and minds of a generation for whom rock 'n' roll was not just music to dance to but the soundtrack of their lives.

That's the story, then, or at least the part of the story that plays so well against the heartbeat rhythm of Paul's life, filled in along the way with lovers, partners, and passions that drove him toward and away from them. In that sense his body of work becomes the musical legacy of one artist's journey through the landscape, the idealized tunes about the times of his life and those who grew up listening to them.

But because all popular music is, in one way or another, despite its subject matter, about idealization, if for no other reason than that its form requires satisfactory resolution, Paul's music is not necessarily only about the life of *his* times. For the boomers especially—Paul's primary audience—his songs articulate the poetics of *their* lives: the events, the relationships, the love, and the heartbreak, all of it reimagined and romanticized through the back roads of their minds. If Dylan was the undisputed poet of the sixties, Paul was its resident diarist, offering impressionistic images of signs on subway walls and tenement halls, of people walking through airports, of the sound of drizzling rain like plipping drips of memories of a loved one far away, of the Mississippi Delta shining like National Guitars, of the open window of love on wounded hearts, of heroes thrown up pop charts, of diamonds on the soles of their shoes.

Paul's musical sophistication and lyrical stylistics distinguish him from the rest of the sixties singer-songwriters he came up with, alongside and above. His songs were never as witty as Phil Ochs's, as exotic as Elton John's, as zeitgeisty as Lennon's and McCartney's, as raunchily self-degrading as Jagger's and Richards's, as self-pitying as Donovan's, or as baffling (or beautiful) as Leonard Cohen's. Nor was his imagery ever as majestic or romantic or apocalyptic as Dylan's; Paul's messages on subway walls and tenement halls added up to little more than disaffected-teen graffiti. And nothing in Paul's work comes close to Dylan's stunning and ultimately uncategorizable "Ramona." In it, comfort comes with the tearful wisdom of one saying good-bye, while for Paul, in his similarly melodic but hopelessly moony "Kathy's Song," wistfulness substitutes for wisdom (or superiority) and the longing for a loved one is cushioned by the comfort of physical distance.

At least part of the reason for Paul's unique style lay with his fifties roots, when R&B almost always elevated women into angels of perfection, where love ruled (while Dylan's country and western roots glorify the ramifications of fallen angels). It is really no mystery why Paul was never able to completely shake his envy for Dylan's musical power and enduring popularity: Paul's melancholy for the past, his desire to build bridges over troubled waters, could never match the courage of Dylan's fierce determination to never look back.

As idealized, sentimental autobiography, then, Paul's songs no matter how beautiful and irresistible, tell only part of the story. They encapsulate the feelings, the emotions, the words of life, but offer little insight into where those feelings were rooted, how those emotions evolved, where those words came from. As is true of all great artists, no matter their medium of expression, their art becomes a mirror that reflects back to audiences idealized images of themselves. Hoping to see inside the artist, these audiences really seek to discover themselves. The magic of Paul's music is in its effortless allure; it lets the listeners hear someone else but brings them, ultimately, to themselves.

Biography, on the other hand, is not a mirror at all, but a window of illumination into the life of its subject. It is the "making of" documentary, the story behind the story, the insight inside the vision.

What follows, then, in this window into Paul Simon's life, is the rest of the story.

PART ONE

Tom & Jerry

1

Two Princes from Queens

PAUL FREDERIC SIMON WAS BORN ON OCTOBER 13, 1941, IN Newark, New Jersey, to Louis and Belle Simon, an immigrant couple from Hungary, where Louis had been a first violinist on the official Budapest radio station. They relocated to the United States in the early thirties, when Jews were being persecuted across Europe, and like many free-world immigrants, upon his arrival in the promised land Louis anglicized his stage name to Lee Sims. Lee was a talented and reliable double-bass player (the "family bass-man" in Paul's "Baby Driver"), and after a brief stint playing for a radio station in Newark and just after Belle gave birth to Paul, he soon had more work than he could handle. He became the regular bassist, and eventually the bandleader, of several resident WOR-AM radio programs and a member of television orchestras for such popular daytime shows as *Arthur Godfrey and His Friends* and the national primetime CBS network television broadcasts of *The Jackie Gleason Show* and *The Garry Moore Show*. Lee also did a stint on country singer Jimmy Dean's national morning show, for which he had to get up at 4 a.m. Whenever Paul was home from school, either sick or on vacation, he glued himself to the big black-and-white TV in the family living room, eagerly hoping to see a shot of the orchestra and glimpse his father in the pit.

Belle, meanwhile, had become an elementary school teacher in the New York City system, a prestige- and benefit-laden position, low in pay but secure, with Christmas and Easter breaks and a long summer vacation part of the package. During the holidays and also in the evenings and weekends when Lee was working, Belle would give private music lessons, specializing in the harp. Like her husband, Belle was a talented musician.

Four years after Paul's arrival, Belle gave birth to a second child, Eddie. Lee moved the family to a predominantly Jewish neighborhood in Kew Gardens, into an attached house on Seventieth Road. Kew Gardens was a fashionable middle-class enclave of Forest Hills, Queens, one of the city's more upscale outer boroughs, populated mostly by former Brooklynites, Bronxites, and refugees from New Jersey, all of whom dreamed of one day living in the suburbs of Long Island. Queens was a stepping-stone to that promised land.

In addition to playing on radio and TV, Lee found steady work in the late forties at the larger ballrooms around the city—each had a resident band or orchestra—culminating in a gig at the most popular midtown Manhattan postwar social scene, Broadway's original Roseland, where he was a member of the house band for twenty-five years. "He used to play there every Thursday afternoon, and some Saturdays," says Paul. "I was seven or eight. If we went to visit my father, we'd say we were going 'into the city.' To go into Manhattan was a big deal. . . . My father was pretty much always in a good mood. . . . Sometimes on weekends he would bring me to Manny's on Forty-eighth Street [the best-known guitar store in New York City], where he bought his bass strings."

The Simons were by now thoroughly integrated into the American lifestyle; Paul has only the vaguest of memories of his family's whispered European history. "Once talking to my parents about my grandfather, whom I never knew [because] he died when my father was young," Paul later recalled, "I found out his name was Paul Simon, and that he was a tailor in Vienna. It wiped me out." Tailoring became Paul's earliest career choice.

But it was one that did not last very long. By the time he was old enough to appreciate just how good a musician his father really was, he showed signs of his own musical talent, notably a singing voice that was especially gentle and sweet, and always on key.

By the early fifties, thanks to the shift in radio formats from live performances to the playing of records and the advent of the "unbreakable" long-playing album format, new, sleeker four-speed phonographs (playing 16, $33\frac{1}{3}$, 45, and 78 RPMs) had begun to appear in every household, often as a bass-heavy unit set in the living room and encased in a coffinlike mahogany box, with smaller 45-RPM players with self-contained, tinny-sounding speakers reserved for the children. Eleven-year-old Paul was lucky enough to get one of these, together with a set of 45s he especially liked that included a musical version of *Alice in Wonderland*. Naturally, he was quite excited when his teachers at P.S. 164 announced they were going to feature him in the upcoming spring/summer school production of the famed children's story.

It was welcome news for his parents. Paul was one of the smallest boys in his class and had already begun to show signs of a classic "short" personality, compensating for his lack of height by learning how to street-fight, a necessary survival mechanism for little guys, especially Jewish boys in the New York City public school system. His aggressiveness alarmed his teachers, who thought it wise to channel some of his excess energies in a more productive fashion, and thus cast him in *Alice in Wonderland* as the scampering, clock-watching White Rabbit.

Paul became obsessed with learning his part. He played his recorded versions of the songs over and over again in his room, trying to match the cute vocal timbre with his own voice. One night during these private rehearsals, as Paul sat on the bed cross-legged singing to himself, his father, already dressed in his tuxedo and about to make his way into Manhattan for the Roseland gig, happened to walk by the room; he stopped outside the door to listen to his son and couldn't help but notice how pure his natural tenor sounded and how well he kept in tune. "That's nice, Paul. You have a nice voice," he said as he peeked his head in. It was a signal moment for the boy, who idolized his father and was proud of his connection to show business. The compliment was enough to make Paul think he really might want to become a singer instead of a tailor.

Meanwhile, at rehearsals Paul discovered that he was competing with another boy in the show for both attention and accolades. Taller and thinner, with curly hair and an unusually sweet and high voice, Arthur Garfunkel had been cast as the effervescent Cheshire Cat.

The two boys already knew each other. They were neighbors, and although they weren't yet what might be called friends, they'd nod casually to each other whenever they passed in the halls or saw each other on their way home from school. Arthur lived in a house that was similar to Paul's and only three blocks away, but their interests were a million miles apart. Whereas Paul had become something of a "name" in the schoolyard for his physical intensity, a small but gritty concrete-hoops and softball player, Artie had no interest in sports or any type of what he considered roughhousing. At least part of the reason was that in spite of his height, he was too frail for contact games and left-handed, and self-conscious about both. As he later recalled, "Left-handed people are off the mainstream. . . . I sang to justify my weirdness in the neighborhood."

Indeed, being left-handed in a right-handed world was not easy for any kid engulfed in the rigid right-hand New York City school system. Its entire teaching methodology, from its one-armed chair-desks to the officially approved style of forward-slanted cursive writing, was designed to favor right-handed pupils. Studies have been done about the alienation experienced by left-handed baby boomers whose "affliction" was blamed for every social disorder, including (eventually) politically left subversiveness. For Garfunkel, this subtle but forced social ostracism pushed him even more toward his natural tendency as a loner, leaving him more interested in the sweetness and solitude of poetry than in the roughhouse world of competitive street sports and their imagined link to gang culture.

Nevertheless, the two boys became real friends, especially after they realized they were *both* lefties living in a righties' world, which became evident at rehearsals. They soon discovered they both liked to sing on stage and liked the sound of each other's voice almost as much as they liked their own. Paul's ears really lit up one day during rehearsals, when Artie was called upon to sing at the regular school assembly in the auditorium, a special honor among the students. Artie performed "They Tried to Tell Us We're Too Young," a pop ballad that had become a 1951 chart-topper for Nat King Cole.

It was a song he just loved to sing. Sometimes on the way to school, either alone or with another friend, he would break out into his own soft and slow version of it just to amuse himself, cuddling up to the high notes as he looked both ways before crossing the street. Jesse Colin Young, another classmate who would go on to have a significant musical career, remembered, "I used to walk home from school with Artie when we were friends and he would sing that song in that beautiful high voice."

When Artie did it for the kids in the auditorium that day, the girls, especially, responded in a way Paul had never seen before, certainly not like the audiences on TV that politely clapped for his father's music. These girls *squealed*. "Artie was the most famous singer in the neighborhood," according to Paul. "My first recollection of him was in the fourth grade, when he sang in the assembly and all the girls were talking about him. After that, I decided to try singing, too. I said, 'Hey, I want to cut in on some of this myself.' "

When he, too, was asked to sing a song for assembly, he chose "Anywhere I Wander," from the musical film biography *Hans Christian Andersen*, which had become a number-four hit single for pop crooner Julius LaRosa. It was an unusual choice for Paul, not really his kind of music. R&B was already where the action was for him. As he later recalled:

> My clear recollection of the first time I ever heard rhythm and blues was when I was listening to the Yankees, sitting on my father's lap. I'm a New York kid, so I am a Yankees fan. When I was at the peak of my passion for the Yankees . . . I would score the games as I listened to them on the radio . . . the

game would come on in the afternoon, and I would be on
the back porch of my house in Queens getting my score all
set up . . . I didn't want to miss a thing so the radio would be
on twenty minutes early. The game wasn't on yet, but on that
station was Martin Block and the Make-Believe Ballroom. The
kind of popular music he was into I couldn't stand. It wasn't
rock and roll and I didn't like it. It was corny, grown-up music,
but one day he says, "Now here is a record I'm getting a lot of
requests on, but I have to say this record is so bad that if it's a
hit, I will eat it." That record was "Gee," by the Crows.

In the storied stormy history of rock 'n' roll, several songs are
credited with being the "first" rock 'n' roll song, but "Gee," released in
June 1953, was among the very first "race" records to reach the radio-
ready ears of white kids in New York City, despite Block's obvious
disdain for it.

After "Gee," Paul became obsessed with the sound of R&B, a
passion fulfilled by Alan Freed, the legendary deejay who came to
New York's WINS in early 1954 via Cleveland. Freed championed
"Gee" nightly on his eleven-to-one show, thereby introducing a new
sound and a new world to the city's eager teens.

Freed's move to New York City caught a wave when he realized that promoting R&B into the mainstream was a potential gold
mine. He quickly took over "management"—in other words, became a party to payola—from such groups as the Spaniels, whose
1954 version of "Goodnight Sweetheart, Goodnight" he used as his
nightly close, a gesture that pushed it up Billboard's "race music"
charts.

Freed called his radio program *The Moondog Show* (after the
Moonglows) but soon found himself being sued by a blind white
street musician who had become a fixture on the streets of New
York clad in Viking costume; he happened to be a serious classi-
cal musician with several copyrights under the name of "Moondog."
Forced to make a change, Freed came up with the "Rock and Roll
Jubilee," thus coining the name for the type of music he featured
on his show, mostly R&B, mixed with an occasional Chuck Berry
twelve-bar blues tune, a piano-and-guitar mix of country chords and

provocative lyrics—1955's "Maybelline," for instance—that spoke directly to the audience of teenagers who listened to Freed every night in their rooms after dinner while they did their homework. Soon other acts were added to Freed's mix, including the very white and very southern Everly Brothers, who exploded onto the national scene in 1957, a year after Elvis became the great R&B integrator, with their recording of "Bye Bye Love." It was this song more than any other that would soon convince Paul once and for all that he wanted to sing and be a part of the exploding teen-rebel phenomenon that was rock 'n' roll.

"New York became a pool of sounds, but only one station was playing rock and roll, the station Alan Freed was on," he would say. "But he wasn't on every day of the week, only six days of the week, so on Sunday, I would look for rock and roll on the radio and the closest thing I could find to it was gospel, a church station. I had never heard gospel music, but it sounded kind of close to what Alan Freed was playing . . . early rock and roll drew from a lot of different elements."

Musically minded teenage boys all over the city tried to emulate the new mix of sounds they were hearing on the radio, and they would group together in threes and fours on street corners after school and on Friday and Saturday evenings, in a small circle facing one another to sing a cappella, or "doo-wop" style, meaning without instrumental accompaniment. In those days almost no one played any instrument other than piano, and even that only because most immigrant parents, including Paul's, insisted that their children take lessons. Paul reluctantly took his, but soon enough his father bought him his first guitar, hoping he would be more motivated to learn how to play it than he was to play the piano, for which he had shown no real interest. To get him started him, Lee showed Paul a few chords, and everything in his world changed. "The main thing about playing the guitar," Paul told *Playboy* in an interview he gave in 1980, "was that I was able to sit by myself and play and dream. And I was always happy doing that. I used to go off in the bathroom, because the bathroom had tiles, so it was a slight echo chamber. I'd turn on the faucet so that water would run—I like that sound, it's very soothing to me—and I'd play, in the dark."

Still, group street-corner harmony was the happening thing, and Paul and Artie were very good at it, especially Paul, who could work out all the vocal parts fairly easily. "We started singing doo-wop with five others, three boys and two girls," Paul later recalled. "I remember the day we discovered how to sing a chord, that if one person sang a note and held it and another person did it too, it was a revelation."

The first song Paul Simon wrote on the guitar, for himself and for Artie, was not all that dissimilar to a popular song of the day by Richie Valens, "We Belong Together." It shared the same three or four chords, the basic C–A-minor–F–G pattern that his father had shown him, which was the structural basis of so many pop tunes. Once he had the song, he ran to Artie's house with his guitar and played "The Girl for Me." "We were twelve or thirteen," Paul later remembered, "and in its own way that song was our local neighborhood hit." According to Artie, they actually made a recording of it "in one of those booths at Coney Island for twenty-five cents." (Before they recorded it, to make sure the boys wouldn't forget the song, Paul's father wrote out the words and the chords, by hand, on a piece of paper. That paper is now in the Library of Congress, the first officially copyrighted Paul Simon and Art Garfunkel coauthored song).

"The Girl for Me" proved so popular that Paul worked out additional harmonies for three other teen-age street-corner Carusos to back them up whenever they sang it, and soon other groups began to do it as well until it was one of the most popular Queens neighborhood doo-wop tunes. Filled with pledges of lifelong love and predictions of always being true to each other set to a simple but appealing melody, "The Girl for Me" was perfectly suited to the gentle sweetness of the voices of its two lead singers.

Not long after, they dropped the other singers and reverted to being a duo, singing popular songs they heard on the Alan Freed radio show, with Paul working out the harmonies on the guitar and the two of them singing at school dances and nearby talent shows.

Paul and Artie were both academically gifted and both were accepted into Parsons Junior High School's special program for the best local students, in which three years of studies—grades seven, eight, and nine—would be combined into two. Unfortunately, the school was not located in their relatively safe middle-class environs, and it was necessary for them to walk ten blocks to get to it, which they always did together, to avoid being shaken down by the neighborhood's local tough-kid teens. More times than either want to remember, they had to give up their lunch money to avoid taking a beating. These walks brought the two even closer together.

Paul soon became so good on the guitar that Lee often brought him along on weekends and let him play with his band. Not knowing any rock 'n' roll, Lee relied on his fifteen-year-old son to take over for that part of the show. It was a thrill for Paul, who often brought along with him a childhood pal who had become a pretty good guitar player, as well. His name was Al Kooper, who would later carve out his own niche in rock 'n' roll. As Kooper recalled: "I was playing occasional gigs with a neighborhood friend, the not-yet-famous Paul Simon, and his father, a society bass player who'd book all kinds of big band jobs. For the first part of the set we'd sit there with our guitars turned all the way down, strumming along dumbly to 'Laura' and 'In the Mood.' Then every hour we'd leap up and it would be [rock 'n' roll dance] time for fifteen minutes. For being the life of the party, I think we were paid fifty dollars apiece. One night we played a prom at C. W. Post College with the square band. (You've got to remember that the *kids* were square in those days, too. They still went for big bands rather than rock 'n' roll on those 'important' occasions.)"

Although the academic coursework at Parsons was extensive, both Paul and Artie still had time to pursue individual interests beyond their shared love of singing. For Paul, it was baseball. Still a rabid Yankees fan (Artie was a Philadelphia Phillies fan because, he later said, he couldn't bear to wear a Bronx-based Yankees hat in Queens), Paul played in the somewhat humiliating, for him, "Under Five Foot" Little League on a team that a year later, in 1955, made it all the way to the regional finals.

Still really a touch under five feet, Paul had inherited his "shortness"—Belle was just under five feet as well and Lee was barely five foot four. Paul was, and always would be, self-conscious about his height, and feared he might never grow any taller (he added only two or three more inches). "Being short had the most single effect on my existence, aside from my brain. In fact, it's part of an inferior-superior syndrome. I think I have a superior brain and an inferior stature, if you really want to get brutal about it."

His shortness wasn't the only problem he was having. His father loved the fact that Paul could play ball as well as he could play music, believing that baseball would add to his physical confidence, but hated the rock 'n' roll Paul played on his guitar, and the more his son gravitated toward it, the more distance it put between them.

While Paul's mother was supportive in the way that European mothers were about their sons, granting total approval to everything they did, Lee felt they were being led around like rats by this Pied Piper Freed character. One day Paul heard a new song Freed played on his radio show, the Penguins' "Earth Angel," a Top-Ten hit song whose aural beauty took Paul's breath away. "Dad, you gotta hear this," his son said, and excitedly put the record on. "That's awful," his father said. What about the words? "They're stupid." No, Paul insisted, the words were *everything*, the metaphor, earth, heaven, angels, all of it. A few days later, while his father was driving the family car, on the radio came Patti Page's "I Went to Your Wedding," a soft adult-pop tune Paul liked. Without thinking, he started singing along. "God, that's awful," Lee said. His feelings deeply hurt, Paul vowed he would never sing in front of his father again. (Despite his intense dislike for rock 'n' roll, Lee may have already begun to see the handwriting on the wall. When he reached fifty years of age, he retired as a professional musician and went back to school to earn his PhD in linguistics.)

After the car incident Paul became increasingly sullen, his demeanor that of someone carrying a too-large chip on a too-small shoulder. Perhaps worst of all for him, Artie, who was tall with blue eyes and blond curly hair, as if Van Cliburn and Tab Hunter had been caught in the fly machine, attracted all the girls at school. His good looks made him by far the more popular of the two. Their physical differences planted the seeds of an extended siblinglike rivalry and narcissistic jealousy that would never completely disappear.

In the fall of 1955, having successfully finished the accelerated study program, Paul and Artie graduated and were put into the regular tenth grade at Forest Hills High school, where they continued to practice their harmonies. As a reward for successfully completing Parsons, and perhaps as a gesture of reconciliation, Lee bought his son a brand-new better-quality guitar, a real instrument on which he could practice. Paul was excited about the new sounds he could conjure up on this guitar, sounds that made the instrument come alive in his hands. Thus encouraged, he began to use his family's tape recorder—an unusual luxury in those days—and working with Artie, recorded all their worked-out arrangements.

What happened next, which some still call the flashpoint of the rock 'n' roll revolution, began quietly in 1956 on Broadway between Fifty-third and Fifty-fourth Streets, at CBS Studio 40 (later to be known as the Ed Sullivan Theater), where, ironically enough, Lee Sims had played for years as a member of the network house orchestra. Lee may very well have been in the pit at least one of the nights when Tommy and Jimmy Dorsey, hosts of a summer rerun show in place of the vacationing Jackie Gleason, booked a singer called Elvis Presley to play live before their half-filled studio audience. Those summer appearances lit a fuse that within months set off a cultural explosion that turned nuclear with Elvis's three subsequent appearances on *The Ed Sullivan Show*. Twitchy, undulating, with long and wild greasy hair, wearing wide-shouldered jackets and white patent-leather shoes, and with hips that moved in a way nobody had ever seen them move before on network TV, Elvis projected an unabashed sexuality that teenage girls found both audacious and appealing. At the same time, Elvis's unique performing style gave young men "permission" to move freely and think freely about dancing, singing, girls, sex, and . . . playing the guitar. As Bob Dylan would later put it, experiencing Elvis as a teenager was like busting out of jail. Paul heard it, too, and was immediately driven back to the guitar to somehow try to find where that magic came from.

For the rest of that year, as Elvis's music dominated the radio airwaves everywhere, Freed kept his small but lucrative atolls alive with the sounds of Fats Domino, Chuck Berry, Little Richard, Jerry Lee Lewis, and the Everly Brothers. From the first time Paul heard them, he realized that if Elvis had the voice, the look, and the fire, Don and Phil Everly had the harmony. Paul knew he could never be like Elvis, he didn't have *that*, but the Everly Brothers—their harmonies were *reachable*.

To prove to himself he was serious about music, he gave up his after-school job at Kitty Kelly Shoes, a cavernous Thirty-fourth Street shoe store in Herald Square, directly across the street from Macy's, where he had acquired the nickname "Lightning" from the floor personnel for his speed in retrieving and returning shoes from the huge stockroom in back. Less than a year later, he and Artie had somehow managed to make their first real record.

Using the name "Tom & Jerry" they called their 45 "Hey School-girl," which sounded similar to the Everly Brothers' "Bye Bye Love," although Paul's and Artie's harmonies were nowhere near as crystal-clear or as sophisticated as the Everlys'.

It wasn't even a new song. Prior to making the record, they had performed "Hey Schoolgirl" all over Queens, for any and all audiences. Satisfied with the reaction it received, Paul, after being blitzed by Elvis and seduced by the sound of the Everlys, decided to journey to Manhattan, to the storied Brill Building, located at 1619 Broadway. The Brill Building was an elevator-and-doorman office tower originally built by the Brill Brothers as a financial hub until the stock market crash of 1929, after which they rented the largely empty offices to the only tenants they could find—music publishers.

Several floors were given over to budding musicians and wannabe songwriters and became a crank-house for pop, a factory for hit-making, where cigarette smoke hung heavy in the halls and piano chords could be heard coming from the open doors of the air-conditionless music rooms.

Paul knew about the Brill Building from his father, and on this brave day he took Artie with him to knock on its office doors with the hope of their being instantly recognized as the next Everly Brothers. Unfortunately, they were the only ones who saw themselves that way. They came unprepared; they didn't even have a tape recording of the song, just Paul's guitar and the desire to play "Hey Schoolgirl" for anyone willing to hear it, which turned out to be nobody. The competition was tough and far more aggressive, consisting of other ambitious outer-borough kids like Neil Sedaka and Carole Klein (later Carole King), both from Brooklyn, and an aggressive young fireball by the name of Walden Robert Cassotto from the Bronx who later changed his name to Bobby Darin.

As long as they were in town, Paul suggested to Artie they record the song right then and there, make some copies, and hand them out to the Brill Building's resident publishers. Chipping in to cover the $25 recording fee, they hustled over to Sanders Recording Studio, a nearby closet-size studio someone had told them about probably just to get rid of them, which more closely resembled one of those "four for a quarter" photo booths, and recorded "Hey Schoolgirl" and another original for the B side called "Dancin' Wild."

Low cost, not privacy, was the main attraction of Sanders, and there was always a hungry promotion man or two lurking just outside the booth's door, looking to snag the next Elvis. This night the boys got lucky when they met one of these sidewalk Svengalis, a song promoter by the name of Sid Prosen, whose already falling star had once before risen to the heavens on the back of Theresa Brewer's pre–rock 'n' roll recording of his 1952 original song "'Til I Waltz Again with You." Brewer's career, however, would not hold up under the onslaught of rock 'n' roll, where harder, tougher (and often black) women like LaVern Baker were muscling out the sweet, white-faced country lasses. He was now searching for a duo that could do for him what the Everlys had done for Archie Bleyer's Cadence Records. He had a tiny independent label of his own, which he somewhat pompously called Big Records, in truth nothing more than an out-of-the-trunk operation to peddle 45s to the new mom-and-pop record shops that were springing up everywhere.

Prosen overheard Paul and Artie recording their song and, when they came out of the booth, dramatically offered to sign them on the spot, telling them he could make them stars—"the next Everly Brothers." Sitting down to talk over coffee, Paul knew enough about the music business from his father to agree to a one-time deal, with the money the record earned to be divided evenly among the three of them. Prosen agreed, but a few days later, as contracts were being drawn up, he called the boys and told them they had to change their names. Unless they were blind, no one was going to mistake Paul Simon and Art Garfunkel for brothers, he explained, and on a record they needed more "friendly" (read "less ethnic") names. Shades of "Lee Simon."

No problem, Paul said. They could use the name they sometimes used in Queens when they were just goofballing, "Tom & Jerry," from the cartoon series. Paul, who was Jerry, now added Landis as his new last name as a sort of tribute of everlasting love to his high school sweetheart Sue Landis (she was "the girl" in "The Girl for Me"). Art, who was Tom, gave himself the last name Graph, after his nickname at school for his mathematical abilities and his habit of using graph paper to chart the rise and fall of pop tunes he liked. Thus Paul and Artie became Jerry Landis and Tom Graph.

Prosen released "Hey Schoolgirl" as both a twelve-inch 78 rpm and a pop-friendly 45 and actually managed to get it played on the Alan Freed radio show, thanks to the $200 he paid the popular and easily bribable deejay under the table, a practice known as payola that would soon end the career of the opportunistic but ultimately not-too-bright Freed. He promptly put "Hey Schoolgirl" in his regular nighttime rotation of songs. Paul and Artie, meanwhile, unaware of the grease that had been applied to the skids of their career, were knocked out beyond belief when they heard their record on the radio.

Freed's power was such that the record quickly jumped onto the national charts. *Billboard*, the so-called bible of the music business, reviewed the single and compared it favorably to the recordings of the Everly Brothers. Their "who-bop-a-loo-chi-bop" chorus* with its Buddy Holly–like hiccup and Everly Brothers–style harmonies jumped onto *Billboard*'s Hot 100 singles chart. It sold a hundred thousand copies and reached as high as number forty-nine, pushing it into regular rotation on every AM pop music station in the country, where it shared daily airtime with the Everlys' current hit, "Wake Up

---

* Paul would often return to this lyric technique in his songwriting throughout his career, in songs ranging from 1968's "Mrs. Robinson" ("koo-koo-ka-choo, Mrs. Robinson") to 1985's "Diamonds on the Souls of Her Shoes" ("ah-waka-waka wak") to 1998's "Bernadette" from *The Capeman* ("wop, wop wop wop, dom dom dom zoom").

Little Susie," Sam Cooke's "You Send Me," Paul Anka's "Diana," and Rick Nelson's "I'm Walkin'."

In November 1957, with their record on the charts, Tom & Jerry caught the ear of a young and ambitious deejay out of Philadelphia by the name of Dick Clark, who had taken over as the host of the fledgling ABC network's afternoon pop program, *American Bandstand*. The show featured the hottest rock acts lip-synching their hits and a regular group of all-white Philadelphia teenagers who danced to the hit tunes of the day and, as a result, became stars themselves.

Clark liked the fresh, clean-cut sound of "Hey Schoolgirl" but decided to test it out before inviting Tom & Jerry to be on his show. One of the keys to *American Bandstand*'s popularity was a feature Clark had come up with called "Rate the Records" as a way to take the pulse of a new recording. A record would be played and then "rated" by three members of the live studio audience. A high test score could send the show's millions of teen viewers out to buy it, and this marketing technique soon made Clark a far more powerful force in the rapidly expanding business of rock 'n' roll than Freed would ever be.

When "Hey Schoolgirl" received a "triple 95," Clark booked the boys for a live appearance on November 22, 1957. On the day of their scheduled appearance, Prosen dressed them in suits and ties he had bought and accompanied them, via train, to downtown Philadelphia, where the show's studios were located. "This was a memorable experience for the both of us," Paul later recalled. "We walked into the dressing room and there was Jerry Lee Lewis, combing his hair!" Paul's jaw dropped when he realized he was in the presence of the magical, charismatic, rough, and raw Jerry Lee, whose recording of "Great Balls of Fire" had raised the temperature of teenagers around the world. To their amazement, Lewis was scheduled to go on before Tom & Jerry were scheduled to make their first network appearance. If Elvis was a pistol, Jerry Lee was a Howitzer. And here they were, innocent and inoffensive little Tom & Jerry, headlining on the same show with him.

The teens in the audience seemed to like them well enough, and the whirlwind kept spinning. Afterward it was straight on to

Cincinnati for a week of personal appearances at a series of "record hops," where they autographed copies of their hit single and the 8-by-10 glossy publicity photos Prosen had had specially made up for this tour. From there it was off to Hartford, Connecticut's, famed State Theater to appear on a mostly black bill headlined by LaVern Baker, one of the many comical missteps Prosen conjured up in his attempt to manage his duo's run for the roses.

And then, all too quickly, it was over. Sid Prosen proved no Archie Bleyer, Big Records no Cadence, and Tom & Jerry no Everly Brothers. Elvis had given rock 'n' roll an iconic look—tall, lean, dark, beautiful, bad, and sexy—none of which could be said suited Tom & Jerry, just a couple of goofy-looking and lucky Jewish kids from Queens. They returned to New York with a grand total of about two thousand dollars they split between them (about 2 percent each for Artie and Paul from record royalties, the other 96 percent staying with Prosen to cover the boys' "expenses").

Artie then told Paul he wanted out. "It was all over my head," he said. "I never would have done it if Paul hadn't pulled me along. I was too fearful of the competitive, adult world of rock 'n' roll." He put his money in the bank and, figuring his musical career was over, turned his attention back to his studies. He wanted to go to Columbia University and major in mathematics when he graduated from Forest Hills High.

Paul, on the other hand, was intoxicated by the whole roller-coaster ride that was rock 'n' roll. With his thousand dollars he went straight out and bought himself a cherry-red triple-quad Chevy Impala.

And continued to write songs, determined to come up with another hit. Only this time, as a solo act.

2

Paul's Mystic Journey

J ERRY WITHOUT TOM WAS FINE WITH PAUL. WITH SID PROSEN, too. He had nothing else going, and urged Paul to continue recording for him, without Art, no problem. Prosen told Paul he believed he could make him a star on his own.

Guitar players were the coming thing, and Prosen recognized that Paul could play better than most of the two-or-three-chord wonders trying to pass themselves off as the next Elvis Presley. As for Paul's diminutive stature, Prosen convinced himself that since music was a radio phenomenon, and with rare exception, most of the time no one really knew what anybody looked like behind the voices that came out of all those transistor radios, this was only a minor hindrance to Paul's future as a rock 'n' roller.

Seventeen-year-old Paul now turned to, of all people, his father for help in writing a really good song. Despite his antipathy for rock 'n' roll, Lee agreed, and, working together, they came up with something called "True or False" and a B-side tune to go with it, "Teenage Fool." Prosen, meanwhile, suggested to Paul that he take yet another new name, so that there would be no confusion or teen mag queries about whatever happened to Tom. And, if the record tanked, it would be easier for him and Paul to cut their losses, maybe even find another Tom somewhere and go back to the duo thing.

So this time Paul became "True Taylor," and "True or False" became a pretty fair imitation of post–Sun Records Elvis. However, with Prosen's unsubtle touch at the controls, the record was neither catchy enough on its own nor copycat enough to make the Elvis connection click, and it died a quick death. Paul then recorded two more tracks for Prosen, both instrumentals, as Prosen suggested, because songs like the Champs' 1958 "Tequila" were now all the rage, and Paul could certainly play as well as those boys. Unfortunately, "Tia-juana Blues" went nowhere and Prosen didn't even bother to press any copies of "Simon Says."

Prosen then fell back on his original safety play, suggesting to Paul that it might not be such a bad idea after all if he was to get back with Artie, and maybe the two could come up with another Tom & Jerry hit. Artie, who had by now matriculated at Columbia, but perhaps missing the glory of rock 'n' roll after all, to Paul's surprise and delight, agreed to resurrect Tom & Jerry. Working together, the two boys came up with a bunch of new songs for Prosen.

But they couldn't rediscover the magic. The new songs—"Don't Say Goodbye" backed with "That's My Story" and "Our Story" backed with "Two Teenagers"—went nowhere. They had little melody and corny lyrics; there was nothing for audiences to grab onto (years later Paul would describe them as "fodder for eunuchs"). After these latest failures, Big Records went under, and that was the end of Sid Prosen in the lives of Paul and Artie.

In the summer of 1960 Paul, or "Jerry Landis," managed to place two solo singles with MGM records, "Anna Belle" backed with "Loneliness." MGM's interest in Jerry Landis may have been the result of Rosen's fire sale of whatever was left of the Tom & Jerry catalogue. In a separate deal, King Records, an independent label out of Ohio started by Syd Nathan, bought the rights to "Hey Schoolgirl" and rereleased it, but this time around it did nothing. ABC Records bought "Surrender, Please Surrender" backed with "Fighting Mad." Then, Paul's precious Impala overheated and blew up right by Artie's house, an avoidably blunt metaphor for the flashy resurrection and fast fizzle of Tom & Jerry.

Artie happily returned to his studies at Columbia, and Paul applied to and was accepted by Queens College, part of the then free City University of New York. Because most students who went to Queens lived at home, it was more like going to an extended high school. Paul majored in liberal arts for one or two semesters (English lit) but soon slipped quietly back into the world of so near yet so far on the Manhattan side of the Fifty-ninth Street Bridge and took to hanging out at the Brill Building, 1590 Broadway (another on-the-street, nondescript office building music mill two blocks south of the Brill), and 1650 Broadway. Everyone involved in the pop music business, or trying to find work in it, inevitably careered through the Brill/1590/1650 bear pit of agents, managers, publishers, songwriters, and studio musicians for hire. It was something of a social scene as well, as everyone quickly got to know everyone else, and whispered tips about who had a good song or who was looking for one became the standard method of spreading information among its inhabitants.

Despite his disappearance from the charts, and his unusual looks, which eliminated him from any serious contention as the next teen heartthrob, Paul's singing ability and guitar skills ensured his quick acceptance by the record pluggers, studio musicians, and songwriters forever on the lookout for the next big hit, no matter who it was or where it came from.

By the summer of 1959 he was picking up regular gigs at $25 a pop to cut demos for the current crop of dozens of hopeful pretty-boy recording stars including Dion (Dimucci) from the Bronx, Fabian (Anthony Forte) out of Philadelphia, and Bobby Vee (Velline) out of Fargo, North Dakota. These were the most talented (or the most marketable) of the next generation of pop idols, whose records offered the neutered remains of a music that had once provided the sound track for the fifties youth rebellion. What had been an exciting cultural phenomenon was now becoming a predictable nickel-and-dime operation, coerced, bleached, and bobby-socked into social submission, with singers as safe, cute, and, for the most part, weak and punchless as decaffeinated coffee (with some notable exceptions, like Dion).

Because most of the new good-looking contenders couldn't even sing, they needed better voices on their demos. Paul, with his uncannily sweet and always on-key voice and his ability to read a song and quickly get to its essence, became a player in that game. His particular skill was also of value to song hustlers looking to show off a new song's hit potential. Sometimes when more than one voice was needed, maybe a girl-and-boy combo, Paul recorded with Carole Klein, whom he had met and befriended during his Tom & Jerry days. Although they worked together only occasionally, Carole toyed with the possibility of teaming up as a duo, but Paul did not want to go back down that dead end. "Carole would play piano and drums and sing. I would sing and play guitar and bass," Paul recalled. "The game was to make a demo at demo prices and then try to sell it to a record company. Maybe you'd wind up investing three hundred dollars for musicians and studio time, but if you did something really good, you could get as much as a thousand for it. I was never interested in being in groups; I was only after that seven-hundred-dollar profit."

Carole's Paul-and-Carole dream ended when she met Gerry Goffin, another college-kid wannabe songwriter; the magic happened, they got married, and in 1960 Carole, now King, and Goffin came up with "Will You Love Me Tomorrow" (originally "Tomorrow"), which that December became a number-one hit for the Shirelles.

Paul's next encounter with the music world came via Al Contrera, a founding member and bass singer of the Mystics, a Brooklyn-born doo-wop group originally known as the Overons. They were managed by Jim Gribble, who signed them to Laurie Records, one of the hotter Brill-based labels. Laurie assigned songwriters Doc Pomus and Mort Shuman to come up with something for the Mystics that sounded similar to "A Teenager in Love," which they had written for Dion and the Belmonts. Using almost the same melody and emphasizing its soft-beat harmonies, they came up with "Hushabye," which went on to reach number nine on the national charts and achieve the coveted position as the closing song on Alan Freed's short-lived, but extremely influential, Saturday night *Big Beat* television show.

Then, for one reason or another, the group's silky-voiced lead singer, Phil Cracolici, left the band. Contrera remembers what happened next:

We were all set to do a follow-up to "Hushabye," a song called "All Through the Night," and the B side, "I Begin to Think Again of You." And another song, too, that we liked, "Let Me Steal Your Heart Away,' that we thought had some potential. The guy who wrote it was a good piano player and tunesmith by the name of Gene Pitney, who would go on to have quite a career of his own.

Our manager, Jim Gribble, who worked out of an office at 1697 Broadway, was always looking for that diamond in the rough. So on any given day there would be dozens of guys and girls hanging out in his office, waiting for him to listen to them and decide if he wanted to put them on a record. Among the crowd that always seemed to be there was this one kid, Jerry Landis, who'd had a hit record with "Hey Schoolgirl" and now was just sort of hanging out, with his guitar, off in a corner somewhere, always practicing and writing down songs. He was always there, kind of small and unnoticeable, among these crowds of eager teens waiting and wanting to be discovered.

Then, when our lead singer, Phil, suddenly left the group, we had to find someone to replace him. Believe me, we tried a million guys, nobody could sing the way we wanted, and then someone noticed little Jerry there in the corner. "What about him," Gribble said. "Okay," we said, "let's try him out." We liked the way he sounded, so we agreed to do the new songs we had with him singing lead.

We spent hours rehearsing the songs, and as we did, we got to know Jerry a little. He was a cool guy, except for us he was a little too nerdy. We were a tough bunch of kids who had come out of Bensonhurst, Brooklyn, a neighborhood where the mob controlled everything. We had all been kid runners for the mob, and we had to break away from them very slowly and very carefully when we decided to go into the city and try to be singers. So we were from the streets, we were tough guys, and we didn't take shit from nobody. And here was Jerry, this little nerdy guy from Queens with a guitar as big as he was, leading us.

Things were going okay, he had a really good voice, but he couldn't hit this one note and it was driving the rest of us crazy, especially Gribble. So Joe made Jerry stand on his head in the corner of the office, telling him that it would help him hit the note. Very reluctantly, he did it, and we all had a really good laugh about it, including, eventually and reluctantly, Jerry.

Still, we had to fire him. It was really a mutual decision, because he just didn't fit in with our personalities. We were too tough for him, and we didn't think we would all look good together onstage. I remember that one of the things that really disappointed him when he was still with us was that when Laurie Records heard the masters, they mixed them down so there was no distinct lead voice. They wanted that group harmony sound, like on "Hushabye," while Jerry thought it was going to be his voice in front and the rest of us in back. But by the time we let him go, I remember him saying something about he wanted to do his own thing anyway, and singing with a group was not it.

The three songs he recorded with the Mystics went nowhere. Then, by himself, he recorded for Amy Records what he thought were the best of the new songs he had written, including "Motorcycle," "I Don't Believe Them," "Cry Little Boy Cry," "Get Up and Do the Wobble" (cowritten with his brother, Eddie, who had also developed into a good guitar player), "Express Train," and "Wildflower," all of these under the pseudonym "Tico & the Triumphs." None of these records did anything. And as "Paul Simon" he recorded "The Lonely Teen Ranger," "Lisa," "I'm Lonely," "Wish I Weren't in Love," "Swanee," "Toot, Toot, Tootsie, Goodbye," "Just a Boy," "Shy," "I Want to Be the Lipstick on Your Collar," "Play Me a Sad Song," "It Means a Lot," "Anna Belle," "Wobblin'," and "Loneliness."

This latest batch was overly derivative from all over the pop map: "The Lonely Teen Ranger," which just managed to break into the back end of the Top 100, benefited from, but ultimately was too similar to, Dion's "Lonely Teenager," while "I Want to Be the Lipstick on Your Collar" was a response record to Connie Francis's monster hit "Lipstick on Your Collar." Paul also tried to get a piece of the novelty action with "Wobblin'," in which he hoped to catch some of Carole King's "Mashed Potatoes" action. He even tried a little Al Jolson ("Swanee," "Toot, Toot, Tootsie, Goodbye").

As frustrating and rat-wheeling as these experiences may have been, Paul's swimming in the deep of popular music made Artie think yet again about returning for another try. Although they were no longer officially a team, or even occasional get-together-to-remember-the-good-old-days kind of guys, they still talked on the phone and talked about music.

In early 1960, on his own, Art changed "Graph" to "Garr" (short for Garfunkel) and made a deal with Jack Gold of Octavia Records, who recorded and released Art Garr's "Private World," backed with "Forgive Me." (Songwriting credits for both "Private World" and "Forgive Me" are not clear. They may have been written by someone named Raphael, which may or may not have been a pseudonym for Garfunkel. It's possible they may even have been written by Paul.) "Private World" was in the style of the newest novelty sound to invade the Brill Building hallways, pseudo-folk music, which had exploded onto the charts as the result of an unlikely group of singers held together by a couple of guitars and, of all things, a banjo: three clean-cut, white college-type kids out of San Francisco who called themselves the Kingston Trio. Bob Shane, Nick Reynolds, and Dave Guard were influenced by the Berkeley crowd, where Jack Kerouac, Allen Ginsberg, and the whole Beat movement had coalesced, and the work of irreverent comics like Lenny Bruce and Mort Sahl, who were performing at the honky-tonk strip joints that dotted San Francisco's Broadway. The Trio also took note of the smirky song stylings of the Smothers Brothers out of San Jose, who became regulars at the Purple Onion, where their act combined the smart-ass humor of Bruce and Sahl, among others, and the style of folk songs.

With their smash-hit recording of "Tom Dooley," the Kingston Trio became the hot new thing, and banjo and guitar groups suddenly sprang up everywhere, including in the halls of the Brill. It also attracted Artie, who thought folk-type music better suited his sweet, chorus-boy vocal abilities than the harder rock 'n' roll or doo-wop.

Nonetheless, all of his efforts fell flat, and he, too, failed to capture so much as a whiff of the sweet smell of the brief but heady success of "Hey Schoolgirl." Even so, he remained committed to the new folk sound.

Still, this latest round of failure led Artie to take the summer off to go to Paris, with little more than a backpack, to experience a bit of European boho street life. As far as he was concerned, anywhere the wind blew, as long as it wasn't back to New York, was good enough for him.

Paul, meanwhile, mostly to satisfy his mother, between stints at the Brill Building slogged through undergraduate school and finally graduated in the spring of 1963. That fall he enrolled part-time in Brooklyn Law School and took a job during the day as a salesman (in full-dress office garb: suit, white shirt, tie, shined shoes) with music publisher E. B. Marks, pushing songs to the various record companies forever in search of good new material for their singers.

It was unglamorous grunt work, and it bothered him that he was once again selling someone else's wares. The feelings of treadmill frustration this job must have aroused were deepened by the fact that his own music had slipped up on the oily sidewalks of commerce and landed him smack on his ass. To Paul, working for E. B. Marks was like working in the shoe store again, and it left him waiting more impatiently than ever for something to break his way.

As it turned out, he didn't have to wait very long.

Artie's wanderlust eventually brought him back to the States and to San Francisco, while Paul had discovered something new in New York's Greenwich Village, where he first encountered the rise of the counterculture and the music that came from it.

The flashpoint of the East Coast folk movement was the first Newport Folk Festival, held in the summer of 1959, which introduced to the beautiful, if barefoot, crowd the hitherto little-known Mexican American folksinger Joan Baez, who awed the crowd with her pristine singing voice and faultless acoustic-guitar playing. Out of that seminal gathering came a new musical sensibility that quickly drifted down to New York City, where, as always, whatever current music fad was blowing in the wind was soon turned into dollars and cents.

As performers like Baez and others soon discovered, however, there was no room at New York's midtown black-tie inns—the Persian Room, the Copacabana, even Roseland—for their style of dressed-down, stoned-out college-kid folk music. The quick and easy solution was simply to take to the streets, specifically the streets of Greenwich Village, and its big circular fountain at the center of Washington Square Park.

For much of the twentieth century the Village was known for its low-rent, high-octane existence, non-mainstream (Off Broadway) theater, backroom jazz clubs, and great bars that fed and quenched the artistic element that through the years made it the creative heart of the city. They congregated around the fountain, sometimes during the week and always on Sundays, where crowds of musicians, poets, students, retirees, teachers, panhandlers, chess players, and residents would cluster to hear free and spontaneous shows.

The rest of the Village was filled with big, roomy, always busy restaurants. One of these, Gerde's, on West Third Street, had been in operation for generations, until, in 1952, eighty-one-year-old Gerde retired and sold his place to three Italian immigrants, the brothers Mike and John Porco and their cousin Joe Bastone. They kept the name Gerde's, even when the city condemned nine square blocks, including Gerde's longtime location, in a back-door deal for a series of depressingly monolithic high-rises for NYU. The arrangement heavily favored the politics and the pocketbook of Nelson Rockefeller, who made a handsome profit from the development.

The Porcos moved Gerde's to 11 West Fourth, close enough to enable them to keep the name and, they hoped, most of their clientele. The only problem was that the clientele had also been kicked out of the neighborhood and forced to relocate to Little Italy, leaving the two-thousand-square-foot Gerde's the favorite hangout of flies trying to avoid getting caught in the sticky curlicues that hung from the metallic ceilings. Fortunately, enough steady customers remained for the Porcos to eke out a living.

Into this peculiar void came Izzy Young, a passionate devotee of all things folk music. In 1957 he opened a storefront at 110 MacDougal and called it the Folklore Center. After Newport '59, it quickly became the meeting ground for every folkie who came to the Village in search of kindred spirits and some bread. Eventually, Young became a sort of informal booker of acts, filling the downtown bars with solo artists who took up little room and maybe even brought in a customer or two. Eventually, Young, working with a Chicago-based club owner named Albert Grossman, produced concerts in Greenwich Village and midtown's Town Hall that featured Peggy Seeger, Sonny Terry & Brownie McGhee, Oscar Brand, the Reverend Gary Davis, the New Lost City Ramblers, Happy Traum, Dave Van Ronk, "Ramblin' " Jack Elliott, and dozens of other folkies.

Young was then approached by an advertising agent, Tom Prendergast, who convinced him the time was perfect to open a regular folk club in the Village, and together they searched the neighborhood for the right venue. When they came across Gerde's and saw all the empty floor space, they approached Mike Porco, tending his own bar, and suggested putting live performers onstage there. They quickly struck a deal; Young and Prendergast would pay for all advertising and promotion, and the salaries (such as they were) of the performers. They would also keep "the door"—the admission fee. Mike could keep all money he made selling drinks and food.

Porco, no fool, realized he had nothing to lose and probably a lot to gain selling beer, soda, hamburgers, and pizza. Thus was born the Fifth Peg, although nobody ever called it that. To everyone on the street it became Gerde's Folk City, and soon enough in the business as the Brill Building of Folk Music, a font of potential Kingston Trios with original songs just waiting to be recorded and turned into million-sellers.

Soon enough, the club was crowded, but the only one making any real money was Mike Porco, so Young and Prendergast bowed out, leaving the club in the hands of Mike, his brother, and his cousin, none of whom knew anything about folk music, but all of whom understood how to turn cash. Mike put on something he called the Monday night hootenanny—a word he had picked up from Young and Prendergast—which meant free-admission nights where anybody could get up and sing. "Hoot nights" quickly became the premier showcase for new talent and the most popular social event in Greenwich Village.

Every Monday crowds came down to hear the well-known interspersed with the unknown, with numbers given out that were chosen at random to determine the order of performers. Porco kept a small notebook to mark down the reactions of the audiences to new talent, and if a performer got a star next to his or her name, he would book them, for pay, for a weekend gig. One such starred act was an unlikely looking but beautiful-sounding duo who now called themselves Kane and Garr.

3

"Kathy's Song"

ROCK AND ROLL GOT VERY BAD IN THE EARLY SIXTIES, VERY mushy," Paul recalled in 1971. "I used to go down to Washington Square on Sundays and listen to people playing folk songs. . . . I liked that a whole lot better than Bobby Vee." Part of what Paul found so energizing on those Sundays was that everyone more or less looked the same, and they looked a lot more like him than like Elvis, Fabian, or Pat Boone. These people dressed in jeans, let their hair grow a little, wore vests or plaid shirts, used glasses if they needed to, and always kept their focus on the song and the guitar work rather than on appearances, which, with rare exceptions (Eric Andersen comes to mind), were not that different from his. And there was little showmanship going on: the spotlight was drawn to the genuine talent that was scattered throughout the three-chord wonders and string-scrubbers fixated on, and unable to get beyond, "Michael, Row Your Boat Ashore."

One afternoon in late 1962, Paul, now back in Queens, happened to run into Artie, who had just returned from San Francisco, his hair a little longer, his jeans a little more faded. He told Paul he intended to complete his studies at Columbia—at least in part to keep his student draft deferment now that the war in Vietnam was beginning to percolate. To do so he was living with his parents in Kew Gardens. The two musicians were once again neighbors, back where they had started.

Paul and Artie hadn't seen each other for a while, and as they talked about what they had each been up to, they realized they had both discovered the "new" music. They quickly agreed it was a kind of sound they would both prefer to perform.

And there was something else they had each discovered and were now eager to share with each other—pot. Weed was the new rage among the folkie set, and the yellowish, pungent smoke could be seen (and smelled) everywhere from San Francisco to the streets of Greenwich Village. It had replaced beer as the staple of the coffee-house set, even at Gerde's, where everyone was openly smoking pot, right under Mike Porco's nose. Even if he knew what it was, which he always insisted he didn't, he wasn't about to stop it, because along with the pot came dozens of orders for hamburgers, fries, sodas, and anything else out of the kitchen that was edible.

So Paul and Artie got stoned together and talked about the old days as well as about the future. Paul had some new songs he had been working on, and soon enough they were playing them together, first alone and then at the Alpha Epsilon Pi fraternity house, near the Queens College campus where, between trips to the Village, Paul liked to sing. At one of his shows he called Artie onstage to join him on some backups and harmonies, the kind they had perfected as Tom & Jerry. As Artie recalled, "The first night we got back together we started singing these songs. We [soon were doing] them at the Frat house because the echo was right."

The other thing they shared was a growing admiration for Bob Dylan. It is no exaggeration to say that without the charisma and the inventiveness that quickly turned Dylan into such a cultural phenomenon—and his music and the whole folk scene behind it into such a huge commercial force—the Village scene would not have lasted even as long as it did, nor attracted the kind of mainstream attention it received. First and most notably it came from the *New York Times*, whose music critic Robert Shelton gave Dylan's initial official Folk City paid engagement, as the opening act for the Greenbriar Boys, the kind of high-tone anointment that, overnight, made Dylan a star. This led to Dylan's landing a recording contract with Columbia Records, all of which took place within months of the Minnesota-born singer-songwriter's arrival in the Village as a complete unknown.

But even before Shelton brought Dylan's talent to the attention of the rest of the world, everyone on the coffeehouse and club circuit, including Paul and to a less obsessive degree Artie, knew who was the best performer on the scene, the one who could most effectively silence the often rowdy crowd at Folk City without saying a word. Up on the tiny stage, with his snap-brim cap opened and set high on his curly-haired head, a guitar held around his neck by a string, a stained, dirty jacket, jeans, and black boots, with no introduction, no hello, no nothing—that was Dylan.

He was the answer for Paul, even if he wasn't exactly sure what the question was. His voice wasn't conventionally sweet, although it was wonderfully rough and indelibly midwestern, with an echo of Woody Guthrie, to be sure, and also, somehow, a hint of Jimmie Rodgers, and his songs were, well, they were not like anything Paul had ever heard before, and he thought he'd heard almost everything. There was a literal quality to them; musical stories poured from him that evaded the certainty of simple love songs, that did quantum leaps beyond anything the Kingston Trio ever did. There was a song Dylan wrote and sang about Guthrie, "Song for Woody," which was shockingly beautiful—it carried a "hey hey" lilt (that a year later the pop duo Paul & Paula would incorporate into their hit song "Hey Paula"), a strong lyrical progression that linked Dylan's future to Guthrie's past, and a powerful blend of sincerity and fearlessness that made it both wonderfully unique and fabulously entertaining.

Short and scruffy, about as noncommercial as could be, Dylan was also Jewish. And as Paul, aka "Jerry Landis" knew, being Jewish in the first wave of rock 'n' roll performers was like being afflicted with some incurable disease. Dylan certainly didn't flaunt his religion, but everyone in the crowd seemed to be aware of it, including Paul.

By late 1963 Paul and Artie felt secure enough to make another try as a professional duo. Their focus this time was not the Brill Building, but Folk City, where they signed on for one of the Monday hoots, billing themselves this time as "Kane & Garr," armed with three new songs that Paul had written: the angst-ridden "The Sound of Silence," which was without doubt influenced by any one of a dozen new Dylan songs (the melody resembles Dylan's "The Times They Are a-Changin'"), "Sparrow," and "He Was My Brother." It was enough to fill out the three-song hootenanny minimum/ maximum.

The simplest (and least listenable) of the three new songs was "Sparrow," a self-conscious English 101 allegory-as-autobiography (Paul is the sparrow) with an overlay of nature-is-God—the last line's "dust to dust" is spoken by "the earth" rather than God, or God depicted as nature, but it was at least melodic enough to get Artie to work on a harmony part that was far more sophisticated than the song itself. "He Was My Brother" represented a leap forward for Paul in terms of songwriting technique. This song was *about* something, capturing the mushrooming passion of the early days of the civil rights movement, and it made crystal clear which side he was on. That it was Dylanesque there can be no doubt, but it does not compare with the level of protest that Dylan was writing during this period, songs like "The Lonesome Death of Hattie Carroll," "The Times They Are a-Changin'," and "Masters of War."

Finally, there was "The Sound of Silence." Overly vague, it was the type of gloom-and-doom song that would become Paul's special niche. With images that don't connect—what *is* the sound of silence?—he appears to be making some sort of "God is dead" statement (there is confusion about when the song was written and what it is about; some claim it refers to the generational impact of the John F. Kennedy assassination, with its crowds of people—ten thousand, maybe more—but Kane & Garr sang it at Folk City for the first time in September 1963, two months before the horrific events in

Dallas). Ultimately, its imagery is obscured by its vagueness, redeemed by the single line about the handwriting on the subway walls
and tenement halls, which is at once vivid, specific, and powerful.
(In several recent interviews, Paul has disavowed the angst factor of
"The Sound of Silence" by explaining that he wrote it in a bathroom,
for the echo off the tiles, and turned the lights off so he could better
concentrate—hence, "Hello darkness, my old friend . . .") Still, "The
Sound of Silence" had a catchy melodic lilt and was redeemed by
the complex harmonies the two had worked out and by the simple
but gorgeous fingerpick that rode under their two voices. Despite
the fact that it really wasn't about any specific issue or incident, at
a time when issues and incidents were driving the increasingly top-
ical Village folk music scene, the song had a way of sticking in the
brain, like a jingle for chewing gum. It was, by far, Paul's best effort
to date. (According to Artie, "The Sound of Silence" was about "the
inability of people to communicate with each other, not particularly
internationally but especially emotionally, so what you see around
you are people unable to love each other.")

On the night Porco had booked them for their first paying gig,
Paul and Artie would play before a largely indifferent but, for Folk
City, polite audience. They might soon have slipped out of the col-
lective memory of the formative years of sixties rock 'n' roll but for
the presence of one member of the audience who thought "He Was
My Brother" had some commercial potential. His name was Tom
Wilson, and he happened to be Bob Dylan's producer at Columbia
Records.

Tom Wilson had been assigned by John Hammond to produce
the just-signed Dylan's first album, part of the by now well-known
legend of the making of Bob Dylan. Hammond was an artists and
repertoire (A&R) executive with a strong background in jazz and
rhythm and blues, and a lifelong resident of Greenwich Village. He
had been responsible for recording many of the great artists of the
thirties and forties for Columbia. When Mitch Miller, the head of the
label's A&R department whose iron grip on Columbia Records kept
virtually all contemporary (in other words, rock) performers off the
label, was finally replaced by Goddard Lieberson, Wilson wasted no
time in reaching out to Hammond and offering him free rein to

help revitalize the label. One of Hammond's first coups was to sign Pete Seeger, whose career had been damaged by the blacklisting of the Weavers. Despite enormous opposition from nearly every executive at Columbia, Seeger was signed, and his 1963 *Live at Carnegie Hall* album became a smash hit (and gave young America "We Shall Overcome" as its civil rights anthem). In September 1961 Dylan met Hammond in the apartment of up-and-coming folksinger Carolyn Hester, whom Hammond had also just signed to Columbia. (Hester signed on because she wanted to be on the same label as Seeger.) Hester asked Dylan to play harmonica on her album. At the sessions, Dylan, who also played guitar and sang a little harmony, caught the ear and eye of Hammond, who invited him to audition to sign with Columbia. Not long after, Dylan played "Talking New York" for Hammond, who signed him on the spot (or as close to the spot as legend allows) and put him on record by that November. The cost of producing Dylan's first album was $402, and it contained thirteen songs, only two of which were originals—"Talking New York" and "Song to Woody." *Bob Dylan* was released in February 1962 and bombed, after which Dylan became known as Hammond's Folly around the offices of Columbia. The second Dylan album, also produced by John Hammond, was released in mid-1963. *The Freewheelin' Bob Dylan* was the one that made Bob Dylan. It contained his version of "Blowin' in the Wind," which had already been covered and was a monster hit for Peter, Paul and Mary, a group conceived and managed by Dylan's manager, Albert Grossman, in the basement of Folk City. Grossman and Hammond did not get along, and to keep Dylan on the label and peace in the family, Hammond bowed out of producing Dylan's third album, *The Times They Are a-Changin'*, and assigned it instead to house producer Tom Wilson, an African American with a background in jazz and a sharp ear for what was new and hip. Recorded between August and October 1963, *Times* was released in January 1964 and affirmed Dylan's place as the king of folk.

One of the things Wilson introduced on Dylan's next album was adding electricity to Dylan's already supercharged recordings (reportedly with the help of Paul Rothchild, who would later produce several folk and, later on, rock acts, including Phil Ochs and the seminal art-rock band the Doors). It became Dylan's first top-ten album, the half-acoustic, half-electric *Bringing It All Back Home*, produced by Tom Wilson in 1965. It introduced the notion of "folk rock" that would soon take over the industry.

By the time Kane & Garr made their singing debut at Folk City, Wilson was a star producer at Columbia. He had been given a free hand to work with any act he wanted and was constantly on the lookout for "the next big thing." One of his rituals was to sit at the bar at Folk City as often as he could, to catch the flow of new talent. He happened to be there the night Kane & Garr made their paid-gig debut, and he liked "He Was My Brother" so much, he wanted to record it.

However, not with Kane & Garr. He liked it for the Pilgrims, a new act Columbia had recently signed that needed material. Out of England, the Pilgrims—Don Sanders, Tony Goodman, and Chris King—were a part of the so-called Christian Beat scene that had sprung up in London but did not catch on in the States until much later, as Christian Rock. Wilson had hoped to find a more secular, timely song that he could use to break the Pilgrims in America, and he believed "He Was My Brother" was that song.

What happened next happened quickly. Paul was still working part-time for E. B. Marks, a music publisher, and his job was to take their catalogue around and show it to A&R men to see if they might be interested in using one of the songs for their acts. Paul had actually met Wilson once before, in his position as publisher's rep, and had tried, with no success, to sell him some songs.

After their show at Folk City, Wilson approached Paul and Artie about acquiring the song, but to his surprise—and perhaps Artie's as well—Paul refused to sell it to him. Instead, he told Wilson that he should give him and Artie another chance, a studio audition, and if he still didn't think they could do justice to it, then he would talk about the Pilgrims. Wilson agreed, and at that session Paul and Artie sang "The Sound of Silence" for him. Hearing it this time, Wilson liked it enough to commit to trying to get the boys a contract at Columbia.

Not surprisingly, Paul and Artie were ecstatic over this turn of events. Not only had they made the big connection, but they had done so with *Bob Dylan's producer*. However, soon enough, they realized the downside of their good fortune. By now, everyone in the Village (if not the Western world) knew they would sooner or later be measured against Bob Dylan, and not just for his singing and songwriting, but also his guitar playing—deceptively minimal yet perfectly in sync with his musical style, not to mention his singular look and his irresistible onstage charisma. In Paul's words: "Dylan and the Beatles and Stones all happened a year and a half to two years before Simon & Garfunkel. I remember thinking at that time, 'There's no room to be original here. They've got the whole pie.' It was like if I could just get a tiny little slice and get in there."

Their audition for Columbia went well, thanks in part to the skills of house engineer Roy Halee, a jovial studio frump who happened to have one of the sharpest ears in the business (perhaps growing up as the son of the Roy Halee who provided the singing voice for all the Mighty Mouse cartoons had something to do with it). Halee provided the perfect mix for the audition he caught on tape. (Also in the control room that day was Jim McGuinn, who would soon change his name to Roger McGuinn and hit it big for Columbia with the Byrds, a group that, more than any other, helped popularize some of Bob Dylan's best songs.)

Satisfied with the results, and at Tom Wilson's urging, Columbia signed Paul Simon and Art Garfunkel. Paul quickly set about to organize the twelve or thirteen songs needed for the first album. As it turned out, Wilson felt that only five of Paul's original songs were good enough to be included on the debut album; the rest were mostly traditional folk songs, somewhat in the style of Dylan's first album—spare, Americana, classic, and, they hoped, universally appealing.

Wednesday Morning, 3 A.M. was recorded in three separate daytime sessions on March 10, March 17, and March 31. To fill out the sound of just one guitar, Barry Kornfeld, a friend of Paul's from the Village, who may have also helped out with some of the writing (he soon became the copublisher of Simon's music), was added as a second guitar, and Bill Lee was brought in by Wilson to play bass. Before the sessions actually began, the selection and order of songs was set. This was a time when rock albums were listened to from the start of side 1 to the end of side 2. They were considered the aural equivalent of a live concert and were planned with meticulous attention to the progression of the songs.

The first track on side 1, "You Can Tell the World," was written by two stalwart folkies, Bob Gibson and Bob Camp. Gibson, an older pre-Dylan folkie who had had his share of troubles with the blacklist in the fifties, was at the time collaborating with Phil Ochs. It was followed by a folkie standard that Joan Baez had been singing in concert, "Last Night I Had the Strangest Dream," by elder folkie statesman Ed McCurdy. Its lilting melody and simple chord pattern made it a good choice to show off Simon & Garfunkel's harmonies. Track 3 was a Paul Simon original, "Bleecker Street," which has been all but forgotten today but at the time was considered by Paul to be one of his strongest songs. That was followed by "Sparrow." Next came a traditional folk tune, "Benedictus." Side 1 concluded with the "The Sound of Silence."

After the implied intermission, side 2 kicked off with what Wilson believed would be the showcase tune of the album, "He Was My Brother." Next came a traditional folk song, "Peggy-O," which Baez had all but made her own and Dylan had parodied on his first album, followed by "Go Tell It on the Mountain," a spiritual that had been adapted as a traditional folk song, "The Sun Is Burning" by Ian Campbell, and Dylan's "The Times They Are a-Changin'" most likely at the insistence of Wilson. Everyone at Columbia was including at least one Dylan song on their albums ever since Peter, Paul and Mary had struck gold with their 1963 recording of "Blowin' in the Wind," the fastest-selling single Warner ever had. The final cut on the album was another Simon original that gave the album its name: Wednesday Morning, 3 A.M."

When the album was finished, Columbia set up a showcase performance for the duo at Folk City. These prepaid and papered showcases were gold for Mike Porco, as the label, hoping to create some word of mouth, picked up the entire tab for such events. Although the album wasn't due out for months—it had to be mixed, artwork completed, and promotional events put in place—the purpose of it was to officially introduce Simon & Garfunkel to the world.

Only, throughout the recording process nobody was sure what to call them. Someone suggested "Art and Paul," but they quickly discovered another duo was using that name. From the outset Paul was adamant—no more fake names, Toms and Jerrys, Kanes and Garrs. It was going to be Simon & Garfunkel or it was going to be nothing.

For its part, Columbia pushed hard for the duo to consider using something else, reminding the boys that even Dylan had left his "ethnic" (Jewish) "Zimmerman" behind for "Dylan." Wilson, however, agreed with Paul and appealed directly to Norman Adler, the second vice president of Columbia Records, who was also Jewish, to make the final decision. "This is 1964!" he declared (although what that actually meant is anybody's guess) at the meeting attended by Paul, Wilson, Adler, label president Goddard Lieberson, and John Hammond. Adler then stood up and added, as if declaring war, "It's Simon & Garfunkel! Next case." (Ian Whitcomb, the British singer-songwriter, wrote in his memoirs about "Simon & Garfunkel": "I thought they must be a firm of lawyers or perhaps kosher butchers. How could they hope for fame and fortune in pop with such an unglamorous group name?" Later on, he changed these references to "a legal firm or upholsterers.")

Although everyone in the Village would later claim to have been at the March 31, 1964, Folk City debut of Simon & Garfunkel, Louis Bass, an observer of the scene, actually was, and he recalled the night this way: "I remember Simon & Garfunkel performing 'Sound of Silence' for the first time at Folk City. They sang it as some sort of college reunion. [In order to fill the house, they had invited a lot of their friends from Queens College and the fraternity house.] At that time I never thought they would make it. They didn't sound as good as some of the other acts. It was the first time they tested out publicly. They went over well because it was all their friends."

Robert Shelton, Dylan's champion, who by now had gained a side bit of fame just for having written his *New York Times* rave of Dylan and had been elevated to the status of seer of the folk scene, was also there that night to see what the fuss manufactured by Columbia's PR team was all about, and he wasn't impressed. "Simon & Garfunkel were uptown guys, Queens guys. . . . I was struck by a kind of Mickey Mouse, timid, contrived side," Shelton later said. "And of course through Dylan, Van Ronk, all those guys, what was really being created was a rough, natural dirty sound. [Simon & Garfunkel] sounded very suburban. Simon always struck me as a suburban type of Dylan."

Not long after, Michael Thomas, a British journalist who was covering the Village scene and who would go on to become a successful screenwriter, reporting for the August 1964 edition of *Eye*, one of the papers that lived and died on the New York culture of the decade, explained that while Simon certainly wasn't the only object of Dylan's disdain, he was, in Thomas's opinion, one of the more deserving:

> Dylan touched everybody at the core of their ambitions. Some, like Ochs and [Tom] Paxton and Tim Hardin, felt his energy and were energized; some, like [Eric] Andersen and [David] Blue, and others like Richard Fariña, the destructive heat of his own life, and Paul Simon, that last great sophomore, were [also] stricken by Dylan.

The Man Himself was there that night, alongside Shelton, who had, since that *New York Times* review, become his buddy. Dylan's mere presence was an acknowledgment that Simon & Garfunkel were being pushed hard by the label they now shared. Indeed, they were the only other so-called Village act that had managed to get signed to Columbia, something that Dylan, never known for his generosity or desire to share the spotlight, probably didn't appreciate. Chances are that Dylan looked on Simon & Garfunkel as somehow diminishing what only he and his talent had been able to pull off.

Moreover, by now Dylan had all but abandoned the Village scene and the packs of wannabe folksingers who had flooded it. In truth, Dylan had done only a handful of paying Village gigs, including three or four (the number is not clear) at Folk City, the rest either showcases or sit-ins with friends. He was already in the process of moving up and away. Here is Shelton's recollection of what happened that night:

> Dylan and I were at Folk City as Simon & Garfunkel came on. Simon cast a hostile look Dylan's way. Onstage, Simon & Garfunkel began to sing ethereal choirboy harmonies that

sounded seriously out of place at Gerde's, home of weather-beaten ethnic songs. At the bar, Bob and I, who had been doing quite a bit of drinking, had an advanced case of giggles over nothing. We weren't laughing at the performance, but Simon was furious. Afterward, Simon acted as though there were a Dylan cabal against him, while Dylan tended to ignore Simon. . . . Although Garfunkel never joined the one-way vendetta, Simon seemed determined to elevate himself at Dylan's expense. On their first album, Simon & Garfunkel recorded "The Times They Are a-Changin'." Looking forward to S&G's second album, Simon was not only emulating Dylan's alienation, protest, and brotherhood, but also directly satirizing Dylan. Simon's "Simple Desultory Phillippic" was a vicious burlesque. Its harmonica playing and shouts for "Albert" left little doubt about its target.

Bob Spitz, one of Dylan's many biographers, also wrote about the incident, confirming that Simon held a long-standing grudge against Dylan because he had talked loudly through the entire show.

Despite (or because of) Dylan's obvious disdain, or jealousy, or anger, or drunken rudeness, or whatever, neither Simon, nor Garfunkel, nor the executives from Columbia were impressed with their debut, and it was decided among them that it might be better to keep the duo away from the performance stage until their album was actually released. They did one or two more nights at the Gaslight that had already been booked, with even more dismal results than their debut at Folk City. Dave Van Ronk remembered those Gaslight shows, and believes that Simon and Garfunkel were signed to Columbia because they still had some leftover pull from their Tom & Jerry days:

When [Simon & Garfunkel] first showed up, they were in a pretty tough situation, because they had already had a Top 40 hit as teenagers, and as far as the music was concerned, they were over the hill, but the mouldy fig wing of the folk world despised them as pop singers. I remember hearing them down at the Gaslight, and nobody would listen. I thought they were damn good, but the people who wanted to hear Mississippi

John Hurt and Dock Boggs wanted no part of Simon & Garfunkel. . . . "Sounds of Silence" actually became a running joke: for a while there, it was only necessary to start singing "Hello darkness, my old friend . . ." and everybody would crack up.

A week after their less-than-spectacular debut, Simon, still smarting over the Dylan incident and the subsequent condescending reception at the Gaslight, became convinced the album was going to bomb, and he didn't want to be around to see it. With Artie opting once more to return to classes at Columbia, Paul flew off by himself to Europe, eventually winding up in Paris, where he supposedly slept on the concrete embankment of the river Seine under the Pont Neuf and busked in the Metro to make some pocket money.

One night after playing a set in the Metro, Paul happened to meet a fellow free traveler sitting next to him on a park bench. The young man's name was Dave McCausland, and he was English. They got to talking, and McCausland told Paul that he was the proprietor of a folk club in the Railway Hotel in Brentwood, Essex, the county to the east of London, and that if Paul was ever passing through, there was an engagement with his name on it waiting for him.

That was enough for Paul. After picking up some money at the American Express office sent to him by his parents, he flew to London and worked his way to Essex. He arrived there on April 11, 1964, and found himself in the middle of the peak of Beatlemania, which had energized the British music scene in a way nothing and nobody had before. As Kenney Jones, of the Small Faces and later the Who, put it, "All of us war babies were living in the rubble of the bombings, in cloudy black and white until the Beatles put all our lives into sunny Technicolor."

Dave McCausland warmly welcomed Paul to his Brentwood folk club at the Railway Hotel in the back room of the pub, where he quickly became a nightly fixture, accompanying himself on acoustic guitar. One thing Paul noticed immediately was the politeness of the crowd. There was none of what Van Ronk had described as the Village's "dirty" scene, the competitive hostility that served as the underpinning for the singers of songs that called for social justice

in the Village of the early sixties; there were no pushy acts wanting
to take his place in line, no Bob Dylan to publicly humiliate him.
Here Simon & Garfunkel didn't even exist; he could become Paul
Kane again and erase the whole ugly experience of his brief time as
a Greenwich Village folkie and the anticipated failure of *Wednesday
Morning, 3 A.M.*

And then he met Kathy Chitty.

She was a pretty office secretary in the daytime and, at night,
the ticket taker at Dave McCausland's club. She lived in Brentwood
with her parents. Born in 1947, Kathy was thin, with mouse-brown
hair cut in bangs and hung down long and loose. She had a British
working-class quietness about her, a sense of modesty that appealed
to Paul, along with her thin, expressive hands and her fabulously
intense eyes. Paul met her the first night he performed in Essex,
after she had watched him from the back of the club, listening raptly
to every song. Afterward, she went boldly to his dressing room and
introduced herself. Whatever young love at first sight is, according to
those who were there, the two of them fell into it fast, hard, and deep.
After that first night they became inseparable, and with each set Paul
sang at the club, he appeared to be singing directly to and only for
her. She was so different from the American girls he had known,
especially the pushy teen ballbusters-in-the-making in Queens who
never failed to take any and every opportunity to tell him he was too
short, too ugly, too broke, and too chubby to be considered the kind
of rough low-brow colt they were interested in breaking.

Soon enough, however, the desire to try to play his music in
London proved too strong for Paul to resist, and after a tearful (on
her part) farewell and a promise (on his part) that he would return,
in the spring of 1964 Paul set out alone to find his place in the
musical storm of England's cultural shift. Paul arrived in London the
very week the Rolling Stones' eponymous debut album knocked *With
the Beatles* out of first place on the British charts.

Here, at the beginning of it all, Paul Kane happily lost and found
himself playing the small folk clubs around London's Soho, until
he began to feel the pull of something that wasn't there—Kathy
Chitty. After playing a club near Liverpool, standing on the station
at Widnes, waiting for the early morning milk train back to London

one night, Paul began to compose, first in his head and then on a scrap of paper, "Homeward Bound," a song filled with images of self-loathing, with its shades of mediocrity and emptiness, all against a lilting, British seesaw speech-pattern melody.

The words flowed like water from a faucet. Next came the moony song he would write for her, "Kathy's Song," in which she got title billing as the longed-for object of the singer's affection. "Kathy's Song" was a major leap forward in every way for Paul. It is built around one specific real-life character (the writer) thinking about another, far away (the girl), as rain falls on the roof—simple as that, but more vivid, real, and moving than the ten thousand people, maybe more, of "The Sound of Silence." In "Kathy's Song" the boy imagines he kisses the girl when she starts each day (there is something charmingly childlike about that lyric). There is also an insecure, confessional feel to the song, the writer admitting that he is afraid his songwriting is not good, with words "tearing and straining" to rhyme, his self-conscious posing poetics nothing compared to the powerful emotions he feels for her. All of it is beautifully wrapped in Paul's lovely fingerpick playing and sweet-voiced singing. "Kathy's Song" is the first great Paul Simon love song, without a single "oo-bop-a-luchipa" to be anywhere found.

One other admirer played an important role during this period of Paul's life. Her name was Judith Piepe, a former social worker who had fled Germany with her parents in 1933, the morning after the night of the burning of the Reichstag. She had seen Paul sing a couple of times in London, playing sets in the numerous clubs around town, and one night when she was with another, younger woman by the name of Joan Bata, who was staying at Piepe's East London flat, she simply walked up during a break and introduced herself to Paul and told him that if he ever needed a place to stay, her flat was available to him. Within a few days, with nowhere else to go, Paul accepted Piepe's offer to sleep there.

Piepe's flat was a precursor to the numerous hippie communes of the late sixties. Piepe had recently converted from Judaism to Christianity, which intensified her natural desire to nurture youthful lost souls. Paul had no problem moving in and quickly found it the perfect place to practice, write, and sing at all hours with nobody ever complaining about the noise. Often after gigs he would come back to the flat at one or two in the morning for dinner, doughnuts, and coffee with evaporated milk that surrogate mother Piepe was more than happy to make for him. When her practical side kicked in, she offered to help get Paul bookings, as she knew every club and every club owner in London. Sometimes Kathy came in from Essex to spend her weekends with him, going to a gig if he had one or sitting quietly alongside him at the apartment while Paul got stoned, played the guitar, sang, and worked on new songs.

After which he and Kathy could lock out the rest of the world and listen to the drizzle of the rain while they made love.

4

The Calm Before the Storm

T HAT SEPTEMBER, TOM WILSON CALLED PAUL BACK TO THE
United States for final preparations before the release of
Wednesday Morning, 3 A.M. Paul, reluctant to leave London, brought Kathy to the United States with him, and when he
arrived, instead of contacting Tom Wilson, or even Artie, he decided
to take her on a five-day motor trip, just the two of them, to show
her as much of the country as he could before he got down to the
business of the album. Out of that excursion came the road song
"America," in which Paul confesses to Kathy, while she is sleeping,
that he is lost, the strong implication being he isn't talking about
where he is, but about *who* he is.

They finally arrived back in New York City, and only after Paul
had seen Kathy off at the airport did he meet up with Tom and

Artie, both of whom were eager to listen to Halee's final mix and to show Paul the album's cover. The top half was a black strip with the words WEDNESDAY MORNING, 3 AM stenciled in white across a black background, and the lower half was a shot of Paul and Artie standing together at a subway station, presumably in front of a wall with the words of a prophet written on it.

The album was released October 19, 1964, and sold a dismal three thousand copies. None of its songs received much exposure on the radio, and the label could not place the duo on any TV shows. To anybody in the rest of the country, the album sounded too New York, while to the Village crowd and its followers, it wasn't New York enough. Either way, it couldn't compete for airtime against the flood of Beatles songs, Roy Orbison, the Beach Boys, and even Louis Armstrong, who had a monster radio hit that fall with his novelty version of "Hello Dolly."

By Christmas, the album was declared dead by Columbia, and Paul, convinced he had no future in America, returned to England, Judith's flat, and Kathy's warm, waiting arms, certain that this time he would remain with her in London forever.

Upon his arrival, the first thing he did was to sublease a room for himself in a small house near Belsize Park in North London. As it happened, Martin Carthy, a folksinging traditionalist, also lived there. The two became friends, and Carthy helped point Paul in the direction of clubs and pubs where he might find work as a singer, and transport cafes where the food was cheap. In a good week he was able to earn as much as twenty pounds (about seventy-five dollars at that time), which covered all his expenses and left a few quid over for pot. It was the life he wanted—a working musician able to survive on his own. Apparently no one knew that Paul Kane was also Paul Simon, one half of Simon & Garfunkel, and that he had made a major-label album in the States (no one in the States knew about it either, or so it seemed), and he preferred it that way.

Eventually he discovered that Lorna Music, a small music-publishing company situated in London's West End and run by Alan Paramor, Leslie Lowe, and Peter Pavey, had licensed a song of his from E. B. Marks Music in America, Paul's publisher (under the pseudonym Paul Kane). The song, "Carlos Domingues," had been recorded by Val Doonican on his latest album and done very well, selling about 90,000 units.

One afternoon Paul decided to pay a visit to Lorna Music, to thank them for using his song. Les Lowe graciously invited Paul to come have tea and talk about his music. As Lowe later remembered, "This young American sat there, in our tiny, cramped office, took off his duffle coat and took out his guitar and started to play strange songs. I was very impressed and I had no doubt that Paul's work was unique. So I took him in to meet Alan Paramor."

That meeting resulted in Lorna Music's signing Paul to a British publishing and recording contract. The first step was to make a few demos, which they did at Regent Sound Studios on Denmark Street. The demos were passed around and led to several gigs in the Soho section of London, along Greek Street's cellar-club row, where he soon became a fixture on the folk scene flourishing there.

That May, Lowe managed to get Paul a record deal for a single on the Oriole label. Paul chose to record "He Was My Brother," which had been on *Wednesday Morning, 3 A.M.*, and his own version of "Carlos Domingues," using the name Jerry Landis (the publishing credits remained as originally registered to Paul Kane). The song attracted some attention and helped to keep Paul working the folk-club circuit, where he met lots of musicians and hung out at the all-night dives on Frith Street, almost always with Kathy, silent and close, one arm slipped through Paul's, her head leaning on his shoulder as he talked music and sipped espressos into the first hours of daylight.

Back in New York, Artie was more than a little surprised when he received a call from Paul asking him to come to England and hang for the summer. Having finished his spring-semester classes at Columbia, Artie, energized by the sound of Paul's voice and the stories of how easy and fun life was in London, decided to take him up on the offer, but only if they could meet first in Paris, still Artie's favorite city. Paul said he had no problem with that but told Artie they shouldn't stay away from London for too long, and that his friend Judith Piepe, who was now fiercely determined to push Paul to stardom, would surely let Artie stay at the commune/flat and help him as well.

Besides being housemates, Paul and Carthy ran into each other frequently on the pub tour circuit; they had gotten to know each other's music and often shared songs. Carthy had originally learned "Scarborough Fair," a traditional song about the festivities in the lovely seaside resort of Scarborough, on Yorkshire's craggy north-eastern coast, from an Ewan MacColl and Peggy Seeger book of traditional songs called *The Singing Island*. Carthy often played it for Paul, who fell in love with its lilting melody and spent weeks trying to give it a more contemporary sound, using Artie's high harmonies to infuse it with a spectral beauty and a contemporary Everly Brothers feel that Carthy's solo vocals simply couldn't match.

> I had a very strong liking for English traditional music . . . and Martin Carthy was probably the best player, the most musical of the players. [His] arrangement of "Scarborough Fair" is sort of how I remembered how he did it. Everybody did "Scarborough Fair" and everybody did "She Moved through the Fair" [a popular Irish ballad sung by a groom eagerly anticipating his wedding day]—those were two really big songs.

Artie fit easily into the communal atmosphere of Judith's come-and-go flat and was soon studying the guitar for hours on end with Caroline Culpepper, who was also staying with Judith, working on songs with Paul, especially on the harmonies for their more contemporary version of "Scarborough Fair."*

The summer flew by, and as August wound down, Artie announced that he had to go back to New York to start classes at Columbia. Paul said he understood. More than that, to everyone's surprise, no one more than Kathy, Paul said he was going back, too. He was under pressure from his parents to return to school and his studies to be a lawyer. Whatever the reason—guilt, club fatigue, homesickness, or a combination of all three—he also loved

---

* Bob Dylan, too, was a big fan of Carthy; he had met him and heard him play "Scarborough Fair" and borrowed from it lyrically and melodically for his highly similar, if rougher-hewn "Girl from the North Country." Here is Dylan's version: "If you're travelin' through the North Country Fair . . . remember me to one who lives there, she once was a true friend of mine." And Simon & Garfunkel's prettier, more folksy, and harmonically sophisticated version: "Remember me to one who lives there, she once was a true friend of mine."

the good side of being with Artie, his best friend growing up and his singing and songwriting partner. Paul, wounds sufficiently licked, now felt ready to rejoin the real world and leave his dream of being a London-based folk-music star behind.

For their last night in London, Paul, Kathy, and Artie went with Judith to the Flamingo Club on Wardour Street to see the Ian Campbell group perform. However, by showtime, the group had failed to arrive, and the club's promoter, Curly Gross, desperate to put something onstage, asked Paul, by now a well-known local performer, if he could do a last-minute fill-in. Without hesitation, Paul took his guitar—he always carried it with him—and went up on the small stage. He performed "A Church Is Burning," "Leaves That Are Green" (which sounds quite similar lyrically and melodically to Phil Ochs's "Changes"), and "The Sound of Silence," all unfamiliar to the audience. Then he brought Artie up to sing "Benedictus," which became a fitting "farewell forever to London" for the boys. Later, Paul would describe these days as among the happiest of his life. Indeed, he was able to make a living off his songs, playing the small British pubs and clubs he loved, sleeping late, singing into the night, and making love to his muse. It was, he said, all he could ever want.

Paul lasted one semester at Brooklyn Law School before he packed it in, knowing, as he had all along, that it was going to be music or nothing. His last day at school was January 18, 1966, and the next day he boarded a flight back to London, for what he thought would be a two-week vacation to visit Kathy and Judith, before returning to New York City, where he hoped to move to Manhattan and resume his music career.

What he didn't know was that during his absence, Judith had put together a ten-song tape from the hours of music Paul had recorded at Lorna Music and taken it to the BBC, hoping they might play one or two on the air. At the time the BBC held a monopoly on radio broadcasting in the UK, though "pirate" stations that beamed into the mainland from ships moored at sea were at their heels and would eventually lead to the formation of Radio One. In 1965, however, the BBC's staid Light Program was the only station where pop music could be found, aside from the more adventurous Radio Luxembourg, broadcast on a strong signal from Europe. Judith had her work cut out for her, calling the BBC every day, until they agreed to play a couple of the songs on the *Five to Ten* show for two weeks. *Five to Ten* was a five-minute morning slot (that came on at five minutes to ten o'clock) that immediately followed *Housewives' Choice*, which had twenty million listeners, and was followed in turn by *Music While You Work*, another enormously popular program on the BBC.

The shows that featured Paul's demos aired in March 1965 and were an instant sensation. The BBC was overwhelmed with letters and phone calls from listeners wanting to know where they could buy "Jerry Landis" records. The uniform response was that there was only one recording available, the single Oriole recording of "He Was My Brother."

Since making the record, Oriole had been acquired by CBS, whose London branch was, at the time, little more than an outlet for its American catalogue (the company was unable to use the name "Columbia" in the UK, as it had already been registered as the name of a record label by EMI, hence the record label was called "CBS"). Since it was prohibitively expensive against any possible profits to remove all the labels from the "Jerry Landis" singles, CBS decided instead to quickly record a new Paul Simon album and hope to sell that instead. To make sure it was done right, and having no one in London they trusted to do it, Columbia sent Tom Wilson over the pond to produce it. (Wilson is uncredited on the album, which lists Reginald Warburton and Stanley West as producers. They were, in fact, Levy Studio house engineers. This was the first and only time Paul worked with them.) Paul and Tom had a happy reunion, and Tom, too, wound up staying at Judith's flat in the East End. With the details of the recording date set, Paul settled in for a longer stay in England. Kathy couldn't have been happier.

Early in June 1965, at the Levy Studio on Bond Street, Paul laid down twelve tracks, accompanying himself on his own acoustic guitar, recorded live under his single-miked voice. It took all of one hour for Paul to record the entire album at a total cost of sixty pounds (about two hundred dollars), not including the ninety pounds Paul received as an advance for the songs and the liner notes, which read like gibberish and may have, in fact, been a conscious parody of Dylan's early, nearly indecipherable album liner notes. For the cover, Paul chose a gorgeous picture of himself and Kathy sitting cross-legged on a London "narrow street of cobblestone" in what may be the only existing photo of them together, and which resembled to a remarkable degree the Bob Dylan–Suze Rotolo Village Street cover of his 1963 album, *The Freewheelin' Bob Dylan*. Paul: "To be twenty-two years old and to have your girlfriend on your album cover, that was *it!*"

These songs would later become the heart of the Simon & Garfunkel repertoire; they were, in order of appearance, "I Am a Rock," "Leaves That Are Green," "A Church Is Burning," "April Come She Will," "The Sounds of Silence" (This was the only time it was titled as "The *Sounds* of Silence." All previous and subsequent Simon & Garfunkel versions list it as "The *Sound* of Silence."), "A Most Peculiar Man," "He Was My Brother," "Kathy's Song," "The Side of a Hill," "A Simple Desultory Philippic," "Flowers Never Bend with the Rainfall," and "Patterns." (For the session, Paul rewrote some of the lyrics to "He Was My Brother," changing one of the lines to make the song more specifically about the death of Andy Goodman, one of the three civil rights workers killed in Mississippi the year before and a former Queens College classmate of Paul's.)

Later Paul would claim that the song had originally been written as a tribute to Goodman, who had been murdered on June 21, 1964, although his body wasn't found until the following August. But he could not possibly have written the song for that reason, because he and Garfunkel sang it nearly a year earlier at Folk City, and it was first recorded by them on March 17, 1964, three months *before* the murders took place. Years later, in February 1984, in an interview with *Playboy*, he inexplicably said this about it: "One of the only times I did it [write issue-specific songs] was in "He Was my Brother," which was about Andrew Goodman, a college classmate who was killed in Mississippi during the Civil Rights Movement," but clearly the song was written *before* the murders took place.

To celebrate the recording of his first solo album, and a single, "I Am a Rock" backed with "Leaves That Are Green," Paul spent his advance money on a used Sunbeam convertible to tool around the countryside with Kathy.

That July he was invited to appear on Britain's most popular and important music show, watched by virtually everyone under twenty-five. *Ready Steady Go* was a rough equivalent to what *American Bandstand* had been to Tom & Jerry in the fifties. The producers wanted him to do "I Am a Rock," but a shortened version—this was the era of live TV—so that P. J. Proby, a huge British star at the time, could close the show with his current hit, "Let the Water Run Down." Paul, refusing to be upstaged, did his entire song, which meant that Proby's would have to be shortened. No one at the station, most of all Proby, was happy about it, but Paul couldn't have cared less. "I Am a Rock" failed to chart as a single, and the album missed being ranked as well.

Despite poor sales, Paul believed the album was its own reward and righted many of the wrongs that he had suffered in the States. When Jackson C. Frank, another expat folksinger who had since become a good friend, asked Paul to produce and play second guitar on what would be his only album, *Jackson C. Frank*, Paul happily agreed. For the first time in his career, talented musicians were looking for him and his talent. It was a great feeling and made him realize that even if this was as far as he was going to get in his career, it was a major vindication, a long way from stocking shoes in Herald Square.

And then, in the proverbial overnight of show business lore, everything in Paul Simon's and Art Garfunkel's lives changed completely and forever, without either of them having the slightest inkling of how or where or when the signs of that change had first emerged.

That fall of 1965, while Paul was still in England playing, sleeping late, and zooming around in his Sunbeam with Kathy by his side, back in the States, out of the absolute nowhere of pop oblivion, a new 45 release of "The Sound of Silence," studio-altered by Tom Wilson, was climbing up *Billboard*'s Singles chart like a high-flying rocket headed straight for the astronomical Top Ten.

PART TWO

Simon & Garfunkel

5

The Sounds of Simon

THE YEAR 1965 WAS A WATERSHED FOR AMERICAN POP music, marked by a cultural shift that saw the swift end of the Village folk scene. Its coffin was nailed tight by Bob Dylan's "Like a Rolling Stone," the single he chose to release from his groundbreaking album *Highway 61 Revisited*. With that record, Dylan succeeded in shifting the sound of the sixties from his modern, purist version of post-Guthrie country and western–influenced folk music to what would come to be known as folk rock. In the summer of '65 "Like a Rolling Stone" was played on the radio constantly, bombarding the coming-of-age boomer generation with his decade-defining question that rejected all the pseudo-intellectualism he and everyone else under thirty had been fed from day one: not "What does it mean?" or "What do you think?" but *"How does it feel?"* The six-plus-minutes-long single built around that emotional inquiry broke all the rules of radio and record cross-promotion and buried once and for all the entertainment business know-it-alls who thought they had so brilliantly manufactured the very quality that had given folk music its appeal—its socially aware, anticorporate, liberal-leaning sincerity—by manufacturing "folk stars," some as great as Leonard Cohen, some as awful as Sonny Bono. "Like a Rolling Stone" also forced Columbia Records to wake up to the fact that its old A&R policy was obsolete, and it became, virtually overnight, the label every rock star wanted to be on. Simultaneously, Tom Wilson became one of the most powerful and influential producers in the business.

Indeed, Wilson, it appeared, had the golden touch, a unique ability to catch on record the direction in which the cultural winds were blowing. Looking for a follow-up to "Like a Rolling Stone," he found it in, of all places, Simon & Garfunkel's *Wednesday Morning, 3 A.M.*, an album that had been presumed dead and buried in Columbia Records' potter's field of also-rans and never-was's. He was first alerted to its potential when a Boston-based late-night WBZ-FM deejay—who catered to Cambridge's ample college demographic—picked up a copy of *Wednesday Morning, 3 A.M.* and at precisely that day and time played "The Sound of Silence."

It proved the perfect song for the perfect time, and overnight it was picked up by other FM stations up and down the East Coast, all the way to Cocoa Beach, Florida, where it caught the students coming down for spring break. When a local promotions man for Columbia went down to the beach to give away free albums of new artists, all anybody wanted was Simon & Garfunkel. The rep had to call Wilson to find out who the hell *that* was. Wilson asked which specific song they were asking for and was told "The Sound of Silence." He immediately found a copy of the track and listened to it. Over and over again. Yes, it was okay, he thought. Yes, it had a certain something, but it was really too soft, he thought, to be a hit. Then he put on a copy of the Byrds' recording of Pete Seeger's "Turn Turn Turn," their second number-one hit after covering Dylan's "Mr. Tambourine Man" and the less successful "All I Really Want to Do," all released in 1965.

And that's when he got it. "The Sound of Silence" needed to be remixed, rocked up, put to a beat with a McGuinn-type guitar. Wilson brought together some of the same studio musicians that Dylan had used for "Like a Rolling Stone"—Al Gorgoni on guitar, Bob Bushnell on bass, Bobby Gregg on drums (whose opening snare drum shot remains one of the most immediately recognizable sounds of sixties rock)—but, ironically, not Paul's friend Al Kooper, who, despite his early dislike for Dylan's voice, had added the crucial organ part to "Like a Rolling Stone." Correctly, Wilson felt Kooper was too closely identified with Dylan's sound to use him for the remix of "The Sound of Silence."

Wilson overlaid a strong bass, an electric guitar, and a drum part with the snare mixed way up, and when he thought he had what he wanted—Paul Simon's lyrics, Artie Garfunkel's harmonies, the Byrds' clang, and a taste of Dylan's electric sound—he released the single to every college FM rock station in the country, and a week later to everybody else.

And he didn't tell Paul and Artie what he'd done until after he'd remixed and released the record.

Back in the States, Artie had returned to Columbia University to finish his master's degree in architecture when he got the call from Tom Wilson about "The Sound of Silence." Paul, meanwhile, was still in England, making occasional trips to Paris and Denmark to work their club circuits. That September in Denmark, he picked up a copy of *Billboard*, and as he had done every week for years, going all the way back to the days of "Hey Schoolgirl," he turned to the singles charts. He froze when he saw "The Sound of Silence" at number eighty-six. He then bought a copy of *Cashbox*, another industry trade magazine, and saw the same thing.

Back in England a few days later, while hanging with Al Stewart at the flat, he received a call from an excited Artie about what was happening. A day later a copy of the single arrived in the post from Tom Wilson. He immediately put it on Stewart's phonograph, listened to it intently, and as Stewart later recalled, "[Paul] was *horrified* when he first heard it . . . [when the] rhythm section slowed down at one point so that Paul and Artie's voices could catch up."

Paul hated the remix but loved the success. The following week, he picked up the latest editions of the two magazines and saw that the song was in the low thirties. That's when he knew it had a shot to go to number one.

By January 1966, it had, indeed, reached the top of the charts and earned Paul and Artie a gold record for selling a million copies. That was when Paul Simon, who'd just turned twenty-four, got on a plane bound for New York. Good-bye Judy's flat, good-bye folk clubs, good-bye Paul Kane, and good-bye Kathy Chitty, whom he would not speak to or hear from or see again for the next twenty years.

In the end even Kathy could not compete with the chance to stand alongside Dylan.

The winter of '66 was bitterly cold in New York City, with snow up to the shins in Queens, which always seemed the last borough to be plowed. "I had come back to New York," Paul later recalled,

> and I was staying in my old room at my parents' house. Artie was living at his parents' house, too. I remember Artie and I were sitting there in my car one night, parked on a street in Queens, and the announcer [on the radio] said, "Number one, Simon & Garfunkel." And Artie said to me, "That Simon & Garfunkel, they must be having a great time." Because there we were on a street corner [in my car in] Queens, smoking a joint. We didn't know what to do with ourselves.

Paul had anticipated being greeted on his return to New York like a conquering hero, which, to say the least, did not happen. Nothing was quite right about it. He thought he and Artie had broken up this time for good, and now this, a partnership he hadn't wanted rekindled as a result of a remix he had not made whose enhanced performance he did not like. *What were all those guitars doing burying not just the vocals but his own beautiful fingerpick? What had they done to his song?*

The idea for the remix had been Wilson's, but its execution fell to Roy Halee, Columbia's resident engineer, who had a remarkable ear for mixing and who would soon become irreplaceable for the revived Simon & Garfunkel and later for Paul and Artie individually. According to Lou Christie, a wildly popular and immensely entertaining stage performer who was one of the staples of AM Top Forty in the early sixties, via a string of hits that included the catchy "Lightnin' Strikes" and "Rhapsody in the Rain," Halee was the crucial element for any creative artist trying to make hit records at Columbia. As Christie recalled:

> I met Roy when I moved over from MGM, where I had had a great run, to Columbia, at the urging of Clive Davis. Roy Halee was assigned to be my engineer, and I was struck by the way he worked. He was very relaxed, but he had a depth that other engineers didn't have. It became clear to me early on that he was an artist himself. He locked right into the sensitivity I was trying to find as a singer. Roy's mixing was incredible. He saved a couple of my recordings just by mixing them his own way. He was a nice, easygoing, plain-looking, slightly overweight, red-headed Irish guy. He reminded me of a football player, for some reason, and when he was on a session we all sort of rose to the occasion. He was a special talent, inspirational in his way.*

If Paul couldn't figure out what to do about Artie and the whole Columbia Records situation, he didn't have much time to think about it. No sooner had he arrived back in New York and gotten high with Artie than CBS demanded a new album from them, to ride the success (and imitate the sound) of their hit single. At their insistence, it was to be called *Sounds of Silence* (the *s* on "sounds" added, presumably, to emphasize there were two voices, even though the original recording also had them). Because there was no time for Paul to write an album's worth of new material, he rerecorded with Artie most of

---

* Paul "immortalized" Halee in his 1965 "A Simple Desultory Philippic (Or How I was Robert McNamara'd into Submission)," which first appeared on *Parsley, Sage, Rosemary and Thyme*. The song is a lighthearted gerund-rhyming pop list that pokes fun at Dylan, Mick Jagger, Phil Spector, Lou Adler, Barry Sadler, Lenny Bruce, Roy Halee, and Art Garfunkel (". . . been Roy Haleed and Art Garfunkeled . . .").

the songs from the British *Paul Simon Songbook*, plus four new ones. As with all five Simon & Garfunkel albums, *Sounds of Silence* was conceived more as a unified-theme album than a series of songs, a miniconcert, as it were, that reflected where Paul and Artie were in their individual lives, creatively and personally, and their progression as a pop-rock duo.

Sounds of Silence was recorded at the CBS studios on Fifty-second Street and in Nashville and Hollywood. Side 1 opened with the remixed "Sound of Silence," followed by "Leaves That Are Green," similarly electrified, and then a new song, "Blessed," which Paul had written in Judith Piepe's flat, about being caught in a rainstorm and finding shelter in a church. "Kathy's Song" came next, and although it was rerecorded, Paul insisted that this song retain its acoustic purity and that he sing it solo. This was followed by "Somewhere They Can't Find Me," which sounds very similar to "Wednesday Morning, 3 A.M." Side 1's final track was the only cover on the album, Davey Graham's "Anji," a song Paul had heard while living in London and liked very much.

Side 2 began with "Homeward Bound," Paul's melancholy ode to Kathy inspired by his wait that time at Widnes Station, here beautifully reworked and harmonized. "Richard Cory" followed, adapted from the poem by Edwin Arlington Robinson, with an original Paul Simon chorus lyric (the song would later be recorded by the Belfast band Them with still-unknown lead singer Van Morrison). It was not uncommon for folk rock to adapt poems to music. This was part of the folk tradition, and although "Richard Cory" was an okay attempt, other, more purist-rooted folkies were doing it much better. One thinks immediately of Phil Ochs's great adaptations of Edgar Allan Poe's "The Bells" (1964) and Alfred Noyes's "The Highwayman" (1965). Phil was a major part of the Village scene, and both his music and his politics were an obvious influence on this phase of Paul's singing and songwriting. Next on the album came "A Most Peculiar Man" and "April Come She Will," both from *Songbook*, then "We've Got a Groovy Thing Going" and "I Am a Rock," two songs intended for but left off of *Songbook*. "According to Artie," Paul said at the time, "it is my most neurotic song. I don't know whether that is true or not. It's a song about loneliness." (Interestingly, both "Richard Cory" and

"Most Peculiar Man" are about suicide, hardly standard Top-Forty material.)

Wilson passed the producing chores over to Bob Johnston, with Roy Halee once again engineering. To flesh out the electric rock sound that had worked on "The Sound of Silence," Wilson hired then session guitarist Glen Campbell, who had gained a reputation as a studio musician, having worked with many of the best acts in the business, including a turn with the Beach Boys, and the great session drummer Hal Blaine, who had previously worked with Elvis ("Can't Help Falling in Love), the Beach Boys ("I Get Around"), and most important for this album, the Byrds' remake of "Mr. Tambourine Man."

So eager were Wilson and Columbia to capitalize on "The Sound of Silence," they had the album in stores by January 17, 1966, less than three weeks after Paul's return to the States. A week later, the reworked "Homeward Bound" (backed with "Leaves That Are Green"), the first single from the album, immediately jumped onto the *Billboard* Top Ten. It was followed by "I Am a Rock" (backed with "Flowers Never Bend with the Rainfall"), which reached number three, despite a groundswell of critical disdain for the duo and their relentless songs of pseudo-depression. The academically oriented fellow Queens native "dean of rock critics" Robert Christgau dismissed the song as just that—pseudo fill-in-the-blanks—writing that he preferred the then current pop tune "Paper Cup" by the 5th Dimension because "it says far more about Alienation than Paul Simon's 'I Am a Rock' ever did."

Christgau wasn't alone among critics in feeling that Simon & Garfunkel were not the real thing, from their goofily unsmiling album covers to their prettified approach to teenage angst, that they were imitators, what Peter, Paul and Mary were to Bob Dylan (and what Simon & Garfunkel was to Paul Simon): commodified, slicked-up pop posing as folk rock, which itself was already a homogenized version of folk.

Paul's insecurities, always lurking beneath his thin skin, especially after Dylan's monumental *Blonde on Blonde*, released that same year, led him to realize that the *Sounds of Silence* was already passé, light-years behind Dylan's tougher, bluesier sound that attracted so many imitators, not the least among them Simon & Garfunkel. Paul insisted he had no interest in being the next Bob Dylan (or Dylan soundalike). "I didn't want to be Dylan," Paul recalled later. "He was so good. Frankly, I never would have written 'The Sound of Silence' had it not been for Bob Dylan. But soon after that, I said, 'You can't be that. He's that. You are . . . I don't know what. But you're not that. Don't be that."

The only problem was that all Columbia wanted from Simon & Garfunkel was *exactly* that, Dylan-lite, a duo stylistically pre–*Blonde on Blonde* Dylan that could potentially outsell him by twisting just a little bit more toward Top-Ten pop. Already, Simon & Garfunkel had surpassed Dylan's total record sales (pre *Blonde on Blonde*), and as far as Columbia was concerned, they, not Dylan, had the makings of a great moneymaking machine.

Almost before they knew it, the label put Simon & Garfunkel on the road. In those days the rock concert scene, with few exceptions, featured amalgams of hit makers, much like the old Alan Freed fifties shows, updated with fashionable new deejays. On the East Coast it was Murray the K, who had smartly dubbed himself "the Fifth Beatle" during the first throes of American Beatlemania and was now putting together profitable (for him) living jukeboxes he called "Music in the Fifth Dimension—*total audience involvement!*"—to capitalize on his self-proclaimed "Fifth" status and to imitate the relatively repetitive rotation of "progressive" FM by serving up his show five times a day, for nine days, to pot-drenched teen audiences in movie theaters scattered around the tri-state area. Paul and Artie were doing a two-song set on one of these shows that included such disparate stars as Mitch Ryder, Wilson Pickett, Smokey Robinson and the Miracles, Cream, the Who, the Blues Project, the Blues Magoos, the Young Rascals, Lou Christie, and, to add an element of Bob Dylan, Phil Ochs. (The show rotated Ochs, Simon & Garfunkel, the Blues Magoos, and the Young Rascals on different nights, to give audiences a reason to come back more than once. These acts were considered the stars of the lineup.) And a movie.

On top of all this, Columbia executives decided to catch as much of the Simon & Garfunkel wave as they could while it was cresting, and they rereleased *Wednesday Morning, 3 A.M.* It reached number thirty on the pop charts, which made Paul wince because it seemed to him an inferior and out-of-order follow-up to *Sounds of Silence*.

Even worse, someone had picked up the rights to all the old Tom & Jerry recordings and the various post–"Hey Schoolgirl" recordings they had done and released them. Paul, with the backing of Columbia Records, sued the distributor and quickly had them pulled, thus preventing further distribution, but it was another clear sign that the Simon & Garfunkel feeding frenzy was getting out of control and that no one was there to stop it. As if on cue, Mort Lewis entered the fray.

Lewis had made his bones in jazz as Dave Brubeck's manager in the fifties. Living in San Francisco in the sixties, Lewis witnessed firsthand the explosion of the Kingston Trio and the commercial potential for this new style of pop folk music. The Trio signed with Capitol Records, and Lewis, at Columbia's behest, immediately began looking around for a similar band. When he saw the Brothers Four perform in a small club, he signed them on the spot by promising he could get them a recording contract at Columbia. Unfortunately for them, and for Lewis, the purist four-part harmony folk sound that was their signature quickly became passé, mauled by the big boots of the Beatles and the subsequent British Invasion.

Lewis then looked for a more contemporary group, heard Simon & Garfunkel (at, of all places, one of those Murray the K shows), went backstage, and told them what they wanted to hear, that the real tour money for them was not in multiple-act shows that demanded three and four performances a day, but in something that was still, at that time, a largely untapped source of revenue: college campus concerts. Lewis was quick to point out what the boys already knew, that doing Murray the K shows was considered promotion for their records and therefore paid them little or no money. He promised to change all that, beginning with a booking on *The Ed Sullivan Show*, which was then the ultimate venue for any musical act in America.

On January 17, 1966, Lewis made good on his promise when the newly signed Simon & Garfunkel appeared on *The Ed Sullivan Show* at the same CBS theater where Paul's father had played in the orchestras of many of the biggest television shows of the fifties. And now here he was, Paul Simon and his partner Artie, singing "I Am a Rock," with all of the song's late-adolescent self-importance that they could muster.

Three months later they appeared on *Hullabaloo,* the West Coast rock-show equivalent of Britain's *Top of the Pops,* where they lip-synched "Homeward Bound." Not long after, again as Lewis had promised, Simon & Garfunkel did their first major college concert, at Tufts University, where they performed all the songs from their first hit album and a couple from their forthcoming one. They quickly became the top live campus act in the country, usually dressed in suits and ties, or sometimes turtlenecks, capitalizing on and extending what Robert Christgau described as their "outcast visionary" personae.

On every campus they played, audiences loved them, but not the same way they did the Beatles or the Stones (neither of whom played colleges). Simon & Garfunkel's core crowd was more cerebral, overwhelmingly made up of awkward-stage-of-life boys and the kind of girls who loved them in spite of or maybe because of it. Paul remembered this about those tours:

> Simon & Garfunkel had a peculiar type of groupie. We had the poetic groupies. The girls that followed us around weren't necessarily looking to sleep with us as much as they were looking to read us their poetry or discuss literature or play their own songs. . . . I wound up going back to the room and smoking a joint and going to sleep by myself. Most of the time, sometimes not.

Everything they touched now turned to gold records. On some of the bigger tour dates, Simon & Garfunkel had a group called the Cyrkle open for them. The Cyrkle (named by John Lennon) was a guitar-driven band, led by Don Dennemann and Tom Dawes, who had come together while attending Lafayette College in Pennsylvania. They began as a frat-rock band, the Rhondells, before being signed by Beatles manager Brian Epstein, who decided they could be the American Beatles (which is how Lennon came to give them their name). Epstein managed to get them booked as the opening act on a couple of dates on the Simon & Garfunkel tour. Soon enough, Paul offered them "Red Rubber Ball," a song he had written years before and had originally done with Bruce Woodley, of the hit band the

Seekers, who had offered him one hundred pounds back in Paul's London scuffling days to collaborate on a song the Seekers could record in the band's quest for a hit. Their version suffered a quick death, but the Cyrkle's recording of "Red Rubber Ball" went to number two in America and prompted the Seekers to rerelease their version of it after their smash single soundtrack recording of "Georgy Girl."*

That April, ABC-Paramount, which still held the legal rights to a couple of Paul's earlier recordings, released "That's My Story," an old Tom & Jerry single, and it too charted, reaching number 123. Two months later "I Am a Rock," backed with "Flowers Never Bend with the Rainfall," was released, the second time "I Am a Rock" was put out on a 45. That, too, did well. And in September came "The Dangling Conversation," another song from their forthcoming album, backed with "The Big Bright Green Pleasure Machine," which reached number 25.

After this run of singles and their unbroken string of sold-out college campus appearances, on October 10, 1966, Simon & Garfunkel released their third album, *Parsley, Sage, Rosemary and Thyme*. The title of the album was a line from the opening track "Scarborough Fair/Canticle," which was, despite what the credits say, not written by Paul Simon. It was the same traditional song that Martin Carthy, Paul's friend in London, had recorded on his 1965 debut album *Martin Carthy*. "It was never my song," Carthy said later, with a fair amount of bitterness, meaning that it had never become his signature and, once it had become a hit for Simon & Garfunkel, became one of theirs.

> It was there for anybody to do. The only thing I resent is that [Paul Simon] said he wrote it. He took enormous pains to learn it when I wrote it down word for word for him. It's as

---

* Several other groups covered "Red Rubber Ball," including Eggchair, which was included in the 2004 film *Dodgeball: A True Undercover Story*; it was covered by the Diodes in 1977, and Simon & Garfunkel recorded a live version of it on the 1982 album release of their concert in Central Park.

much his song as it was mine, but his way of getting it wasn't
entirely honourable, I think.

Interestingly, Carthy and the song were also a source of inspiration for Bob Dylan during his visit to Great Britain in 1962. Dylan
at least acknowledged Carthy in the sleeve notes of *The Freewheelin'
Bob Dylan*, the album that contained Dylan's version of the song he
called "Girl from the North Country." According to Simon biographer Patrick Humphries, there was much resentment in England
and in the Greenwich Village folk scene among those who felt the
credit for the song on *Parsley, Sage, Rosemary and Thyme* should have
read "Traditional, arrangement Paul Simon." Ever since the Tom &
Jerry debacle, Paul was extremely careful about protecting his copyrights and may have felt that because the song was in the public
domain he could legally copyright his arrangement of it and collect
songwriting royalties for it. The feud between Carthy and Paul lasted
until 1998 when Paul, while performing in England, invited Carthy
onstage to perform the song with him at the Hammersmith Apollo
and graciously acknowledged Carthy's contribution to it.

The rest of the album was made up of recycled tunes, most of
them from Paul's London period, and from the opening track it
carried a sense of melancholia about it. "Scarborough Fair," with
its "remember me to her" lyrics and its minor-key melody, suggests a sense of longing, and after "Patterns" and "Cloudy" comes
"Homeward Bound," which articulates that melancholia; clearly Paul
had Kathy on his mind, or at least had her on his mind when he
wrote these songs, an echo of longing that had apparently resur-
faced during the making of the album (but apparently not enough
to get in touch with her). The album then took a slightly upbeat
turn, with "The Big Bright Green Pleasure Machine"; "The 59th
Street Bridge Song (Feelin' Groovy)," which Paul had written in his
London flat; "The Dangling Conversation," which he had written in
his bathroom and which Artie never liked, believing it was far too
pretentious (even for them); "Flowers Never Bend in the Rainfall";
"A Simple Desultory Philippic (Or How I Was Robert McNamara'd
into Submission)"; Paul's less-than-vivid parody of the current Bob
Dylan sound, "For Emily, whenever I May Find Her," which Paul

wrote in a single sitting; "A Poem on the Underground Wall," with obvious allusions to "The Sound of Silence"; and, to bring it all back home, "7 O'clock News/Silent Night," one of a very few overtly political, antiwar songs to make its way onto any Simon & Garfunkel album. Protest music was by now dead in the water, and neither Paul nor Artie nor Columbia Records wanted any real part of it, although this last cut very effectively blended a beautifully melodic version of the traditional Christmas carol "Silent Night" with the voice of a newscaster reading horrific headlines about the war in Vietnam, the civil rights struggle, and other disturbing images that played extremely well against the beauty of the Christmas song. Once again, Bob Johnston produced and Roy Halee engineered.

Eleven days after its release the boys resumed their college concert gigs, where their image as the "weird," "alienated," and "poetic" duo was made even more vivid by *Parsley, Sage, Rosemary and Thyme*. Mort Lewis shrewdly continued to burnish their antiestablishment image by withholding them from the many TV variety and talk shows that wanted them, unless they could choose their own songs and play a long, uninterrupted set. As Lewis knew all along, on those terms there would be no takers.

In one gigantic leap, it felt like, Simon & Garfunkel had become the number-one folk-rock act in America, but Paul, as ever, was keenly aware of which way the wind was currently blowing. Already harder-sounding groups were making their presence felt—English groups like the Who and Cream, which he had first heard in his London pub-crawl days, were now beginning to make solid inroads in the States. He wondered how long he and Artie could survive in that crowd, how long they could remain relevant, how long they could make a living, if not a life, out of playing the songs of, and assuming the roles of, Simon & Garfunkel.

Then something happened in Monterey, California, that changed everything again.

6

A Gathering of the Tribes

L IKE ALL SEISMIC SHIFTS IN MODERN POPULAR CULTURE, THE events that signal the beginning of something new and different also signal the end of something else. Most of the time, when commerce catches up with culture, culture moves on. Such was the case with the 1967 Monterey Pop Festival, a musical event that demonstrated in no uncertain terms how far ahead at the time culture was from incorporation and, indeed, at the same time how far behind the corporation was from the culture.

Monterey's celebration of the so-called summer of love—its cultural landmark the release of the Beatles' monumental *Sgt. Pepper's Lonely Hearts Club Band*—was one such shift that brought the suits with the deep pockets running to catch up and cash in. In that sense, there was something very new and different about what happened at

Monterey and also something very old and familiar; the festival was a leap as significant as Elvis's appearance on *Ed Sullivan*, and even before the crowd had dispersed, the corporate money behind it wanted it to look as noncommercial as possible to increase its commercial value. With rock 'n' roll especially, this was the oldest story in the book. The hustlers who sold 45s out of their trunks to record stores did not consider themselves cultural revolutionaries, no matter how liberating the music they hawked was. They saw it strictly in terms of hot product and cared only about how much they could make off of it. Behind every Elvis Presley, there was always a Colonel Parker.

Monterey wasn't the spontaneous gathering of West Coast hippies that the celebrated documentary filmmaker D. A. Pennebaker's 1968 *Monterey Pop* presents but a canny business deal that started not in the open countryside of upstate California but downstate in the business offices of Hollywood with Ben Shapiro, a small-time record packager looking for a way to make a score by figuring out how to cash in on the new cultural phenomenon of "free love." He was working with a young wannabe mover and shaker by the name of Alan Pariser, and the two came up with the idea of funding a "music mart," an event to showcase new acts, with a few bigger names sprinkled in as drawing power, a wet dream of ancillary merchandising, mostly T-shirts and posters, almost all the profits from which would go to them as a way to recoup their investment and make a few bucks.

They quickly raised fifty thousand dollars in seed money by selling their idea to the major record labels that were always looking for ways to increase sales and along the way maybe even trip over the Next Big Thing. With the money in place, Shapiro and Pariser booked the relatively inexpensive Monterey Fairgrounds for the weekend of June 16 through June 18. The San Francisco alternative newspaper *The Oracle* had first announced the event, cleverly dubbing it "A Gathering of the Tribes." It was a great name, and it stuck.

The first "tribe member" signed to Monterey was also the unlikeliest (but the easiest to get): Indian sitar player Ravi Shankar, a friend of George Harrison. The second addition was not a performer, but equally if not more important: Derek Taylor, the Beatles' former publicist, who had a well-deserved reputation as the hippest and smartest PR man on the scene. His job for the "gathering" was a familiar one for him: to preserve the innocence of the event while helping to develop a highly workable business model that would result in a fat return on the investors' money.

Taylor's joining the project doomed the original notion of a "free love" gathering. He quickly put together an artistic committee—a "steering committee" as he called it—made up of the top names in pop and rock, including head Papa John Phillips, Paul McCartney, Brian Wilson (who, despite being on the steering board, felt that the Beach Boys would look too awkward and old-hat to appear with the rest of the acts on the bill), Brian Jones, savvy PR man and comanager of the Rolling Stones Andrew Loog Oldham, Smokey Robinson, Donovan's music attorney Abe Somer, and Paul Simon.

Phillips, always sharp and with a nose for money (and its antithesis, cocaine), quickly took charge of the committee and brought in Mamas & Papas producer Lou Adler to help organize the event. Simon, excited by the prospects of the event, was especially adamant that it be modeled after the jazz festivals of Newport and Monterey and run on a nonprofit basis.

Adler was the founder and president of Dunhill Records and also its primary producer, and the label was the home of the Mamas & the Papas, whose string of hit singles and albums had made Phillips and Adler mansion-rich. Adler was a man of talent and experience. Before the Mamas & the Papas, he had worked his magic with Jan and Dean, Sam Cooke, Johnny Rivers, Barry McGuire, and Scott McKenzie. He was a veteran who knew his way around the scenes. The committee unanimously agreed that Adler and Phillips would be cochairs and that Derek Taylor would also head the publicity division.

Adler, nothing if not commercially attuned, quickly outmaneuvered Shapiro and Pariser with Phillips, Paul Simon, Johnny Rivers, and record producer Terry Melcher putting up equal sums of money, and succeeded in totally removing whatever remained of them from their own project and assumed total control and last-word approval over any and all aspects of the festival. Adler believed that Shapiro's vision of a "free" showcase for new talent was impractical and that sales of T-shirts would not produce a decent profit. Instead, he wanted to headline his own roster of talent along with other established

Top-Forty bands to ensure a big gate. In Adler's view, charging admission was where any real money was going to be made.

Soon after that, Adler, Phillips, and Taylor met with the Monterey city fathers and somehow convinced them that despite their revised plan, the festival was still intended as a charitable and educational event. Even as all of that was taking place, a bitter disagreement erupted between the San Francisco–based bands, who considered Monterey their turf, and the L.A. music industry reps. The SF boys fancied themselves the counterculture's real thing and had signed on from the beginning when Shapiro and Pariser had approached them with their original concept. Now they bitterly resented the usurpation of the festival by the L.A. group, whom they (rightly) believed were interested in profit. Led by the Grateful Dead, the SF bands vowed to make it as difficult as possible for Adler and company to pull off what had turned from a small fair into a huge spectacle.

Finding himself up against the SF contingent's brick wall, Adler knew that he couldn't get rid of them because they were among the biggest draws in the region, but also that he couldn't give in to their demands that the festival remain nonprofit. A frustrated Adler finally turned to New Yorker Paul Simon, who he considered was from a neutral turf and whose reputation was delicately balanced between commercial hit maker and purist folk-rocker, and asked him to serve as the committee's ambassador of goodwill to try to make peace with San Francisco's long-haired hippie bands.

Paul packed his bags and went up north to pay a personal call to the Dead's famous house on Haight-Ashbury, which Paul described as the spookiest place he'd ever seen, and where, during his visit, perhaps in an effort to ingratiate himself, or just out of his curiosity, he was offered a chance to try LSD for the first time. Although he accepted the gift of the tabs, he did not take acid that night, but even so, it gave him enormous credibility among the Dead, and that alone signaled something of a breakthrough in the negotiations. By the end of the weekend Paul had succeeded in assuring a skeptical Jerry Garcia and the others that Adler's heart was in the right place and that what was good for Monterey was also good for San Francisco's rock bands.

Having proved himself capable of getting along with the byzantine hierarchy of Haight-Ashbury's counterculture leadership, Paul convinced the Dead to go along with Adler's proposals. The other SF bands then fell into place.

While in San Francisco, Paul began an intense relationship with Denise Kaufman, his first real girlfriend since Kathy Chitty. Kaufman was the ex-girlfriend of another Bay Area resident, Jann Wenner, who at this point had yet to publish his first issue of *Rolling Stone*. The always intense Wenner, struggling to break into publishing with his magazine concept, was infuriated that Kaufman had taken up with, of all things, a rock 'n' roll *performer*, even though he and Kaufman were no longer seeing each other. As if trying to get even, Wenner, who was assigned to cover the festival for the British music publication *Melody Maker*, later wrote enthusiastically about how Jimi Hendrix had smashed his guitar better than Pete Townshend, but he put the blade between Paul's shoulders when he wrote that "Paul Simon will not be remembered as an outstanding lyricist." (Later that same year, in 1967, Wenner launched *Rolling Stone* and continued to punish Paul and Simon & Garfunkel by refusing to cover the band in his magazine. It would take years for this rift to heal.)

In the end, all the original bands that had signed on with Shapiro and Pariser played Adler's festival, although in the hugely successful movie, very few of the SF bands were included, with much of the footage devoted, not surprisingly, to the Mamas & the Papas; Shankar, who closed the film (but at the festival the closing act was the Mamas & the Papas); the Who; Jimi Hendrix, one of two unknowns to emerge from the festival a star; and Janis Joplin, another unknown singer, who, thanks to her astounding performance, was immediately signed to a record deal by Clive Davis, the new head of Columbia Records. Davis was one of several label heads who attended the festival at the urging of Lou Adler, who promised they would find more new talent there on one stage than anywhere else in America.

Simon & Garfunkel went on relatively early Friday, at 9:30, to close the first night, because a curfew had been imposed by the San

Francisco police as one of the conditions that Adler had agreed to in order to get them, yet another group vying for power, to allow the festival to take place. Paul and Artie did "Homeward Bound," "At the Zoo," "For Emily, whenever I May Find Her," "The Sound of Silence," "Benedictus," and "Punky's Dilemma," and for their final number, a rousing version of a song they normally didn't perform, "Feelin' Groovy," arranged in a gorgeous, rich rondo of "ba-dah-dah-dahs" that showed off their immaculate harmonies, all of it underscored by Paul's always precise fingerpicking. "Feelin' Groovy" was the only Simon & Garfunkel song to make it into the eventual movie of the festival, but it was enough to help broaden their appeal and prove they were closer to pop than folk and capable of playing before large, noncollegiate audiences. At Monterey, as part of the backstage machinations leading up to the festival's successful run, Paul had proved to be a skillful negotiator and an important part of the production team. Onstage, together with Artie, he made a crucial commercial leap forward for Simon & Garfunkel.

The entire festival confirmed Adler's vision of a huge financial windfall, with more than fifty thousand paying customers showing up for each day's program, almost all of whom bought food and souvenirs. To maintain peace with the San Francisco contingency, as promised, Adler saw to it that considerable sums of money were donated to various local and national charities. Paul had all of his profits from the festival, approximately fifty thousand dollars, donated to a Harlem-based project that taught guitar to children.

Although it was never the intention on anyone's part to do so, Monterey had played a key role in changing the style and presentation of rock 'n' roll. The cultural fallout from the show was swift and powerful. News of the three days and nights of continual music traveled quickly, with reporting of the event crossing into the mainstream media. It was the first time that such a grandly conceived rock festival had ever taken place, and it served as a forerunner for Woodstock, a landmark all its own.

Directly off their appearance at Monterey, Simon & Garfunkel were booked for a return visit to the enormously popular and influential CBS weekly prime-time show *The Smothers Brothers Comedy Hour*, an appearance that further established them as a major mainstream act. In every way, then, 1967 was huge for Simon & Garfunkel.

But 1968 would prove even bigger, twelve months that would turn them into the hottest performing act in contemporary rock. As great as they were onstage, they benefited enormously from the dissolution of the Mamas and the Papas, the end of the touring phase of the Beatles, Bob Dylan's withdrawal from the scene after his motorcycle accident, and the drug-fueled disarray of the Rolling Stones. There was all that, and a couple of songs, with one unforgettable hook that sounded like a cross between a sneeze and a tease—*coo-coo-ca-choo*—that Paul reluctantly agreed to provide for an improbable film comedy about a young, disconnected, and disenchanted college grad who is seduced by an older woman and then sleeps with her daughter.

7

The Graduate

BOB DYLAN'S SO-CALLED MYSTERIOUS MOTORCYCLE ACCIDENT in July 1966 near his home in Woodstock, New York, brought the same kind of near hysteria to his fans that the untimely death of James Dean did to his fans eleven years earlier; the only difference being that Dylan was not actually dead, nor, for that matter, all that seriously injured. Later on, it would be suggested by more than one biographer that the accident presented a timely opportunity for Dylan to remove himself from the spotlight for a while and away from the irresistible excesses that had not just burned him out but nearly killed him.

By the time Dylan, until then American rock's primal voice and spiritual leader—the "voice of his generation"—stepped back, the music scene had removed itself as well, away from New York City, that is, Dylan's and rock 'n' roll's East Coast locale, to Los Angeles and San Francisco. If L.A.'s cultural influence outlasted the Bay Area's, it was due in large part to the self-destructiveness the drug culture had brought to Frisco's bands, while over the course of the next few years L.A. would serve up an appetizing and commercially viable brand of soft rock whose main features had been largely abandoned by the sociopolitical musical scene of the sixties: melody, harmony, and musicality, and, most remarkably, a complete lack of political protest. Dylan's abandoning the competition, as it were, sparked a shift in geographical and musical tastes that would have far-reaching consequences for all successful rock acts, none more than Simon & Garfunkel.

Dylan may have left the scene, but his reputation remained and cast a long shadow, and the more those he left behind tried to step out of it, the darker and more intense they and their music became. Paul Simon was widely considered one of the few legitimate challengers to Dylan's vacated throne (if not strictly as a rock poet in the *Like a Rolling Stone* vein then surely as a pop star stylist à la *Positively 4th Street*). But if he was to succeed in this lofty ambition he knew he would have to do it as a one-man band, not as one half of a duo. As long as he kept his partner, he was never going to be recognized as an individual or even a songwriter. With Simon & Garfunkel, most fans had no idea, and couldn't have cared less, who did the writing and who didn't. They were a unit, and Paul had come to the unpleasant realization that as long as they were together, there was nothing he could do about his dilemma.

After Monterey, Columbia Records wanted more new product from the duo, and they wanted it now. As the "summer of love" faded into memory, protest music, antiwar songs, and calls for revolution fell away, not because no one cared about Vietnam, but because those who did were less inclined to buy music from the likes of Phil Ochs and his fellow protest merchants. Two years before, the charts welcomed songs like Barry McGuire's novelty "Eve of Destruction," but by the second half of 1967 that type of music was dead in the corporate waters. Columbia, Dylan's label, wanted simple, sweet, laid-back songs from its biggest-selling mainstream act, Simon & Garfunkel.

While they waited for another album, the label released several singles from *Parsley, Sage, Rosemary and Thyme*, including "Fakin' It" backed with "You Don't Know Where Your Interest Lies" (the B side, released only as a single); "Scarborough Fair/Canticle," backed with "April Come She Will"; and a single track, "The Star Carol," which was included on *A Very Special Christmas*, a Columbia promotional album created exclusively for Grant's discount store chain. Every one of these 45s sold at least a half million units.

In January 1968 Simon & Garfunkel did a Kraft Music Hall special called *Three for Tonight*, during which they performed ten songs, mostly from *Parsley, Sage, Rosemary and Thyme*. The show was hosted by Victor Borge and featured Nancy Wilson (the third member of the "Three"). Paul, meanwhile, continued working on songs for their next album, which he wanted to call *Bookends*. No one knew it at the time, but Paul believed it would be the last album he would make with Artie before breaking up the act, a fitting "bookend" to the musical career of Simon & Garfunkel.

At the same time that Paul and Artie were promoting *Parsley, Sage, Rosemary and Thyme* and preparing to record *Bookends*, a young comic turned director by the name of Mike Nichols was about to make a second feature film as a follow-up to his audacious debut, the award-winning and groundbreaking adaptation of Edward Albee's immensely successful 1963 play, *Who's Afraid of Virginia Woolf*. This time, he wanted to go in a completely different direction.

Nichols had begun his career as one half of the comic duo Mike Nichols and Elaine May, their act an outgrowth of the theater work they both specialized in when they attended the University of Chicago. Both Nichols and May had a flair for comedy, and while still fully matriculated undergraduates, they each joined the Compass Players, an off-campus performance group that was the nucleus for what would later become the seminal improvisational group Second City and, still later, television's *Saturday Night Live*.

Nichols was the child of a German mother and a Russian Jewish father who had immigrated to America just before the start of World War II, and he grew up in an atmosphere of sophisticated Old World European intellectualism. May was a native of Philadelphia, whose parents were performers and directors in the local Yiddish theater.

The comedy duo they formed thrived on the successful blend of his wit and her slapstick. When they graduated from the University of Chicago, they took their act to New York City, where their humor fit easily into the improvisational, jazzy rhythms that were the heartbeat of Greenwich Village in 1960.

Their shows quickly became the talk of the town, and the "evenings" they put on in small clubs became the hottest and most difficult ticket to get. By October 1960, less than a year after arriving in New York, they were set to open on Broadway, in *An Evening with Mike Nichols and Elaine May*. The show drew raves from the critics and lines for tickets that snaked around the block. The success of *An Evening with Mike Nichols and Elaine May* established them as major theatrical stars.

However, by the time the show closed in July 1961, the two were barely talking to each other and ready to dissolve the partnership. The real-life tensions between the two performers had worked for them onstage, putting a comic edge to their routines. Offstage they had developed a mutual antipathy.

On his own, Nichols quickly found work as an actor, first, of all places, in Elaine May's original Broadway-bound play *A Matter of Position*. She may not have been able to work alongside him onstage, but she respected his talent. However, during rehearsals they fought constantly, and before the show even opened on Broadway, Nichols quit. Shortly after, Broadway producer Arnold Saint-Subber, who admired Nichols's stage presence and ability to create a scene out of the merest of physical gestures, urged Nichols to try his hand at directing. That led to several seasons of his staging successful Broadway productions, several by the equally witty and equally verbal Neil Simon, who proved a much better fit for Nichols than May did. In 1963 Nichols directed Simon's *Barefoot in the Park*, which made stars out of its unknown leads, Robert Redford and Elizabeth Ashley. That spring Nichols won the coveted Tony Award as best director.

In the audience one night was producer Larry Turman, who had recently read Charles Webb's *The Graduate*, a funny and smart novel of alienation and affection and thought if a movie could be made of it, it would be as close as anyone could ever get to making a film out of *Catcher in the Rye*, the sardonic novel by the reclusive J. D. Salinger, who adamantly refused to sell to Hollywood. Even after Webb's novel failed to catch on with the public, Turman was determined to find a way to film it.

After several failed attempts to have a screenplay developed—writers just couldn't find the handle of the story—Turman sent Nichols the original novel. He read it and immediately saw the link to both Holden Caulfield in the novel's main character, Benjamin Braddock, and, even more important, to himself. The book had the same type of clever razor's-edge humor that Nichols and May had had onstage and developed into an art form. He agreed to direct the film and help develop it, but when Turman tried to get a deal, even with Nichols attached, he was, not surprisingly, turned down by every major studio. As far as the studios were concerned, Nichols meant nothing to the bankability of any production because he was out of Broadway, not Hollywood, and directors were rarely able to make that crossover successfully. In addition, Turman had no real, workable script for his film.

Nichols, tired of waiting for *The Graduate* to get a green light, returned to Broadway to direct Murray Schisgal's *Luv*, a three-character comedy that proved to be another smash and won Nichols his second Tony Award as best director. At the same time, Jack Warner acquired the rights to film *Who's Afraid of Virginia Woolf*, starring that madcap comedy team Richard Burton and Elizabeth Taylor—inspired casting, to say the least. As it happened, Burton had been on Broadway, in *Camelot*, at the same time as *An Evening with Mike Nichols and Elaine May*, and he and Nichols had become good friends. When Warner was having trouble finding a director for the daring screenplay adaptation by the brilliant Ernest Lehman, both Burton and Taylor recommended Nichols. Warner, which had always worried that the film might be too downbeat for general audiences, leapt at the idea, believing Nichols could find the laughs in the drama. (Apparently Warner had no idea the original play was fraught with laughter and was funnier than most comedies ever are on Broadway, right up to its unexpectedly gruesome final twist. The caustic wit of its comedy makes its dramatic undertow all the more powerful.) Nichols jumped at the chance and told Turman he would have to wait for at least one picture and could use the extra time to pull the production together.

Eventually, Nichols's film of *Who's Afraid of Virginia Woolf* broke box-office records and was nominated for thirteen Academy Awards, including Best Director for his first attempt at film. Now he was suddenly hot in Hollywood, and Turman was able to make a deal for *The Graduate* with Joe Levine, who wanted it for his Embassy Pictures, making it an independent, rather than studio-driven, film, one of the key reasons it looks and sounds the way it does. In 1967 no studio would have been comfortable with the level of sexual tension that permeates *The Graduate*.

Nor would anyone think to make a movie about an aimless, introverted, well-to-do college graduate with a clean-shaven face and short hair whose angst weighed a ton but whose demeanor was slight to the point of near invisibility. Or that such a movie could be a hit. At a time when the youth-oriented pop culture was headed for a new high, *The Graduate*, with its clever, intense, and extremely witty screen adaptation by Buck Henry, was as much a contrast to the "big" films that year—William Wyler's Streisand-fueled *Funny Girl*, Stanley Kubrick's massive yet intimate *2001: A Space Odyssey*, and Carol Reed's musical extravaganza *Oliver!*—as Simon & Garfunkel's softer sound was to the sounds of the Rolling Stones, the Beatles, and the Who.

During the 1967 filming of *The Graduate*, Nichols rented a house in Hollywood that had once belonged to Cole Porter and tried to immerse himself in everything that related to Benjamin Braddock's world. First thing every morning he would get up and turn on the phonograph to listen to what had lately become his favorite group, Simon & Garfunkel. He especially liked *Sounds of Silence* and *Parsley, Sage, Rosemary and Thyme*, which he would play all the way through before leaving the house for the short drive to the Paramount lot, where the interiors of the film were being shot. At night, when he'd return from that day's shoot, he would again turn on the phonograph and listen to Simon & Garfunkel until he fell asleep.

As Nichols later remembered, "My brother had sent me the album *Parsley, Sage, Rosemary and Thyme*, and I played it every morning. About the second week, I said to myself, 'Schmuck, this is your score!'"

It should come as no surprise that Nichols felt a connection to Paul Simon's music. Both were Jewish and the children of European immigrants. Both had enjoyed early success with a partner with whom relations offstage easily became fraught. Both had gone out solo, and both had been drawn to the Village of the early sixties by the intensity of its creative pull. Both were, in a sense, creative misfits: Nichols wanted to direct movies before he had ever filmed a single bit of footage, and Simon wanted to be a rock star even though he didn't look the part. And each in his own way perfectly reflected the personality of Benjamin Braddock, especially as seen through the characterization of him by the then unknown Dustin Hoffman. Hoffman had the comic precision of Nichols and the physical schlubbiness of Paul Simon, and Benjamin, as played by Dustin Hoffman, bore more than a slight physical resemblance to Paul.

Nichols met with Columbia Records and asked its chairman, Clive Davis, if he could use some Simon & Garfunkel music in his film. Davis was immediately receptive to the idea: "When I heard about the project I felt there was real potential for a best-selling soundtrack album. Soundtracks do not always do well; their success often depends more on the extent of the movie's appeal than on the quality of the music itself. Still, when Embassy asked if we wanted the soundtrack rights, I grabbed them; the movie had all the ingredients of a big box-office hit."

Which is precisely why Paul Simon was wary about any involvement in it. At the age of twenty-seven, he had finally made it into the upper echelon of rock, after a decade of one-shot wonders, hard misses, and spectacular hits, and he had done it, he believed, by maintaining his integrity via his songwriting, which, he felt, had kept him spiritually closer to Bob Dylan than to, say, Bobby Darin. Movies meant selling out, Paul believed, until he agreed to meet with Nichols. Impressed with Nichols's manner and his quick wit, and with his finely tuned bullshit detector on full alert (detecting bullshit was, after all, what the whole film was all about), Paul read the script and consented to write one or two new songs for the film.

By now Paul and Artie had chosen William Morris as their booking agency. They had been brought to it by Wally Amos, who was a friend of Tom Wilson's. (Amos would soon leave the agency and open his own management company on the West Coast. He would later gain fame as the founder and distributor of Famous Amos cookies.)

At the time, William Morris was one of the most synergistic agencies and was always looking for ways to intermingle their clients—in other words, put musicians with moviemakers. The Morris people thought this would be a great opportunity to get Simon & Garfunkel into the lucrative field of movie music—soundtracks were big business—even if Nichols was not a client (he was represented by Sam Cohn at ICM). After Amos left the agency to start his own management business, Simon & Garfunkel were handed to the venerable Leonard Hirshan, one of the most powerful William Morris agents, whose roster included some of the biggest stars in the business, including Anne Bancroft, who happened to be one of the stars of *The Graduate.* Hirshan negotiated a deal with Embassy for Paul that paid him $25,000 to submit three new songs to Nichols and Turman, two of which they could choose and use in the movie, with any soundtrack royalties to be paid at point of sale.

By now, of course, Nichols had already begun cutting sequences in his head to "The Sound of Silence" and "Scarborough Fair" as a way of trying to find the rhythm of his sequences and his comedy.

A couple of weeks after the deal was struck, Paul gave Nichols two new songs, "Punky's Dilemma" and "Overs," neither of which Nichols liked for the movie.

At a meeting with Paul and Artie he asked them if they had anything else. According to Nichols, "They said no, then they went off and talked for a few minutes, came back and sang *Mrs. Robinson.* I looked at them and said, 'Where the hell did that come from?' Paul told me they were working on a song called *Mrs. Roosevelt.* They filled in with *dee de dee dee de dee dee dee* because there was no verse yet, but I liked even that."

Artie remembered that magic moment a little differently:

"Paul had been working on what is now 'Mrs. Robinson,'" Artie later recalled. "But there was no name in it and we'd just fill in with any three-syllable name. And because of the character in the picture we just began using the name 'Mrs. Robinson' to fit . . . and one day we were sitting around with Mike talking abut ideas for another song. And I said 'What about

A publicity photo
of Tom & Jerry,
circa 1957.

A sixties poster advertising
the Murray the K
revue in which
Simon & Garfunkel
appeared in rotation.

Paul Simon and Al Kooper in the studio. They were childhood friends growing up in Queens.

Simon & Garfunkel on the *Ed Sullivan Show*, 1966.

One of a series of photos taken for the cover of *Bookends*.

Simon in the forefront; unhappy Garfunkel in the background.

From the photo
sessions for the
cover of *Paul
Simon*, 1972.

Paul Simon and his son Harper, circa 1972.

Artie's "surprise" appearance on *Saturday Night Live*, October 18, 1975.

Paul Simon with Carrie Fisher and her father, the singer Eddie Fisher.

Simon & Garfunkel performing live in Central Park, September 19, 1981.

The night "We Are the World" was recorded in Hollywood, January 28, 1985 (left to right: Lionel Richie, Daryl Hall, Stevie Wonder, Quincy Jones, Paul Simon).

Paul, unplugged and solo, March 4, 1992.

Ruben Blades, Paul Simon, Ednita Nazario, and Marc Anthony in a 1998 publicity shot for *The Capeman*.

Paul Simon and the Gospel Gathering, November 11, 2007 (clockwise from top: Luther Vandross, Andrae Crouch, Paul Simon, and Jennifer Holliday).

"Mrs. Robinson."' Mike shot to his feet. 'You have a song called "Mrs. Robinson" and you haven't even shown it to me?' So we explained the working title and sang it for him. And then Mike froze it for the picture as 'Mrs. Robinson.'"

As it turned out, only two lines of actual word lyrics appear in the film, about Mrs. Robinson and Jesus's love for her.

During production, Nichols realized he had gaps in the sound-track that needed to be filled in, most notably in the long montage when Benjamin passes the summer swimming in the family pool and sleeping with Mrs. Robinson, culminating in one of the film's great edits where Benjamin climbs onto his raft in the pool and winds up in bed on top of Mrs. Robinson. During the long and difficult sixteen-day editing of this sequence, Nichols and his editor, Sam O'Steen, used "The Sound of Silence" and "April Come She Will" as their rhythmic guide, a metronome of sorts, to make it work. According to Nichols, one of the role models he used was Bernard Herrmann's score for *Psycho*. He got what Hitchcock had tried to do—connect the visual dots for the audience using the lead pencil of music.

When they finally finished, Nichols decided he wanted to put those two songs on the soundtrack the same way he had used them to help sequence the shots, and to add "The Sound of Silence" in the opening credit sequence as well, when Benjamin's passivity—a personality trait that became a crucial part of the film—is brilliantly illustrated by watching him stand on an airport lateral mover, not moving but being pulled along by it, moving but not moving.

Despite his clever use of the songs, Joe Levine, who controlled the purse strings, remained adamantly opposed to putting pop tunes in the film that had no direct relation to the story, but he changed his mind when he saw the footage of the opening credit sequence.

Clive Davis, meanwhile, wanted to have a soundtrack album in the stores the same day the film opened, but Paul rejected that plan. There was only one snippet of a new Simon & Garfunkel song in the final cut of the film, and two older songs, which together would hardly constitute a soundtrack. Fearing that stretching the material into a whole album would offend his fans and compromise his own integrity, Paul remained firmly opposed to the idea.

Davis, however, refused to take Paul's no as the final word. "Are you *sure* there's not enough material?" he asked. "This could be an absolutely giant album."

Again Paul said no.

Davis then sent Ed Kleban, the Columbia A&R man who was, at the time, in charge of soundtrack and Broadway show albums, to see the film and give his opinion as to whether there was enough there for an album. Kleban came back and told Davis that he agreed with Paul. "There just isn't enough music. You can't come out with an album that has only fifteen or eighteen minutes of songs from older albums on it."

Davis called Mort Lewis to argue his case but came up against the same stone wall. Lewis repeated Paul's position, that the boys felt strongly that an album had to have at least eleven cuts; anything less would be an insult their fans. Davis emphasized that this was to be a soundtrack album that would likely reach an audience much wider than they already had. When it became clear that Lewis was not going to budge, Davis called Paul to try one last time to get him to change his mind.

They had a long talk, during which Davis assured Paul the album would be released and packaged strictly as a soundtrack, that the cover would be a scene from the movie rather than a picture of Simon & Garfunkel, with a credit stating that the album contained "Songs by Paul Simon, performed by Simon & Garfunkel." Finally, Davis guaranteed Paul that its release would not cause even a single day's delay of their highly anticipated new album, which would contain the full version of "Mrs. Robinson" if that was okay.

"Look," Paul said. "We've been working on the *Bookends* album a long time, we love it, and we think it's a major creative breakthrough. We don't want to wait six months to release it." Again Davis assured Paul that that wouldn't happen. Furthermore, he suggested to Paul what might happen if both albums hit the top of the charts simultaneously, something that hadn't been done since the Beatles exploded in 1964, when every album they made, including the soundtracks to their movies, went through the roof. After talking it over again with Artie, Paul agreed to a January 21, 1968, release of the soundtrack, a month after the film opened. In addition to Paul's songs, sung by

Simon & Garfunkel, the album contained several tracks of incidental music that was also used in the film, composed by Dave Grusin and produced by Teo Macero.

As Davis had predicted, *The Graduate* soundtrack album and the release ten weeks later of *Bookends* (April 3) fed off each other, for an initial combined sales figure of over five million units.

Nonetheless, neither Paul nor Artie was happy with Columbia Records *or* with Davis. To begin with, Davis had wanted to raise the list price of *Bookends* one dollar (above the then standard retail price), which especially outraged Simon. Davis's rationale was that the label was including a large poster with the album and the extra dollar was needed to cover the cost. Paul laughed at that explanation. He knew that Davis wanted to beef up the label's flagging bottom line, and charging a premium on what was sure to be that year's best-selling Columbia album was the way he intended to do it.

Davis, for his part, was offended by what he perceived as their lack of gratitude for what he believed was his role in turning them into superstars (the actual music itself seemed, to Davis, almost beside the point).

This much was true: after the two albums were released and went through the roof, Simon & Garfunkel became the biggest duo in rock, not just in America but all over the world. Paul was pursued by dozens of producers and directors wanting either to use his songs in their movie or to have him write original songs for them. Among those who came calling was Franco Zeffirelli, who wanted Paul to write the music for Zeffirelli's upcoming movie about Saint Francis of Assisi, *Brother Sun, Sister Moon*. Paul turned him down. John Schlesinger wanted him to do the music for *Midnight Cowboy*, starring Dustin Hoffman, who had since become a friend of Paul's. Paul turned him down as well.* Hoffman was slated to do a Broadway show called *Jimmy Shine*. The producers asked for two original songs from

---

* Schlesinger eventually chose "Everybody's Talkin'," written by Fred Neil and performed by Harry Nilsson, and the song reappears throughout *Midnight Cowboy*. Other songs considered for the movie included Nilsson's own "I Guess the Lord Must Be in New York City," Randy Newman's "Cowboy," and, reportedly, Bob Dylan's "Lay Lady Lay." Warren Zevon's "He Quit Me" was also on the soundtrack.

Paul. No. Leonard Bernstein approached him about collaborating on a sacred mass. That offer he couldn't refuse, but after a few weeks of working with Bernstein, Paul withdrew from the project, finding it perhaps too far afield from his comfort zone.

Davis, meanwhile, not wanting to risk losing his best-selling act, struck a compromise with the boys: he would kill the price increase and give them a higher royalty rate if they agreed to a contract extension. After much negotiation, Paul and Artie agreed to the new royalty rate and the contract extension.

Bookends became Simon & Garfunkel's best-selling album to date, thematically and musically reflecting the duo's growth and development as singers, songwriters, and makers of exquisitely listenable pop/rock. The second side featured only two original songs that had not already been released as singles, in this era of radio-play-means-everything. *Bookends*, like the Beatles' 1967 LP, the innovative, massive, and mind-bogglingly gorgeous *Sgt. Pepper's Lonely Hearts Club Band*, was a "concept album." After *Sgt. Pepper*, concept albums became the de rigueur long form of recorded rock music presentation. Several major groups, including the Byrds (*Sweetheart of the Rodeo*), the Rolling Stones (*Their Satanic Majesties Request*), and Iron Butterfly (*In-A-Gadda-Da-Vida*), all had at least one, although none except *Bookends* enjoyed anything like the success of the Beatles (who were already abandoning the form after the comparative failure of *Magical Mystery Tour*).

Paul, feeling especially auteurist in the Dylan style of the day, saw himself as the "author" of an album-size work that functioned at once as a personal and an artistic statement; ideally this loosely autobiographical series of songs would also become commercially successful. Working with Roy Halee as his engineer, Paul played the studio like a guitar.

Even before he had begun writing it, Paul had told Artie, "I'm going to start writing a whole side of an album—a cycle of songs. I want the early ones to be about youth and the last song to be about old age, and I want the feel of each song to fit." John Simon was credited for production assistance on "Save the Life of My Child," the album's opening cut after a Moody Blues–like "Bookends Theme" overture. John Simon recalled:

> I was learning on the job, and so were they. We had Bob Moog, who had invented the Moog synthesizer, the first model of which was as big as a small car. So on "Save The Life of My Child," the bass line is me playing the Moog synthesizer and Bob Moog was in the studio showing us how to get these sounds and things.

The dramatic "Save the Life of My Child" is a beautifully conceived mosaic of street life that in many ways anticipates Paul's 1998 Broadway show *The Capeman*, with its drugs, violence, and mother-and-child life-and-death drama. A close listening to the song reveals an even stronger biographical link—Simon & Garfunkel can be heard singing "The Sound of Silence" within the cacophony of sounds at the end of the song. The next track, "America," creates a cinematic vista that tells of the singer's search for a literal and physical America that seems to have disappeared, along with the country's beauty and ideals. "America" is as strong a protest song as any that came out of the sixties (with Kathy making yet another appearance, this time as the singer's companion, which links the song autobiographically to "Homeward Bound"). "Overs" appears to take a leap forward in time, to the dissolution of a marriage, a disintegration of love that may also be about Kathy. "Voices," Artie's aural concoction, is by far the weakest track on the album. Side 1 concludes with "Old Friends," an imagined meeting of two old friends looking back on their youth, a kind of pledge (or wish) that they might stay together forever.

Side 2 opens with an entr'acte of the *Bookends* theme and then sharply changes course with "Fakin' It," a throwback to Paul's earlier songs of alienation and distrust (and, as some have suggested, his relationship with Artie). A more elaborate reworking of "Punky's Dilemma," which had been left out of *The Graduate*, follows, and then comes a fuller version of "Mrs. Robinson," which became an enormous hit single and would go on to win two richly deserved Grammys for Simon & Garfunkel and Roy Halee—one for Best Record of the

Year, the first time a rock 'n' roll song would win that honor, and the other for Best Contemporary Pop Performance by a Duo or Group (the album soundtrack won another one for Paul for Best Original Score Written for a Motion Picture). "Mrs. Robinson," with its wild range of references, including, famously, Joe DiMaggio, gave the album another layer of autobiographical reflection, via Paul's lifelong devotion to the New York Yankees. Also in the song was an explicit homage to the Beatles: The "coo-coo-ca-choo" from "Mrs. Robinson" is the same "coo-coo-ca-choo" from "I Am the Walrus." Next came "A Hazy Shade of Winter," and the album's conclusion, "At the Zoo," which completes the "cycle of life," a childlike song he intended to turn into a children's book.*

Without question, *Bookends* was Simon & Garfunkel's most accomplished album to date, the best produced and a breakthrough in terms of Paul's songwriting, a record that would stand the test of time and actually get better when the backdrop of *The Graduate* eventually faded from memory. Paul agreed, telling *Playboy*, "*Bookends* was our first serious piece of work, I'd say. I still like the song 'America.' 'Mrs. Robinson' is a little dated now, but 'Where have you gone, Joe DiMaggio?' is an interesting line for a song that has nothing to do with Joe DiMaggio."

---

* Paul and Artie were asked to perform "Mrs. Robinson" live at the Eleventh Annual Grammy Awards, telecast nationally on May 31, 1969, from the Beverly Hilton Hotel. At the time, the Grammys were not considered by younger audiences to be a meaningful award, because of the Grammy organization's attitude toward rock 'n' roll (most of the voters were from the Frank Sinatra generation). After several meetings, Simon & Garfunkel agreed to make a video out of "Mrs. Robinson" for the show (the video had them romping around Yankee Stadium—"Where have you gone, Joe DiMaggio") rather than using excerpts from *The Graduate*. The other nominees for Record of the Year were "Hey Jude" by the Beatles, "Harper Valley P.T.A." by Jeannie C. Riley, "Honey" by Bobby Goldsboro, and "Wichita Lineman" by Glen Campbell. The other nominees for Contemporary Pop Duo or Group were "Hey Jude," "Child Is the Father of the Man" by Blood, Sweat & Tears, "Fool on the Hill" by Sergio Mendes, "Goin' Out of My Head/Can't Take My Eyes Off of You" by the Lettermen, and "Woman, Woman" by Gary Puckett & the Union Gap. Nichols went on to win an Oscar for Best Director for *The Graduate*, but "Mrs. Robinson" was ineligible for Oscar consideration because, according to Academy rules, a Best Song had to be written exclusively for the film in which it appeared. Which, of course, it was.

Indeed, with *Bookends*, for the first time Paul had the opportunity and, thanks to Columbia, the production budget to show off his maturity as a songwriter and a singer, and as an uncredited producer. *Rolling Stone's Record Review* called *Bookends* "a kind of snapshot album of American life in the late Sixties." And while Garfunkel's songs and voice were moving center stage, his harmonies were being slowly pushed to the back of the bus. The delicate vocal balance that first thrust Simon & Garfunkel into the spotlight was breaking down, and without it there was no longer any need to remain together.

As 1968 came to a close, Simon & Garfunkel were at the top of their game, two princes of contemporary music as popular as the Beatles and the Stones. And yet, before anyone else had even the slightest inkling of it, either at the label or in the listening audience, Paul wanted to break up the act and go solo. To him, *Bookends* was the end of Simon & Garfunkel.

8

A Time It Was

IN THE LESS THAN THREE AND A HALF YEARS BETWEEN OCTOBER 1964 and March 1968 Simon & Garfunkel had recorded four studio albums and *The Graduate* soundtrack and sold a total of more than six million units. They had placed nine singles in the *Billboard* Top Thirty, including two number ones, and had become one of the most sought-after concert acts in the world. Whenever and wherever they played live, they received 90 percent of the box-office gross against an already hefty guarantee. By the end of 1968 Paul and Artie were both very rich young men, and their lifestyle reflected this new wealth.

Paul purchased a one-bedroom high-rise apartment on New York's tony Upper East Side, overlooking the river, about a block from Gracie Mansion, the mayor's official home. Paul kept the place sparsely decorated, with rose-orange wall-to-wall carpeting and a giant hobbyhorse its main item of furniture. To one interviewer allowed into his sanctum Paul explained his current way of living like this: "I don't like to waste time on food, clothing, shelter, possessions—I don't even own a car." This was a far cry from the kid with the cherry-red Impala who liked to bomb around Queens. Quietly, at the same time, however, he acquired a large Long Island estate.

Still, as far as the public was concerned, Paul fit perfectly into the role of unpretentious aesthete with a professed lack of interest in all things material, living on an allowance of seventy-five dollars a week from his business manager, fortified with a stack of credit cards.

Part of the reason for Paul's low-key public image was his desire to reflect what he believed was inside of him, or more accurately, what he wanted to be inside. He resisted being a rock 'n' roll star and publicly disdained the term "poet" because it was forever attached to Dylan, whom he envied for his obvious talent and resented for both the early Village heckling and the tough realization that he would never be as widely respected as His Bobness:

> [A]bout being a poet, I've tried poetry, but it has nothing to do with my songs. And I resent all the press-agentry. But the lyrics of pop songs are so banal that if you show a spark of intelligence they call you a poet. And if you say you're not a poet, then people think you're putting yourself down. But the people who call you a poet are people who never read poetry. Like poetry was something defined by Bob Dylan. They never read, say, Wallace Stevens. That's poetry.

Garfunkel also moved to the East Side, but closer to midtown, into an elegant one-room studio. When asked about his new, far more lavish lifestyle, he, too, tried to play it down, wary of appearing too far removed from the duo's hippie / college student fan base, or not really what he and Paul claimed to be: one of them rather than one of their parents. In his words:

> Mostly Paul and I like to play it very cool. We like to pride ourselves on how few celebrities we know. I know I don't live

very glamorously. On a typical day, I get up around noon, don't eat anything, and then go downtown and do little jobs or buy something. Or there's a favor I want to do. Like there's a friend in Australia who wants me to pick up some tape cartridges. Next, maybe I'll meet Paul at our manager Mort Lewis' office. Mort's a gourmet and he's always trying to persuade us to go to some fancy restaurant. But we sit and turn him on. We insist on going to some cheap-looking luncheonette with a lot of plastic and fluorescents and Formica-topped tables. And there I eat something like hamburgers with mayonnaise. At night . . . we'll go see a friend . . . and then afterward we'll find another cheap luncheonette with Formica-topped tables and eat some breakfast things. And then maybe we'll go back to Paul's and listen to something he's working on or some records and have some conversation and coffee. Or I'll go home and read and listen to some records . . . or maybe some girl will call up and drop by. I mean I never have dates or call up a girl and meet her and take her out, that whole bit. It's completely out of my behavior pattern. I can't plan and I don't want to commit myself. Most of the girls I see are those who drop by—or call up and drop by.

Formica and females—that was Artie's pronounced self-image at this, the height of his improbable rock-star fame. If Paul wanted to be seen as a poet, Artie proudly played the role of the proletarian prince, something Paul could not help but resent about his partner. To Paul, the music was everything, while to Artie it was merely a transport to what he perceived as bigger and better things all wrapped up in wealth and comfort. The chasm between them was barely crossable; what happened next would separate them wider than the Grand Canyon.

It began innocently enough with Mike Nichols, who had played a crucial role in turning the boys into superstars and who liked to be driven around New York City in a black limo, making it easier to navigate the city's heavy traffic. One day in the spring of 1968, he was on his way to pay a visit to Artie when he saw him walking along the street near his apartment. Nichols lowered the blacked-out window and shouted out to him. Artie smiled and came over to the car, at which point, like a process server, Nichols handed him a script. He told him he wanted him and Paul to play supporting roles in his next film, a screen adaptation of Joseph Heller's runaway best-seller, *Catch-22*. For the sixties generation, the Simon & Garfunkel boomers, the book had come to epitomize the grim absurdity not just of what was happening in Vietnam but of all wars, and did it with a cool satiric overlay.

The ironic humor of *Catch-22* fit neatly into Nichols's directorial wheelhouse, and he had acquired the rights to the novel soon after it was published, believing it would be the perfect follow-up to *The Graduate*. He wanted Artie for the role of Captain Nately, the sensitive, rich young man. And for the considerably smaller role of Dunbar, he said he wanted Paul.

Both eagerly accepted Nichols's offer. Artie was already a big movie fan, and Paul fancied himself something of a real-life Benjamin Braddock. Although rock and film had proved an uneasy alliance (despite, or more likely because of, Elvis Presley's dreadful movies), Paul thought he might actually be able to make the leap to acting as a way to expand and deepen his image as a serious artist. For Artie, the film represented what he believed was his best chance to step out from behind the long shadow of his short partner and establish himself as a star in his own right.

All of it was fine, until they began working on their next album, which both Columbia and Nichols wanted them to complete before production on *Catch-22* began, which, under the best of circumstances, would not be an easy undertaking. And then the machinery of Hollywood filmmaking kicked in. The role of Dunbar was eliminated early on from the film's shooting script, as it became increasingly clear that Heller's expansive and ironically comic novel's literary brand of black humor was going to be impossible to re-create on the screen. As a result, before Paul spent so much as a single day on the set, his role in *Catch-22* was eliminated. (It's possible Nichols never really wanted Paul but was afraid if he didn't offer roles to both Simon and Garfunkel, he might not get either.) Artie later explained Paul's dilemma as being like a kid let into candy store but not allowed to have so much as a single taste of anything.

The decision by Artie to stay with the movie without Paul came just as they were about to begin recording *Bridge over Troubled Water*, their fifth, and as it turned out final, original Simon & Garfunkel album for Columbia. It was difficult for anyone in the studio not to notice the growing rift between Paul and Artie. Some thought Paul's jealousy over Artie's split loyalties was the primary issue, and the rift deepened when the filming of *Catch-22* became mired in its own inescapable dilemma, which, ironically, gave the film's title a further poignancy as a production that couldn't find its way out of an ever-expanding production schedule. Although originally slated for a three-month shoot in Mexico, it would in fact take a year to complete, adding greatly to the amount of time Artie had to take away from being in the recording studio with Paul.

While production on the film dragged on, so did work on the album, with Clive Davis pressing Paul to somehow finish it so they could all capitalize on their Grammy Award wins, the phenomenal sales of *Bookends*, and the remarkable feat of having the top three album positions on the national charts: *Bookends* (number one), *The Graduate Soundtrack* (number two), *Parsley, Sage, Rosemary and Thyme* (number three).

Ironically, what was originally what Paul had wanted, to break out on his own and take over all but the harmonies for *Bridge over Troubled Water*, now made him angry and sullen, not because of the added burden, which he welcomed, but because of the sense of betrayal. Several of the songs on the album explicitly point the accusatory finger of abandonment at Artie. To some, the finished album had a whiff of homoeroticism about it, as much of it seemed to be about the romantic breakup of a couple even though it was made absolutely clear by Paul, through his lyrics, that the breakup was with Artie, and "the other woman" was the movie he had gone off to make.

In May 1969, Davis finally got what he wanted, although it was not the complete album. Instead Paul delivered the first single from it, "The Boxer," which many still consider the greatest Simon & Garfunkel song and recording they ever made. The opening is gently pretty and extremely youthful, a cut-time descending fingerpick that recalls, for this briefest of moments, the early, pre-percussive sound of the original, pre-remixed Simon & Garfunkel's "Sound of Silence." But that feeling serves only as the briefest of introductions to the epic five minutes and nine seconds that follow. The opening verse, with its expression of the fear of artistic limitation (reminiscent of the self-criticism Paul wrote in "Kathy's Song"), here "a pocket full of mumbles," is followed by the grim observation that we are all creatively "blind," or spiritually bankrupt, that we see only what we want to see, and "disregard" everything else is a startling run of words, beautifully phrased with off-rhymes (rest, jests, resistance, promises, boy, told) in a pattern of broken iambic meter that galvanizes the rhythm section as well as the narrative; the meticulously structured *da-da-dum* of the words fits seamlessly into the same drumbeat that falls into place after the tumbling acoustic intro.

According to Chris Charlesworth, a British rock writer and editor, the song was originally assumed to be a continuation of Paul's long-standing self-inflicted "feud" with Bob Dylan, and in that sense it was seen as an attack on him—Dylan was known among the Villagers to be a fairly good amateur boxer, and the chorus of "lie lie lie" that permeated the song's chorus was taken by some as pointing a finger at Dylan's abandonment of folk (in other words, his lying about his music and his intentions). In hindsight, this seems utterly nonsensical. (Charlesworth agrees.)

The next verse of "The Boxer" connects with the album's recurring theme of abandonment, set in an autobiographical, back-to-the-beginning frame. The singer is a "poor boy" leaving home—as Paul did when he went to England—surrounded by strangers in a railway station, probably a reference to Kathy (and "Homeward Bound"). Once at his destination, the narrator lays low (Judith's house, which he shared in the East End?). Looking to fit in, he tries to join the clique of artists he found there. The song then switches locales again, back to New York, but the only offers he gets there are from streetwalkers, an allusion perhaps to bands only into making money, that "whore" themselves out. The song then breaks into a vocal-and-instrumental run of lie-lie-lies; they are not so much accusations as a bridge, a fade in cinematic terms, that becomes, for the moment, a purely nonchronological exultation—the joy of singing.

Next, the singer laments the passing of years and the acknowledgment of changes—Artie's leaving to make a movie—and sighs to acknowledge abandonment as nothing new in his life, that the more things change, the more they stay the same. Finally, the singer longs to go home—yet not home; to somewhere where the harsh New York winters won't bleed him dry. Mexico, perhaps? All of which resolves with the vision of a boxer—a fighter—who wants desperately to get out of the ring but, despite the beating he has taken, remains in the fight; he is what he is, and will somehow make it through.

The song's extraordinary lyrics are accompanied by Paul's precise and immensely appealing fingerpicking around the chords of C, Am, G, F, Gm and D, and a compelling percussive-driven arrangement, a cacophony of deeply echoed strings, the great Charlie McCoy's powerful bass harmonica, trumpets, what sounds like a million drums, and the Bach-inspired instrumental "lie lie lie" chorus (which, according to David Fricke in his notes to the 1997 compilation release of the Simon & Garfunkel Columbia albums, was written by Garfunkel).

In an interview Paul gave to *Playboy* in 1984, he talked about the song, acknowledging it was fraught with separation anxiety and overlayed with a bit of inspired messianic narcissism for good measure:

> I was reading the Bible around that time. That's where I think phrases such as "workman's wages" came from, and "seeking out the poor quarters." That was biblical. The thing is the song was about me: everybody's beating me up, and I'm telling you now I'm going to go away if you don't stop.

The single track of "Bridge over Troubled Water," the last to be recorded for the album and the first to be finished, took two weeks to post-produce. Paul had originally written it on guitar and decided midway through to have it transposed for piano to include the added gospel flavor he was after and to better match Artie's solo voice (the final mix was done later in New York City). When Paul first showed Artie the lyrics for "Bridge," he told him that Artie should be the one to sing it, but Artie said no because he felt it wasn't right for him.

Paul couldn't believe it; here was a gift-wrapped beauty that Artie was dismissing. "He couldn't hear it," Paul said later on.

He felt I should have done it, and many times on a stage, though, when I'd be sitting off to the side and Larry Knechtel would be playing the piano and Artie would be singing "Bridge," people would stomp and cheer when it was over, and I would think, "That's my song, man. . . ." In the earlier days when things were smoother I never would have thought that, but towards the end when things were strained I did. It's not a very generous thing to think, but I did think that . . .

I was twenty-one when I wrote it [and] it was [my] most mature song of that period. . . . It came so fast and when it was done, I said, "Where did that come from? It doesn't seem like me." [After Artie consented to sing it] it became his signature song. There are two great versions. One is Artie's and one is Aretha Franklin's. I was influenced [in writing it] by the Swan Silvertones, and I heard it as a gospel song. Artie sang it the white choirboy way, which was extraordinarily beautiful. But neither of those voices are my voice, so in a way that song's a mystery because it sort of drifted out of my hands.*

There's eleven songs on *Bridge over Troubled Water,* but there were supposed to be twelve. I had written a song called "Cuba

---

* There are two *other* great versions of the song. A gospel-inspired cover version by Aretha Franklin, taken from *Aretha Live at Fillmore West,* reached number one on the U.S. R&B chart and number six on the pop chart. It later won the Grammy Award for Best Female R&B Vocal Performance in 1972. In 1999, BMI named it the nineteenth-most-performed song of the twentieth century. *Rolling Stone* named it number 47 on its list of "The 500 Greatest Songs of All Time." Elvis Presley recorded it in Nashville on June 5, 1970, and it was released on the 1970 album *That's The Way It Is.* He included it in his set list for his next engagement in Las Vegas, which included the filming of the 1970 documentary *Elvis—That's the Way It Is,* and it was included in the original theatrical release. During this summer season in Vegas, Paul Simon attended one of the shows, and after seeing Elvis perform the song, he was reported to have said, "That's it, we might as well all give up now." Other hit recordings of "Bridge over Troubled Water" include Buck Owens's and Johnny Cash's, which appeared on his 2002 *American IV: The Man Comes Around.* Spanish singer Camilo Sesto covered the song as "Puente Sobre Aguas Turbulentas," and the Jackson Five recorded a version for their third album.

Si, Nixon No," but Artie didn't want to do it. . . . He wanted
instead to do a Bach chorale thing, which I didn't want to do.
We were fightin' over which was gonna be the 12th song, and
then I said, "Fuck it, put it out with eleven songs."

Artie relented and produced one of the greatest Simon &
Garfunkel vocals ever recorded. The single, despite its length of
five minutes, ten seconds, was released by Columbia only because
Dylan had had a hit in 1965 with his even longer "Like a Rolling
Stone," which broke the barrier of the three-minute length a song
could be, a limit imposed by commercial-thick AM radio stations.
"Bridge" quickly rose to number seven and stayed in the Top Ten for
most of the summer.

Still waiting for the completed album to be ready for release,
Clive Davis suggested they appear in a live prime-time TV special,
to be called *Songs of America*, to which they agreed, Paul from New
York, Artie from Mexico. They did two live concerts as a warm-up,
one in early November at State College in Wichita, Kansas, where
they performed mostly older tunes, and one the following week at
Miami University in Oxford, Ohio, during which they introduced to
audiences for the first time several of the songs that would eventually
be included on *Bridge*.

The idea for the program grew out of what had originally been
intended as a guest spot on *The Bell Telephone Hour*, a hugely popular
sixties network TV series. In those days, TV programming was still
mostly dominated by a single sponsor, which often "owned" the hour
and delivered ready-to-broadcast programming on a complicated
barter-and-profit-share basis.

Paul eventually came up with an idea that would make the TV
show far more than a version of their live concerts. At Artie's suggestion, Paul talked with Charles Grodin, who happened to be one of
the costars of *Catch-22*. Grodin, who would receive equal onscreen
writing credit along with Simon & Garfunkel for the special and who
also directed, was a gifted actor and a fine writer. From the start
he urged the boys to try something different, to make the most of
their hour on television, to produce a show that would do more than
simply promote themselves as a singing duo. "If you're going to get

an hour on TV, instead of doing an ordinary show, let's think up something that would be different," he told them.

Did they ever. They came up with a filmed documentary-style show about how they saw themselves in sixties America, and saw America in the sixties, with footage interspersed of John Kennedy, Martin Luther King, Jesse Jackson, Ralph David Abernathy, and Robert Kennedy, bits from Woodstock and newsreel footage of Vietnam, with only the last quarter of the show live concert performance footage, and even then not a single song was performed in its entirety. It was one of the most daring shows ever presented on network television.

Only, it wasn't presented on network television, at least not in the form in which they gave it to Bell Telephone. Sensing there might be trouble with it, Paul and Artie waited until just a week before it was scheduled to be broadcast to turn their finished show over to Bell, in all its raging rock 'n' rolling glory, which, not surprisingly, the sponsor rejected out of hand.

Paul's reaction was immediate and visceral: "So we said, 'You mean to say that there are people who will object if we say you must feed *everyone* in this country?' and they said, 'You're goddamn right someone would object. You'll have to change this: it's not going on.' And we said, 'Well, too bad then. It's not going on, because we're not changing anything.'"

The standoff resulted in Paul and Artie having a difficult meeting with the CBS censors, who, as it turned out, were surprisingly sympathetic to the content and helped create a re-edited, slightly toned-down version with more music that somehow got past Bell and was broadcast the night of November 30, 1969.

The show began with aerial shots of what looked to be Vietnam that cross-faded into overhead shots of American highways, Pittsburgh, the New Jersey Turnpike, poverty shacks, police, African American poor, and garbage heaps against a soundtrack of the recorded version of "America," beginning with "Kathy I'm lost . . ."—the Kathy here less Paul's lost love than the America that had ignored the troubled souls of its own children. The opening line of spoken dialogue is Paul, underneath the song, saying, "I can feel it in the air that there is something great going on all around, and that I have a feeling I'm just missing it." Cut to footage of Paul and Artie in the backseat of a car, discussing music ("this harmony thing," as Paul describes it), Beethoven's defiance of a ban against "parallel fifths" (chords), and the upcoming bicentennial of Beethoven's birth. Or at least Paul is. Artie seems to alternate between bafflement and disinterest. When Paul mentions the bicentennial, Artie offhandedly asks if it's next Thursday, as if he thought they were talking about a meeting. Then he adds that someone else's two-hundredth birthday is coming up. Paul asks who, and Artie replies, "America's." After a silence, Paul says, in what was sure to outrage Bell Telephone, "You think it's gonna make it?" Two things stand out about these scenes: First, their strong resemblance to Dylan's 1965 documentary, made by D. A. Pennebaker, *Don't Look Back*, where handheld cameras record in vérité style the conversations of Dylan and those closest to him. The second is that the presence of the camera notwithstanding, Paul, very edgy and toothy, and Artie, Ivy-tweeded and crew-necked, never look at each other when they talk, which suggests to the viewer that they are talking *at* one another, not *to* one another, and that the lines of communication have already broken down, a theme that will play through the rest of the show.

In the next sequence, Paul and Artie are trying to work out a harmony sequence, and when Artie suggests that Paul sing a different melody line, Paul, with obvious anger and a notable lack of tolerance, admonishes Artie for not letting him (Paul) figure out the chords first. Then he tells Artie that he'll worry about the melody (Roy Halee, credited as the audio consultant for the film, is seen directing this rehearsal session). Next comes a fully orchestrated rehearsal session for "So Long, Frank Lloyd Wright," which, without dialogue, becomes fascinating to watch; it is one of the best sequences of the special.

Back in the studio to record the vocals, Artie asks Paul if the cameras will inhibit him, and once again Paul turns on him, practically sneering as he says, "Do you ever see these cameras inhibit me? I *live* with these cameras." That sends Paul into a revealing side reverie in which he says that he is constantly amazed at how he can write without visuals, that his words evoke pictures without a camera. During the recording of the song, iconic boomer childhood images lash by—*The Lone Ranger, Flash Gordon, Howdy Doody, American Bandstand, The Arthur Godfrey Show*, Mickey Mantle, Lenny Bruce, President Truman playing the piano, Adlai Stevenson, a long sequence built around JFK during which the music segues into "Bridge over Troubled Water," Martin Luther King marching in the South, RFK campaigning in '68, Cesar Chavez, and RFK's last train ride as his coffin was brought home—as "Bridge" crescendos to its gorgeous climax. It is an altogether beautiful sequence, evoking the mythic childhood heroes of the boomers, and presumably Paul and Artie, and the real-life heroes of the sixties, especially the Kennedy brothers and Martin Luther King, all of whom were murdered in ways that the Lone Ranger and Flash Gordon could never be. This reminds the viewer of Paul's question about whether or not America can "make it." The sequence ends with rolling shots of the Kennedy train that recall the opening shots of the documentary, where the camera "rolled" across Vietnam and America.

And on it went for the rest of the hour: a gum-chewing Paul playing a blistering "At the Zoo" on acoustic guitar, looking as if he were composing it as he went along, intercut with Artie on the phone taking care of business, helping to book a concert for the following week (or so it appeared); Artie in the car espousing what sounds like a New Age philosophy of love; Paul talking about the impact of the three days of peace and love and the feeling of belonging that took place at Woodstock; a peace sign made by skywriting planes above the New York City skyline; a montage of the Woodstock Nation intercut with brutal scenes from the Vietnam War, all of it with "Scarborough Fair" playing underneath; Paul and Artie discussing the lunacy of Vietnam as they saw it; a segment on the war on poverty at home in America and the "Poor People's Campaign" intercut with Cesar Chavez leading farm workers in protest to the tune of "El Condor Pasa"; congressional hearings to the tune of "Punky's Dilemma"; spectacular live footage of Paul in a fringed jacket, preternaturally thin, with long hair combed straight down, giving his baby-fat face the look of a painted egg, and Artie equally thin, his blonde hair tousled Dylan-style; Paul rehearsing "Bridge over Troubled Water" with Larry Knechtel, who would become part of Paul's regular backup touring and recording band, killing on the piano; Paul despairing over the state of the world; Paul and Artie in their dressing room counting off the night's order of songs on their fingers, with Paul muttering out loud "How long can this go on?"; a camera-follow onstage, Artie in open-necked red sweater, Paul the same, only in yellow, bursting into a driving acoustic version of "Mrs. Robinson" (the first actual performance footage of the show and the first time they had played together before a live audience in more than a year); an interview with Artie in which he says he can't see himself doing this "five years from now" because it's not spiritual enough; Paul chiming in saying that being a professional songwriter is not enough.

Asked if he would like to be president, Paul waffles, saying some days he would and some days he wouldn't. He'd like to "straighten it all out," meaning, presumably, the country, and he muses that he just doesn't have the time because he must devote himself to developing as an artist; Paul and Artie sitting on the side of a hotel bed singing "Feelin' Groovy," with Paul playing a lovely fingerpick accompaniment, followed by Paul, alone, lying on the bed picking off a strong minor-key version of "Mystery Train," and rock-star shots of them flying first-class; Artie expressing his fear of still not being able to sing well enough in front of a live audience before performing "For Emily" to a gorgeous twelve-string fingerpick by Paul that approaches the symphonic approximation he always loved to do onstage; a beautiful concert performance of "The Boxer"; Paul backstage musing about why he writes songs ("because they're nice, for the pleasure of the rhythm, because they express what I feel, because they relieve tensions when I do"); a concert version of "Homeward Bound," followed by a bringing-it-all-back-home live version of "America," and climaxing with a great acoustic version of "Sound of Silence" as the camera pulls back for the closing credits, under "Song for the Asking."

Although today the show looks relatively tame, in 1969 *Songs of America* had a startlingly radical feel to it, more Woody Guthrie than Greatest Hits, its visual style edgy and jump-cut for an hour usually filled with the music of Perry Como, Bing Crosby, and Andy Williams.

Not surprisingly, the next day a tidal wave of negative reaction came pouring in to the network and Columbia Records that left Paul angry and hurt and regretting ever having committed to doing anything for television in the first place.

By now, the clock was almost wound down and out on Simon & Garfunkel. There were already hard feelings between them over

Catch-22, and further tension from the TV show because Artie did not want to push the political button so hard—he didn't want Simon & Garfunkel to become known as protest singers; he just wanted to make beautiful music. Shortly before Christmas, with the album finished, Paul knew it was over between the two. "At that point," Paul said, "I just wanted out."

The breaking point finally came when both Paul and Artie found the one thing they couldn't get from each other—female love and companionship. A few months earlier, Artie had met Linda Grossman, a sometime actress who had recognized him getting out of a cab on Fifth Avenue with Simon & Garfunkel's manager Mort Lewis, who was on his way to a recording session for "The Boxer." Artie invited her to come along. "I was ready . . . my rhythm was already going. I think I asked her to marry me about the second sentence." Smitten with Grossman, a former architecture major and graphic artist now interested in acting and living at the time in Boston, Artie was willing to commute back and forth to be with her, a further reduction in his already minimal available time, which left Paul simmering with anger.

At the same time, Paul's relationship with Peggy Harper, who happened to be married at the time to Mort Lewis, became even more intense when she separated from Lewis and announced her intention to get a divorce—so she could marry Paul. He had pursued the southern-born former airline stewardess relentlessly, despite his personal friendship and professional relationship with Lewis, who nonetheless continued his close association with Simon & Garfunkel (and Paul, after the coming official breakup of the duo). Paul and Peggy married in late autumn 1969.

Peggy was in the studio when Paul and Artie recorded "Bridge over Troubled Water," done in California to make it easier for Artie to get there from Mexico. For the duration of those sessions, Peggy and Paul rented a house on Blue Jay Way (the same house that George Harrison had earlier rented and had written "Blue Jay Way" in), with Artie barely coming around to visit. As Paul recalls, following the release of *Bridge over Troubled Water,*

[T]here was no great pressure to stay together, other than money, which exerted really very little influence upon us . . .

we didn't need the money. And musically, it was not a creative
team, too much, because Artie is a singer, and I'm a writer
and player and a singer. We didn't work together on a creative
level and prepare the songs. I did that. When we came into
the studio I became more and more me, making the tracks
and choosing the musicians, partly because a great deal of
the time during [the making of] *Bridge*, Artie wasn't there. I
was doing things myself with Roy Halee, our engineer and coproducer. We were planning tracks out, and, to a great degree,
that responsibility fell to me.

I viewed Simon & Garfunkel [and Roy Halee] as basically
a three-way partnership. Each person had a relatively equal
say. So, in other words, if Roy and Artie said, "Let's do a long
ending on 'The Boxer,'" I said, "Two out of three" and did it
their way. I didn't say, "Hey, this is my song. I don't want it to
be like that." . . . "Fine," I'd say.

Bridge over Troubled Water was finally released on January 26, 1970.
Of the album's eleven songs, the obvious standouts were, besides the
exquisitely captured title track, "The Boxer"; "The Only Living Boy
in New York," Paul's sad and beautiful solo farewell to "Tom," Artie's
alter ego; "Bye Bye Love," their homage to the Everly Brothers; and
"Song for the Asking," a plaintive, this-is-who-we-were farewell to their
audience and to each other.

Bridge over Troubled Water landed at number one its first week and
eventually racked up more than nine million sales in its initial vinyl
release, making it the biggest-selling album, worldwide, to date. A
brief British tour followed—more than that was not necessary to promote what was already a smash—and then one final stop that brought
everything back home to Forest Hills, Queens, where, at Paul's insistence, ten thousand dollars of their profits was to be donated to
California-based farm workers' advocate Cesar Chavez.

In the bowl of the famous stadium, beneath the floodlights that
customarily shone down on the world's greatest tennis champions,
they played out their own final game, running through their many
hits and some new songs from *Bridge*, and finished with a scorch-
ing, killer version of the Penguins' "Earth Angel," the song Paul

had first heard so long ago on Alan Freed's radio show and that had so taken his breath away in the bedroom of the house he grew up in, a few blocks from where, now, he and Artie stood, drowning in applause.

On March 16, 1971, the thirteenth annual Grammy Awards took place for the first time on the West Coast, at Hollywood's storied Palladium Theater, hosted once again by the venerable Andy Williams. The event was broadcast live, on ABC's national TV network. That night Paul and Artie had an awkward reunion of sorts when they both attended the event, side by side but creatively light-years apart, even though it had been only months since they had last performed together at Forest Hills. Artie, who had just finished filming *Carnal Knowledge* and was awaiting its release, had thought about maybe doing a little mathematics teaching in a private school in a tony section of Connecticut but wound up spending most of his time in Los Angeles with Linda Grossman, putting together songs for what would be his first solo album.

The Grammys that year were significantly different in that for the first time the winners were not announced in advance. It was hoped that a bit of suspense, Oscars style, might help increase the ratings for the TV broadcast.

It proved to be a bittersweet night, as Simon & Garfunkel's "Bridge over Troubled Water" swept all the major awards. Record of the Year went to the single "Bridge over Troubled Water," beating out such heavyweight contenders as James Taylor's "Fire and Rain," the Carpenters' "Close to You," and the Beatles' "Let It Be." It also won Best Arrangement Accompanying Vocalists and Best Engineered Record. Grammys went to Paul and Artie and Roy Halee for producing. At that moment, the three of them stood together onstage, Paul and Artie finding it difficult to look into the eyes of one another.

Album of the Year went to *Bridge over Troubled Water*, with separate Grammys going to Paul Simon as the songwriter for the album and the single. "Bridge" also won for Best Arrangement Accompanying Vocalists (Larry Knechtel, one of Paul's favorite studio musicians, a veteran of album sessions with Elvis Presley, Ray Charles, the Doors, and Paul), Best Engineering (Roy Halee), and, finally, Song of the Year.

That June, *Catch-22* opened to mostly negative reviews, except for the *New York Times*' Vincent Canby, whose positive review was not enough to save the film, which quickly disappeared from screens and proved a disappointing follow-up to Nichols's groundbreaking *The Graduate*. Nichols then offered Artie one of the major roles in his next film, *Carnal Knowledge*, in which he would costar with Candace Bergen, Ann-Margret, and the ultrahot Jack Nicholson. Artie accepted with great enthusiasm.

Into the seventies, rapid and unexpected changes that all but buried the decade before percolated through the heat of rock 'n' roll. Jimi Hendrix, Janis Joplin, and Jim Morrison all died suddenly, within a year of one another. The Beatles split up for good. And now, Simon & Garfunkel were ready to announce that they, too, were going their separate ways.

Paul, who had recently given up all recreational drugs, even cigarettes, and was in analysis, with Peggy's support, took it upon himself to make the split-up official. "Peggy made me feel like I should do it myself, and take the responsibility," he said later. "If it's good, it's yours and if it's bad, it's yours. 'Go out and do your thing and say "This is my thing."'" Paul placed a call to Clive Davis. "Before others find out," he told Davis, "I want you to know I've decided to split with Artie. I don't think we'll be recording together again."

That spring, Paul appeared, without Artie, on Leonard Bernstein's recording of his "Mass" and appeared solo at a benefit held at Shea Stadium to commemorate the thirtieth anniversary of the bombing of Pearl Harbor.

Not long after, Paul received a phone call from George Harrison, with whom he had become friends after renting the former Beatle's house. Harrison, drawing on his own experience with the Beatles, urged him to use this opportunity to see what he could really do as a solo performer.

Paul listened intently, thanked Harrison for the call, hung up, and knew it was real. He was, at last, "the only living boy in New York."

PART THREE

Simon without Garfunkel

9

So Long, Frank Lloyd Wright

AS THE SIXTIES CROSS-FADED INTO THE SEVENTIES, THE HOPE and glory of the past decade's worth of peace-and-protest music played comfortably alongside the good-time music of the new day. Bob Dylan, the Beatles, the Stones, and the Who had sat comfortably on turntables alongside the Four Tops, James Brown, and Sly and the Family Stone (all of whom could be categorized as makers of either social protest or nonpolitical rock 'n' roll, or both—the beauty of the sixties' boundary-blurring catholicity of taste). This was the great innovation of the relatively new FM bandwidth, where songs of every type and theme could be played directly one after another—a musical/broadcast form that, ultimately, would not last, as stations began to specialize in formats designed for specific target audiences and narrower and higher-priced commercial demographics, all part of the swift co-opting and incorporation of the once socially rebellious rock 'n' roll. Money became the single most important factor, not only to radio stations and record labels, but to the musicians themselves.

Money was always important to Simon, coming from an immigrant family where there had never been a lot of it and where his father, a successful, working musician, eventually chose to leave the business altogether because of the difficulty of having a good enough and steady income. Early on, Paul had taken the appropriate steps to deal with the financial uncertainty inherent in the music business. With the exception of three of his songs controlled by publisher E. B. Marks, written when Paul was in college and peddling his wares at the Brill Building, he owned all of his own songs, and publishing was where the real money in music was. It was the reason he made far more from Simon & Garfunkel albums than Artie, who received only performance money for songs he hadn't helped to write.

As soon as he had started earning significant money, Paul had enlisted the services of Michael Tannen, who specialized in helping successful musicians get the money that was coming to them. According to veteran producer Mike Appel, "Tannen quickly became Paul Simon's guru."

Among Tannen's other clients were the Rolling Stones, John Lennon (without the Beatles), and Stephen Stills, but Paul quickly became his key client. According to rock writer Fred Goodman, Paul first met Tannen "when Simon & Garfunkel hit it big in the mid-sixties. . . . Tannen's acumen helped make Paul Simon one of the wealthiest artists in the business." More than just a financial manager, Tannen had also helped to deliver Simon songs to many of the industry's biggest artists, including Barbra Streisand (whose recording of "Punky's Dilemma" pushes the envelope on absurdity), Elvis's wondrous version of "Bridge over Troubled Water," the Hollies' "I Am a Rock," Frank Sinatra's ultra-cool "Mrs. Robinson," Joan Baez's sincere "The Dangling Conversation," Harpers Bizarre's "Feelin' Groovy," and even, ironically, Dylan's plainly weird take on "The Boxer."

Among musicians, only George Harrison seemed to encourage Paul's desire to go solo. "I'm really curious to hear your [first solo] album," George told Paul, "because now you sort of know what [you] are like individually, and I'd like hear what you're like individually."

George's advice was appreciated by Paul, but he may have also heard within it the slightest caution that perhaps the magic of Simon & Garfunkel was a product of the duo. This feeling, or fear, was that perhaps he could not write by and for just himself.

Although he tried almost every day, nothing came, until one night he found his inspiration in the most unexpected of places, his favorite local Chinese restaurant. Looking over the menu, he saw the colorful description of one of the main dishes staring him square in the face: "Mother and Child Reunion." That somehow coalesced a vague idea he had been playing around with for a while, since the family dog had been killed a year earlier in an auto accident that nearly took his and Peggy's lives, as well. He had wanted to write about the elements of love, loss, and salvation, without being mawkish or, as ever, too specific. "Mother and Child Reunion" gave him a title, after which the song came relatively easily.

A new musical sound had begun to penetrate the still fairly well-integrated FM airways—reggae music, exemplified by the great Bob Marley and his seminal band the Wailers, and the equally compelling Jimmy Cliff, both out of Jamaica. (Cliff would gain worldwide recognition after appearing in Perry Henzel's brilliant 1972 film, *The Harder They Come*.) While reggae had not as yet fully caught on in America, in England it was already a sensation when Paul lived there. It was black street music with rough lyrics and sensational rhythms, played with an emphasis on the two-four beat run by a heavy electric bass that gave it its harder edge and joyful sound.

Paul had experimented with the sound earlier, in the Simon & Garfunkel track "Why Don't You Write Me," a Vietnam War–inspired song about a soldier not wanting to be forgotten while fighting a war no one wanted to remember. It was buried among the bigger, instant classics of the *Bridge* album, but its rhythm strongly appealed to Paul, and, now reinvigorated with the notion of writing a song with a reggae beat, he flew to Jamaica to find and hire Jimmy Cliff's backup band and take them into the island's fabled Dynamic Studios to cut the track. While he was there, he came up with a second reggae-inspired song, the classic "Me and Julio Down by the Schoolyard," the result of a loop of rhythm he had made while cutting "Mother and Child Reunion," and to which he later added lyrics.

From Jamaica it was off to Paris to record "Duncan," Paul's playful, rhythmic ode to religion, salvation, and masturbation (or the religious salvation of masturbation), with Los Incas supplying the musical background, and then "Hobo's Blues," with Stephane Grappelli, the talented violinist who had worked with Django Reinhardt in the Paris of the thirties. And then to San Francisco, where Roy Halee was now living. Columbia Records showed its appreciation for his long string of hits by building a studio for him when he moved to the Bay Area. Paul wanted to run some of his new songs by him and get a firm commitment from Halee to help produce the first Paul Simon solo album, which he was determined to finish by the end of the year.

After putting down tracks in Jamaica, Paris, New York, and Los Angeles, he finished recording them in San Francisco with Halee supervising, expanding his acoustic sound by using some of the best studio musicians he knew, who also happened to be some of the best in the business, many of whom would go on to have celebrated solo careers of their own. They included some he'd never worked with before and some who had appeared live and/or on several later Simon & Garfunkel albums, including Larry Knechtel, Hal Blaine, Ron Carter, and Charlie McCoy, with Cissy Houston, Von Eva Sims, Renelle Stafford, and Deirdre Tuck on vocals. The album's final mix and order of songs would be closely supervised by Paul, which made the album as personal as those he had made with Artie. It was almost like starting over, with a new sound, a new set of musicians, and a brand-new slate of songs.

To further distance this album from the five classic Simon & Garfunkels, Paul asked its recording engineer, Phil Ramone, to become the album's de facto producer (with Halee remaining as its "official" producer). Paul was more hands-on for this album than he had been with any of the Simon & Garfunkels. "When I met Paul," Ramone remembered later, "he had [just] started his solo career. He was a guy who totally lived his life in the studio . . . as part of his daily activity."

That March, two years after *Bridge over Troubled Water*, Paul released *Paul Simon* simultaneously in stereo and in the then trendy quadraphonic sound. The cover featured a close-up photo, taken by Peggy, of Paul wearing a fur-lined parka. Nearly unrecognizable, he felt either very cold or very hot.

Side 1 kicked off with "Mother and Child Reunion," which Paul had recorded in Kingston, Jamaica. Its infectious upbeat rhythm served notice that this was a new Paul Simon, tougher, more street, less sentimental, and all the happier for it. Track 2, "Duncan," had been Paul's first choice for the title of the album, an "alter ego" à la Sgt. Pepper, to further make the point that he was no longer one half of Simon & Garfunkel, before he changed it to the eponymous *Paul Simon*. It was recorded in Paris with Paul on guitar, Los Incas on charango (a South American instrument somewhere between a ukulele and a lute), flutes, and percussion. It was followed on side 1 by one of the lesser, filler cuts, "Everything Put Together Falls Apart," with Paul on guitar and Larry Knechtel on the harmonium and electric piano. "Run That Body Down," another minor tune, featured Paul and David Spinoza on guitars, Mike Maniere on vibes, Jerry Hahn on electric guitar, Ron Carter on bass, and Hal Blaine on drums; "Armistice Day" had Paul on guitar, Jerry Hahn on electric guitar, Airto Moreira on percussion, and Fred Lipsius and John Schroer on horns.

Side 2 returned Paul to form, opening with "Me and Julio Down by the Schoolyard," which jumped and moved with a rhythm as hard as a concrete playground, thick with Latin influence and built around a phrase Paul had had dancing in his head for months—"me and Julio"—that he built into the hard-to-shake-off recurring kickoff to the chorus. It featured Paul and David Spinoza on guitars, Airto Moreira on percussion, and Russel George on bass. Next came "Peace like a River," a pleasant if minor throwaway, with Victor Montanez on drums and Joe Osborn on bass. "Papa Hobo" (Larry Knechtel on harmonium and Charlie McCoy on bass harmonica) was followed by the jazz/swing "Hobo's Blues," recorded in Paris and cowritten by Stephane Grappelli, who also played violin on it. "Paranoia Blues" was recorded in L.A. with Stefan Grossman on bottleneck guitar, Hal Blaine on drums, Paul playing percussion, and

John Schroer and Steven Turre on horns. The final track, "Congratulations," was a summary closing of the autobiographical circle song,
an homage to Tom & Jerry's doo-wop days with Paul on guitar, Larry
Knechtel on piano and organ, Joe Osborn on bass, and Hal Blaine
on drums.

Rolling Stone gave *Paul Simon* a qualified rave written by Jon
Landau:

> Paul Simon's long and manicky struggle between his songs of
> endearing but forced whimsy and his confessions of unhappi-
> ness and loneliness is over, with the latter, in fully developed
> and radically different form, the victor. Simon's first solo al-
> bum is also his least detached, most personal and painful piece
> of work thus far—this from a lyricist who has never shied away
> from pain as subject or theme. . . . *Paul Simon*, as an album,
> is not a particularly enjoyable piece of work; in a very real
> sense, it wasn't intended to be. It is a piece of self-expression
> designed to communicate some very unpleasant but very real
> truths about the artist and those who can hear him for what
> he has to say.

At the time, *Rolling Stone* was not only the most important place to
be reviewed by a rock artist, but, for all practical purposes, the only
place. (The rival *Crawdaddy* magazine was not nearly as influential
and would soon buckle under the competitive strength of *Rolling
Stone*, and the *New York Times* was years away from acknowledging
that rock 'n' roll "counted" as part of "all the news that's fit to print."
High Fidelity, one of the few non-rock music publications to review
the album, called it "disappointing.")

A bad review in *Rolling Stone* could hurt a career, even an established one. John Lennon's solo work, for example, was received
far more coolly than Paul's and for the most part was much less
commercially successful, whatever the cause and effect might have
been. Without question, though, a good review in *Rolling Stone* could
then, and now, sell a lot of albums. *Rolling Stone*'s official nod of approval helped push Paul's album to number five on the American
charts (number six in Britain), despite his stubborn refusal to tour

behind it, resisting Columbia's pressure for him to do so, claiming he didn't have enough new songs for a full tour and didn't want to sing any of the old Simon & Garfunkel ones. Nonetheless, the album was outselling the Stones' *Sticky Fingers*, which Paul was more than happy to point out to anyone who asked, including critics, interviewers, and especially record executives. (*Sticky Fingers* wound up by far the bigger seller. *Paul Simon* sold about 900,000 copies its first year; *Sticky Fingers* did an estimated 1.5 million units.) Paul's no-tour dictum had especially infuriated Clive Davis, who'd felt it was too risky for Columbia to release a Paul Simon solo album without a tour. Its success made Paul feel that record executives knew nothing about either the music they sold or the business model they used to sell it.

Even after the album hit high on the charts, Davis pushed Paul to tour, insisting that was all that was needed to turn it from a hit into a monster, but Paul refused. In their biography of Paul, Joseph Morella and Patricia Barey report (without citing a source) that the thought of a tour caused Paul nightmares, that in his dreams he would walk out onstage, and the microphone would be too high for him to reach, that there would be no setup for his guitar, and that he would leave the stage screaming at his manager.

Paul did make one personal appearance that May, during the album's initial release, at a George McGovern benefit in Cleveland, Ohio, to raise money for the 1972 Democratic nominee for president. He performed several songs from the new album—"Me and Julio," "Congratulations," and "Mother and Child Reunion," plus, something he had said he would never do, several Simon & Garfunkel songs, including "Cecilia," "The Boxer," "America," "Mrs. Robinson," "The Sound of Silence," and "Bridge over Troubled Water."

Chris Charlesworth, the British rock journalist who considered himself a friend of Paul's, remembers running into him during this period, when he was trying his best to remain under the promotion radar.

I'd run into him at the Academy of Music, on Fourteenth Street in New York City. I'd be there for *Cashbox*, I was writing for them at the time, and he'd be standing in the back, wearing that same funny fur jacket and hood he'd worn on the cover of *Paul Simon*. I'd go up to him and say, "Hi, Paul," and he'd put his fingers to his mouth as if to say "Don't tell anyone I'm here, I don't want to be recognized." It occurred to me at this time he liked being an observer far more than being a performer, and that fame was rather uncomfortable for him. [He was] always cautious that way and not spontaneous at all, just like in his shows.

"Me and Julio" (backed with "Congratulations") was released as a single and rose to number twenty-two on the *Billboard* charts. A second single, "Mother and Child Reunion" (backed with "Paranoia Blues"), rose to number four on the charts. Clive Davis, however, despite the singles sales, believed the album itself was fading, and he was not entirely wrong. Despite the success of *Paul Simon*, he feared that Paul Simon as a solo act was never going to be as big as Simon & Garfunkel.

And nobody was happy about that fear. Least of all Paul.

10

On Top and Alone

Although past the sales peak of its initial release, *Paul Simon* was still moving substantial units when Columbia dropped a corporate bomb on Paul. Without warning, on June 14, 1972, it released *Simon & Garfunkel's Greatest Hits*, a directly competitive compilation of what was deemed by them to be the best of the Simon & Garfunkel catalogue. Moreover, Clive Davis was pushing Artie to finish and release what would be his first solo album.

Davis would have preferred above all a live Simon & Garfunkel album to push as "new" material, technically true in corporate-speak, meaning never heard on record before, but in truth there were precious few usable live recordings of Simon & Garfunkel. As it turned out, it was a hopeless mishmash of the carefully constructed Simon & Garfunkel albums, something akin to taking random scenes from a filmmaker's body of work, splicing them together, and calling the final product a never-before-seen feature film. Moreover, despite the reputation of the duo as one of the primal voices of sixties folk-rock-pop, it was based on the slimmest body of work. Their output of what amounted to about sixty songs was enough—but just enough—to gain them entry into pop music's pantheon, in much the way Orson Welles was admitted to film's pantheon based on his very few directed films. Compared to the Beatles, who managed to put out more than twice as much original product, there was always a "rare and precious" aspect to Simon & Garfunkel's music. Every song had a specific place in the chronology of their work, and in the era of theme albums, many felt that what Davis and Columbia did was a major sacrilege to the musical legacy of the duo and, by extension, their "precious" sixties.

Despite Paul's and Artie's artistic concerns about piecemealing their work, Davis steadfastly believed the timing was perfect for *Simon & Garfunkel's Greatest Hits*, especially as the two had announced they were going to get together and perform live one last time. Paul's commitment to the George McGovern presidential nomination campaign had deepened, and he convinced Artie that this was an important enough reason for them to have a one-night reunion. To Davis, however, politics appeared to take second place behind promotion.

McGovern's campaign was crucial to the direction of the country, his antiwar stance *meant* something, Paul insisted, and Artie could not disagree with that. But the reality was that Artie didn't need any political causes to motivate him to get back together as Simon & Garfunkel. After having not spoken to Paul for more than a year, Artie was eagerly receptive to Paul's overture.

The event was organized by Warren Beatty, who scheduled it at New York's Madison Square Garden on July 14, Bastille Day in France. All eighteen thousand available seats sold out hours after they went on sale. In addition to the headline names of Simon & Garfunkel, the entertainment roster included Joni Mitchell, James Taylor, and two other significant reunions: sixties neo-folkies Peter, Paul and Mary, and Mike Nichols and Elaine May.

Paul made a couple of TV appearances to tune up, including a visit that June to *The Tonight Show* with Johnny Carson, where he performed "Papa Hobo," and another one in July to *The Dick Cavett Show*, where, after being interviewed by the affable host, he sang "Let Me Live in Your City," a new, unfinished song (which would eventually turn up as "Something So Right").

The Madison Square Garden benefit kicked off with Nichols and May, who scored a bull's-eye with a couple of classic routines from the Broadway show that had made them stars. They were followed by Peter, Paul and Mary, who sang Dylan's "Blowin' in the Wind" and Woody Guthrie's "This Land Is Your Land." Then it was Simon & Garfunkel's turn. Two microphones were set up at the front of the stage, the arena darkened except for a couple of overlapping spots, and the crowd hushed in anticipation. Then, when Paul and Artie, dressed in jeans and T-shirts, took the stage, the place erupted. They waved to the audience and immediately kicked in with "Mrs. Robinson."

"About three bars into the first song," Artie remembered, "I had very strong feelings 'Well, here we are again. This is where I left off.'" They also performed "For Emily, whenever I May Find Her," a rousing version of "The Boxer," "Feelin' Groovy," and amidst a frenzy of cheers and applause, a medley of "Cecilia," "Mother and Child Reunion," and "Bye Bye Love," ending their set with "The Sound of Silence," before being brought back for a killer encore of "Bridge over Troubled Water." Artie finished hitting his signature angelic high notes at the end of the song, and he and Paul left the stage to a standing ovation.

For the moment, all seemed right again between the two, although accounts vary as to the actual success of the "reunion." *Rolling Stone* reviewed the show and reported that Simon & Garfunkel "stood at their mikes looking straight ahead, like two commuters clutching adjacent straps on the morning train."

At the after-party for the performers, fund-raisers, and major donors, Paul and Artie kept their distance from each other. By the end of the evening, it was clear this was not the beginning of a Simon & Garfunkel reunion but what it was announced to be: a one-off, plain and simple, over almost before it had begun.

Nonetheless, and perhaps even to the annoyance of Paul, whose belief that the compilation album would hurt his solo work, the buzz over their joint appearance helped to push *Simon & Garfunkel's Greatest Hits* to number five on *Billboard*'s list of best-selling albums, while "Duncan," released from *Paul Simon* (backed with "Run That Body Down"), only reached number fifty-two on the singles chart.

Then, as if on cue, that October a single from the *Greatest Hits* album was released by Columbia—"America" backed with "For Emily, whenever I May Find Her," which reached number fifty-three in *Billboard*.

At about the same time, Peggy gave birth to a boy; she and Paul named him Harper, which was Peggy's maiden name. A month later, Artie married Linda Grossman in her hometown of Nashville. Paul and Peggy were invited, and despite the fact that they had just had a baby, both attended. At the reception, Paul and Artie spoke to each other in a friendly manner, joking about how two Jewish kids from Queens had wound up with two southern women (Grossman was also Jewish).

That October, Paul released a book of his lyrics, a near-complete collection of his entire body of work except for those songs controlled by E. B. Marks, which would not give permission for them to be included. The title made it clear that Paul wanted there to be no question as to who, of the Simon & Garfunkel duo, was the real creative force: *Paul Simon: As Sung by Simon & Garfunkel and Paul Simon Himself from "Hey Schoolgirl" to "Mother and Child Reunion."* The book was part catalogue and part scrapbook, very much in the style of songbooks of the day.

After his wedding, Artie went back to work on his overdue solo album, for which Columbia spared no expense. They green-lighted a budget that allowed Artie to hire Roy Halee to produce and to put together the best available studio musicians, many of whom had also appeared on earlier Simon & Garfunkel albums and Paul's solo debut. The songs were recorded at Grace Cathedral in New York City and at Halee's studio in San Francisco. In a gesture of kindness, rather than reconciliation, Paul, whose very name on the credits would help to sell albums for Artie, made one brief appearance on guitar and backing vocals.

However, the album was taking forever to finish. According to Clive Davis,

> Artie continued to equivocate. For a while he wanted to combine classical and contemporary music; next he talked of church music, and then of Greek music. At each turn, I tried to push him as far as possible in the direction of contemporary writers. The others were fine concepts, but they were very eclectic and unlikely to reach any sizable audience.

After months of thought, worry, contemplation, and gentle urging from Davis, Artie settled on the following songs for inclusion in his album: "Traveling Boy" (Paul Williams, Roger Nichols); "Down in the Willow Garden" (Charlie Monroe); "I Shall Sing" (Van Morrison); "Old Man" (Randy Newman); "Feuilles-Oh/Do Space Men Pass Dead Souls on Their Way to the Moon?" (Traditional); "All I Know" (Jimmy Webb), which enjoyed some success when released as a single; "Mary Was an Only Child" (Jorge Milchberg, Albert Hammond, Mike Hazlewood); "Woyaya" (Sol Amarfio, Osibisa); "Barbara Allen" (Traditional); and "Another Lullaby," a second Jimmy Webb song.

Artie named the album *Angel Clare*, after the tragic hero in Thomas Hardy's nineteenth-century novel *Tess of the D'Urbervilles*, whose sensibilities he sought to emulate through the timbre of his voice. After a year and a half of on-again, off-again work, the thirty-eight-minute album was released in time for Christmas and did extremely well, surprising many (but not Davis) by surpassing *Paul Simon* in sales, reaching number five on the *Billboard* lists, where it remained in the rankings for twenty-five weeks, with "All I Know" climbing into the Top Ten at number nine.

Although *Angel Clare* cost more than two hundred thousand dollars to produce, it managed to turn a profit and then some, selling close to a million units. It was a vindication of sorts for Artie—proving that he could make a hit record without Simon & Garfunkel—and put even more pressure on Paul, who was determined that his next solo album had to top *Angel Clare*.* In the fall of 1972, after much prodding from Clive Davis, Paul finally gave Columbia permission to announce a major fall tour.

And then, before any specific dates were booked, he abruptly canceled it. He told Davis it was because he was reluctant to allow anything to take him away from his baby son. He had recently moved to a larger townhouse on Manhattan's West Side and had bought a farmhouse in Pennsylvania, mostly to satisfy Peggy, who never felt quite at home in New York City (whereas Paul felt uncomfortable living anywhere else). While some believe it was the shakiness of his marriage that drove Paul ever harder into his music, and himself, others believe it was the other way around, that his work was the only reality he was really comfortable with, the marriage having convinced him once and for all that he was incapable of living a nine-to-five lifestyle.

Indeed, by 1973 Paul had submerged himself into composing a new set of songs for his next album, despite Clive Davis's urging him to make an album of other writers' songs, as Artie had so successfully done. Nonetheless, Davis green-lighted an enormous roster of talent for what would become *There Goes Rhymin' Simon*. Paul decided to record some of the album in England, and there he would record what would become the centerpiece of the new album, a song he titled "American Tune," the melody for which he had borrowed from Bach's *St. Matthew Passion*. The song, one of Paul's more opaque political musings, possibly about the state of the State under Richard Nixon and the Watergate mess, would eventually be ranked as one of his best; *Rolling Stone* rightly named it 1973's Song of the Year.

Paul recorded "American Tune" at Morgan Studios in Willesden with producer Paul Samwell-Smith, the first time since *Wednesday Morning, 3 A.M.* that he did not use Roy Halee as either his engineer or his producer on a title track. He then returned to the States and

---

* *Paul Simon* eventually did outsell *Angel Clare*. It reached number four in the United States and topped the charts in the United Kingdom, Japan, and Norway. In 1986 it reached the million sales mark and was certified platinum.

flew directly to Muscle Shoals, Alabama, which had become the new "in" place for American musicians to record, including Bob Dylan, Aretha Franklin, and eventually the Rolling Stones. Paul Simon first became aware of Muscle Shoals after hearing the Staples Singers' recording of "I'll Take You There." On the record, the Singers are backed up by the Muscle Shoals Rhythm Section, otherwise known as the Swampers. Paul wanted to work with them and wound up using this set of musicians on five of the ten tracks of *There Goes Rhymin' Simon*: "Kodachrome," "Take Me to the Mardi Gras," "One Man's Ceiling Is Another Man's Floor," "Saint Judy's Comet," and "Loves Me Like a Rock."

These songs came fast and easy. Side 1 opened strong with "Kodachrome," originally titled "Going Home," a pointed autobiographical rejection of the establishment, about being the outcast in high school, too small to play ball, and other "short" problems. Here all of it is tossed aside as just so much "crap," suggesting that his real life started when he began to play music. Looking at photographs apparently helps the narrator and the listener look forward, rather than back, rejecting dark nostalgia for carefree contentment. (According to Paul, "Kodachrome" is about nothing beyond its first, scathing sentence about high school.) The next song, "Tenderness," the only song on the album actually credited to Roy Halee (as coproducer), is a simple ballad with doo-wop overtones, enabled by backup from the great Allen Toussaint. "Take Me to the Mardi Gras" is a tribute to New Orleans, for which Paul used the counterpoint falsetto voice of the Reverend Claude Jeter and delayed echo guitar from Jimmy Johnson, and concludes with a Dixieland jazz fade from the Onward Brass Band. "Something So Right" is one of Paul's more accessible introspective musings about the increasingly confused state of his marriage. His emotions are cleverly turned inside out, which makes them clearer to both him and his listeners by the "something so right, something so wrong" wordplay. The gorgeous strings were arranged by Quincy Jones. The side concludes with "One Man's Ceiling Is Another Man's Floor," a title that evokes Simon's New York City vertical-living roots (a similar image shows up again in "Graceland," where a girl who lives in the city calls herself a human trampoline, meaning, among other things, that she makes a lot of noise walking on the floor of her apartment). "One Man's Ceiling" is a relatively rare straight-blues trip for Paul, driven by Barry Beckett's honky-tonk piano. The lyrics lean to the paranoid side.

Side 2 opens with "American Tune," followed by "Was a Sunny Day," a simple calypso to celebrate the Gulf of Mexico, where Paul had recently spent time; it was notable mainly for its early pairing of Maggie and Terre Roche, who would soon become the Roches. This was followed by Paul's love of rock 'n' roll's classic heroes—"Learn How to Fall" was probably inspired by watching his son Harper learn how to walk. "St. Judy's Comet" was also about his son, a lullaby of sorts, which Paul would perform live, with Harper, on *Sesame Street*.* The album ends with "Love Me Like a Rock," which rises to the level of greatness via the vocals of the Dixie Hummingbirds.

There Goes Rhymin' Simon was released in May 1973, and this time, much to Clive Davis's relief, Paul announced he wanted to do a full tour behind it. To warm up, he returned once more to his geographic creative comfort zone, London, where he performed two shows at the legendary Royal Albert Hall, backed by the South American group Urubamba, which included two members of Los Incas, and a gospel group, the Jessy Dixon Singers (both shows were recorded and used as part of a later live album, *Paul Simon in Concert: Live Rhymin'*). Encouraged by the reception, where, really, he could do no wrong, Paul returned to America and officially kicked off his first extended solo tour, *Rhymin' Simon*, in Boston.

As Paul may have feared, early on, there were calls from the audience for Garfunkel—"Where's Art?"—but those soon faded in the wake of the very strong show that Paul had put together. Invariably, by the end of each performance, he brought audiences to their feet.

Columbia, meanwhile, released a steady stream of singles from the album, beginning in July with "Kodachrome" backed with

---

* On the show he also sang " "When I Wake Up in the Morning," "Cowboy Song/Get Back," "Circle/B-I-N-G-O," "El Condor Pasa," and "Me and Julio Down by the Schoolyard."

"Tenderness" and "Love Me Like a Rock" backed with "Learn How to Fall." "Kodachrome" hit number two on *Billboard*'s singles charts, prevented from reaching the top by Billy Preston's monster hit "Will It Go Round in Circles." "Love Me Like a Rock" also reached number two, just behind Cher's novelty hit, "Half-Breed." Paul's singles were so successful that Columbia had to wait until October to release "American Tune" backed with "One Man's Ceiling Is Another Man's Floor." The only disappointment, and it was a major one for Paul, was the relative soft landing of "American Tune," which barely cracked the Top Forty, at number thirty-five.

On the strength of its hit singles, the album reached number two on *Billboard*, topped only by George Harrison's post-Beatle solo work, *Living in the Material World*. (In England *There Goes Rhymin' Simon* reached number four. "Kodachrome" could not be released there as a single due to trademark laws that prohibited the mention of a brand-name product in a song played over the BBC.)

In every way the album was an unqualified international success—it solidified Paul's status as a world-class solo performer and returned him to the top of his commercial and creative game. So energized was Paul by the attendance at his sold-out tours and the sales of the album that between shows he made time to produce an album for Urubamba (*Urubamba*), the Peruvian group formerly known as Los Incas, who had sung on "El Condor Pasa" and who sang backup when he performed "Duncan." And he gave Peter Yarrow a song for his new album, *That's Enough for Me*. "Groundhog" was something he had in the trunk; it was written for the *Bridge over Troubled Water* album but did not make the final cut. On Yarrow's album, Paul helped out with vocals, and three members of The Band—Robbie Robertson, Levon Helm, and Garth Hudson—sang and played while David Bromberg added mandolin and David Spinoza handled the electric guitar.

In April 1974 Columbia released *Paul Simon in Concert: Live Rhymin'*. Live albums were still considered something of a novelty in the seventies, and the production quality of the songs was almost always mediocre compared to the studio versions; despite its fine production, it only reached number thirty-three in the States (and failed to chart in England). The first and only single released from it, "The Sound of Silence" backed with "Mother and Child Reunion," also failed to chart.

Paul's tour finally ended shortly after Christmas, and he returned home to Harper and Peggy. And to the difficult but inescapable realization that his marriage could not be saved.

11

Still Crazy

THE GRAMMY AWARDS FOR 1973 WERE PRESENTED ON March 1, 1974, back in New York City from Hollywood, at the Uris (now the Gershwin) Theater on Fifty-first Street near Eighth Avenue. Paul's *There Goes Rhymin' Simon* was nominated for Best Album of the Year, but lost to Stevie Wonder's *Innervisions*. And although neither performed, both Paul and Artie showed up as presenters. There was one especially awkward moment when Paul and John Lennon together presented Record of the Year to Olivia Newton-John and her producer John Farrar for "I Honestly Love You." Neither was able to attend, and her award was accepted by Artie. It was the first time the two had seen each other for a while. They were polite, but Artie could not resist at least one apparently spontaneous, onstage jab: "Still writing, Paul?" Artie's little dig at

Paul drew a good-natured chuckle from the audience and an icy smile from his former partner.

Weighing heavily that night was the fact that both men's marriages, Art's to Linda Grossman and Paul's to Peggy, were about to end in divorce. Having already proven they couldn't get along in a partnership with each other, they had managed to prove they couldn't get along with the women they'd chosen to be their wives, either.

For his part, Artie had come to realize he had made a big mistake marrying Linda. There were too many cultural differences and not enough emotional symbiosis between his Jewish outer-borough New York roots and those of his Jewish southern-born-and-bred girlfriend. It became clear to both that they could not continue as a couple, that she did not understand the way he wanted to live his life, laid-back and filled with days of solitude. She also realized how much she did not like the world of show business—especially Hollywood, where Artie now spent increasing amounts of time either recording or on the periphery of the film business. Quietly and without much fanfare, they separated in 1974 and finalized their split with a formal divorce the following year. "My wife attacked the tinsel," Artie said later, "the glitter and the trivia of the music business, although that was what had attracted her in the first place. She developed a hatred of the life."

Paul's marital problems were deeper and more complex. They not only reflected the differences in lifestyles between his and Peggy's but amplified his most deep-rooted insecurities. Peggy had once been his soul mate, or so he had believed; more likely he had worked hard to try to make her into a reincarnation of Kathy, and although it may have worked for a while, ultimately he found he could not replicate the magic of that first love. It's true that both women, willingly or not, had played the muse—Kathy for "Kathy's Song," "Homeward Bound," "America," and "The Late Great Johnny Ace," as the girl the singer has been living with in London "the year before the Beatles and the Stones," while Peggy had been the muse for what many consider Paul's greatest achievement, "Bridge over Troubled Water." Peggy also inspired much of *Hearts and Bones* and makes a cameo appearance as the mother of the child from the singer's first marriage in "Graceland."

However, all-night talk sessions with Peggy that had once been filled with guiding-light suggestions about what and how Paul should strive to stay on track to meet his creative goals had now turned increasingly negative. "I had liked that she could be critical," Paul said later, "because I felt that I was someone who was praised too much. And I thought, finally, someone who's honest. But I began not to like it."

And despite the fact that they could afford a complete staff of domestic help if they so wanted, they began arguing about who should do the dishes, who should change the baby's diaper, and other assorted issues that were less about shared responsibilities than part of their not-so-subtle battle over whose life was the really important one, whose needs were more relevant in the relationship, and who meant more to the other. Paul's vulnerabilities, his always fragile ego, and his ongoing insecurities about how "good" he really was (his height, his appearance, his ability to perform without Artie, his writing capabilities—all manifestations of his insecurities that may have affected his ability to sustain a relationship) were not merely sensitive-personality issues, they were the open wounds of self-doubt that Peggy was able to zero in on at will. "Everything I did was put down [by her]. It was as if the fact that I'd earned all that money—that didn't entitle me to anything. I had a sense of worthlessness."

To make matters worse, even as he and Peggy were disintegrating as a couple, Paul was having difficulty recovering from a squash game injury to his left index finger that was so bad he could longer bend it, play certain chords, or run the sophisticated fingerpick patterns that made up so much of his signature guitar work. The two-year-old injury had subsided for a while, but now flared up and once again interfered with his playing, which only exacerbated his doubts, frustrations, and general irritability. John Lennon urged him to go on a macrobiotic diet.

Two years after the birth of his son, in 1975, Paul moved out of their apartment into a Manhattan hotel before acquiring a duplex for himself on Central Park West, with ample room for Harper whenever he visited or slept over. (Paul had been granted generous visitation rights.)

Alone, depressed, with not much more than his guitar, Paul spent long hours by himself looking out the window, and then slowly, very slowly, he started to write down thoughts about the failure of his marriage that would eventually provide the impetus for the songs on his next album, a collection of introspective tunes documenting his return to the crazy loneliness from which he had tried to escape for all these years.

Not very far away was Artie. Following his divorce, the Hollywood rake had moved back to New York and was living on the East Side (an interesting reversal of their earlier days, when Paul was the slick East Sider and Artie the Columbia University Upper West Sider). If they were aware of each other's close physical proximity, and how could they not be, neither made any effort to contact the other.

At about the same time, John Lennon was working with his good friend Harry Nilsson (of Kotex-around-the-head expulsion-from-the-Troubadour fame) on Nilsson's album, after RCA had threatened to drop Nilsson because of poor sales, bad press, and his continuing alcoholism, which made him something of a problem on the road. John went to the executives at the label and convinced them to keep Nilsson by promising to help get the next album finished.

Both Lennon and Nilsson had lately been living it up without their respective spouses; John, temporarily, as it turned out, was separated from Yoko Ono, and Nilsson was between marriages; they both liked to sleep late, breakfast on booze and candy, have fun until late in the afternoon, then try to make music into the night. To help create a good working atmosphere, John, by now a self-styled "New York artiste" (thanks to Ono's influence), turned Nilsson's Manhattan recording studio into something of a living art form, an ongoing soirée for seventies-style New Yorkers—the hipsters, the famous, the formerly famous, the up-and-comers, the wannabes, the beauties, the beasts, and the culture capitalists.

Paul had kept in regular touch with John ever since his finger injury, and now, when John found out that Paul was alone and that Artie was also in town, he called Paul to urge him to get in touch with Artie and to get them both to come down to the never-ending party and help out on Nilsson's album.

Taking Lennon's advice, Paul called Artie, who immediately agreed to come along. The first night they were there, Paul picked up a guitar, and he and Artie began to work out background melodies to one of Nilsson's new songs, but the two were so tentative and nervous and gave off such a bad vibe that the other musicians in attendance stayed away from them. But they kept at it, and by the end of the night they were able to find some kind of sound, if not distinctive Simon & Garfunkel, something decent. However, none of what they recorded found its way onto Nilsson's album.

The evening, however, was not a total loss, as it began a professional and personal reconciliation between the two. The timing could not be ignored; free of their wives, they had managed to rekindle their friendship, reaching backward somehow to a time before they had grown up, to when they were kids, singing together just because they loved doing it, just because it felt so good to hang with a best friend and feel cool and special in the spotlight of each other's lives.

For the rest of 1975 they tried to find their way back to Simon & Garfunkel, but when they couldn't, Artie began working on his second solo album, giving it the double-edged title *Breakaway*, whose themes of separation and loss referred not only to his divorce but apparently to his days as half of Simon & Garfunkel, as well. The album eventually yielded three hit singles—the title song, "Breakaway"; "I Only Have Eyes for You," which became Artie's first number-one single in England; and a duet with Paul, "My Little Town," which, upon its release, reached number nine on *Billboard*'s Top Singles chart. It was a song Paul wrote specifically for Simon & Garfunkel to sing together, in the wake of their mini-rapprochement. "My Little Town" has a tough, driving sound and was definitely the grittiest song on the album.

On *Breakaway* Artie used the help of several of the most talented musicians of the day, including David Crosby and Graham Nash (two musicians who specialized in West Coast "laid back"). According to Artie,

Graham used to sing with me and Paul in the car a lot. We used to do rounds. Graham loves to sing, he's very playful and easy about making music with people. David I didn't know quite as well as I knew Graham. I knew Graham from "The Hollies" days when he'd first come over to America. Working with him was something I had wanted to do for years.

Also appearing on the album were Toni Tennille (of the Captain and Tennille) and Bruce Johnston of the Beach Boys. Once again Larry Knechtel headed a long list of top studio musicians. The album was produced by Richard Perry, who had produced several of Carly Simon's most successful albums. Artie very much wanted to work with Perry, whose producing style and the sound he captured on record were far different from those of Roy Halee. According to Artie,

> I was very much attracted to some of the records Richard's made in terms of his specific sound he gets on backbeat drums, with specific reference to how they read on the AM radio. There are elements in Richard's style that I thought would be very complementary to mine. I think of Richard's records and his production style as bolder than mine, more graphic, made of fewer, bigger elements. And I was interested in that quality. In the studio, I wanted to defer a lot of creative power. I very specifically wanted to say, "You tell me what you think, I'll try it." So, I purposely wanted to give it away and see what would happen. A couple of times I made a couple of films, and as an actor, you know, you do that. You let the director tell you . . . you divide the labor and go in for more specialization of work. That's what I was after, and I'm very pleased. I think all of these instincts were good. It's a good way to grow.

Paul, meanwhile, kept busy by producing the Roches' first album. He also tried, unsuccessfully, to write some music for Warren Beatty's *Shampoo*. Beatty and Paul had become friends during their frequent appearances at political rallies, and he jumped at the chance to get back into the business of movie songwriting. Unfortunately, nothing he wrote for *Shampoo* made it into the movie.*

That July, Paul returned to the recording studio to cut a single called "Gone at Last," intended to be the A side for another new song, "Take Me to the Mardi Gras." He had wanted to sing it with

---

* He wrote two songs for *Shampoo*, "Have a Good Time" and "Silent Eyes," but neither was used by Beatty, who instead used well-known hits by the Beatles and Buffalo Springfield, and a few seconds of one old Simon & Garfunkel tune, "Feelin' Groovy."

Bette Midler, but there was no chemistry between them in the studio. The official word was that they could not agree on Phil Ramone's arrangement, although others suggest it was more personal than that. Instead Paul used Phoebe Snow, whose distinctive voice gave the tune a rhythmic, gospel overlay that helped turn it into a catchy Top-25 hit single.

That song kick-started a manic burst of writing in Paul that resulted in the ten songs, including "Gone at Last," that Paul needed for his new album, which he wanted to call *Still Crazy after All These Years*. Once the songs were completed, however, it took another nine months to finish the album, attributable to Paul's snail-pace perfectionism, prompting producer Phil Ramone to smirkily describe the process as "like [delivering] a baby. . . . I guess you could call it natural childbirth."

For this album, Paul had committed himself to working exclusively with Ramone, whose own talent ensured that something new was going to be brought to the table. The sound Paul was after was softer, more minor-keyed, to give it a melancholic feel to the arrangement of the title track, "Still Crazy after All These Years." The first line of this song, the first track on side 1, is about running into an "old lover" on the street, a lover who could be Peggy (or Artie, or even Kathy)—all of which work in the context of the song.

Essential to "Still Crazy" is Barry Beckett's electric piano, which gives a lounge feeling to the song, likely more attributable to Ramone than to Paul, as Ramone had been "Piano Man" Billy Joel's producer for quite some time. Mike Brecker's sax played throughout like it was reaching for a memory, but to whom and to what is not clearly expressed in the lyrics. Nor does it need to be. The song is stronger because of its ambiguity.

However, there is a sense that we are at least partly on Simon & Garfunkel memory turf, as the second cut on the album is "My Little Town," the same track that appeared on *Breakaway*. This link-by-album gave a clearer insight into exactly who in the song that "old lover" might actually be. The "little town" is now clearly Queens, and all the references to schoolbooks, saluting the flag, and so on appear to be symbols of nostalgia for the days of Tom & Jerry as much as for the years of Simon & Garfunkel.

If "My Little Town" was about Artie, "I Do It for Your Love," the track that follows it, is quite clearly about Peggy (the struggle with loss and a broken heart threads its way through this entire album). Like the rug the singer has bought in the antique store, his love for the girl (or her love for him, or both) has faded.

"50 Ways to Leave Your Lover" is another story entirely. It was originally conceived, according to Paul's brother, Eddie, as a sing-song rhyme for Harper, sung against the electronic drumbeat of a Rhythm Ace. On the recording, Steve Gadd, Paul's favorite drummer, introduces the song with an almost marchlike intensity. Background vocals are by Phoebe Snow, Valerie Simpson, and Patti Austin. When it was released as a single, "50 Ways to Leave Your Lover" became Paul's first number-one single since Simon & Garfunkel's "Bridge over Troubled Water."

"Night Game" is about the death of a baseball player, which sounds like nothing so much as album filler, offbeat and interesting, but not diverting. This was followed by Paul's previously released duet with Phoebe Snow, "Gone at Last." "Some Folks' Lives Roll Easy" is neo-gospel (a trip to heaven, or as Dylan's version put it, "Knockin' on Heaven's Door") and is the kind of journey-through-life song Paul would do far more effectively a decade or so later, during his *Graceland* period. "Have a Good Time" is an easygoing song that fits into the re-laxed nature of the second half of this album. "You're Kind" is the bit-tersweet documentation that returns the album to its central themes. Talking about it with journalist Bill Flanagan, Paul described it as

> a sort of cruel song . . . an indifferent song. Someone treats you real nice and you say "I'm leaving." You could say it's for an arbitrary reason: "I like to sleep with the window open and you sleep with the window closed." Or you could say it was about freedom. It works either way . . . [and] that makes it a better song. There are people who can't stand to be locked in and there are people who don't give a damn and simply decide, "It's better for me so I'm leaving."

"Silent Eyes" is yet another "up to heaven" song, recorded with the Chicago Community Choir, Leon Pendarvis on piano, Tony Levin on bass, and Steve Gadd on drums, and something of an odd choice to close this album, especially in light of Paul's often-stated ambivalence toward organized religion, but it does manage to put a period on the subject, at least for the moment.

The cover of *Still Crazy after All These Years* featured a very seventies-looking, newly single Paul Simon, complete with 'stache and a stylish hat, standing on the balcony of a New York City apartment. For the album sleeve copy, Paul chose a quotation from one of British poet Ted Hughes's most redemptive poems about the struggle for survival.

Breakaway and *Still Crazy after All These Years* were released the same day, October 25, 1975, and both dealt with essentially the same topic of lost love and all its multilayered implications. They are both very good individual works of musical brilliance and original-ity, filled with personal feelings and emotional expression, and were, arguably, the two musicians' most accomplished individual work to date.

Breakaway reached number nine on the *Billboard* album charts, four places below where *Angel Clare* had peaked, but good enough to go platinum (one million units); *Still Crazy after All These Years* debuted at number one. While there was no doubt Artie had done well, Paul was clearly back at the top of his game, a place where Artie could not touch him.

Touring was still something neither Paul nor Artie liked to do, alone or together. Paul did only a limited number of concerts to promote *Still Crazy*, one or two in the States and a couple more in England. Artie did a few solo shows as well, and that was really it for the both of them for the rest of 1975.

Back in New York, with his album still at the top of the charts, Paul quietly (and oddly) begun haunting the city's East Side singles bars, where, in the pre-AIDS, post-Pill seventies, everyone, it seemed, was searching for something or someone to connect with. More often than not he was accompanied by Lorne Michaels, whom NBC had signed out of Canada to produce its newest weekend experiment in an attempt to capture the elusive after-local-news hour and a half so lucrative during the week with Johnny Carson at the helm of *The Tonight Show*. The network wanted to skew younger for the weekend: the stay-at-home just-marrieds, the working couples watching their pennies, the parents of newborns—a product sponsor's demographic dream. Michaels put together the original cast of the "Not Ready for Prime Time Players," which included John Belushi, Dan Aykroyd, Gilda Radner, Jane Curtin, Garrett Morris, Laraine Newman, and Chevy Chase.

Chase, a tall, good-looking comic actor who, when he later moved to the big screen, was considered by many critics to be the heir apparent to no less than Cary Grant, and Michaels, good friends before the show had begun, had gone out of their way to meet with Paul when he was recording *Still Crazy after All These Years* to try to convince him to appear on their new show, a proposition to which Paul agreed, seeing it as a way of promoting his new album without having to go out on tour. He knew this wasn't going to be another debacle like the 1968 special because Michaels and Chase seemed too cool for any of that, and because Buck Henry, the screenwriter of *The Graduate*, who had since become a friend, was one of the show's writers.

"We knew that Paul wanted to promote *Still Crazy after All These Years*," Michaels later recalled,

> so it worked out well . . . throughout that [first] year the three of us [became] very, very tight friends. And we had one heck of a time—it was a lot of fun. Paul is a very funny man, but not in an overtly physical way. By and large he's funny verbally. He's intelligent and articulate. . . . Paul is often sitting with his guitar. Even when he is just talking to you he's picking away at it.

The two became so close that Michaels bought an eight-room apartment in the same building where Paul lived. Michaels's kitchen door opened onto Paul's laundry room.

On October 18, 1975, Paul made his first appearance as the guest host on *Saturday Night Live*. After performing solo, to everyone's surprise (except Michaels's, who was in on the move) he brought out an unannounced guest—Art Garfunkel—and together they did a series of familiar tunes leading up to "My Little Town." The fact that they did more than two songs caused some resentment among the comic regulars, prompting one member of the highly competitive cast to complain to Michaels that too much of that night's show was being given over to that "that folk-singing wimp."

The eighteenth annual Grammy ceremonies took place on February 28, 1976, back in L.A. at the Hollywood Palladium, and were broadcast live across the United States, hosted once again by Andy Williams. Paul's *Still Crazy after All These Years* easily won for Best Album of the Year, while *Breakaway* was shut out. Stevie Wonder had won in 1973 for *Innervisions* and again in 1974 for *Fulfillingness' First Finale,* and would win again the following year for *Songs in the Key of Life.* During his acceptance speech, Paul jokingly thanked Wonder for not making an album that year.

The evening was a major triumph for Paul, and also the last major live TV appearance he would make for nearly five years.

He had had a decent run with Tom & Jerry, a fabulous run with Simon & Garfunkel, and a sensational run as a solo singer-songwriter. Together, these three distinct phases of his career added up to nearly twenty of his thirty-five years. In American popular music this was almost unheard of, Frank Sinatra turf. The Beatles, by comparison, had had about six years before they fell apart and into relative oblivion for years before their return to the forefront of the public's musical taste. Elvis had had even less, three years or so before he was drafted, his blue suede shoes gone forever, traded in first for army uniforms and then for capes that made him look more Gorgeous George than Elvis Pelvis.

Now, for Paul Simon, chronicler of street youth, the agony of teenage love, and cracked-up marriages, the peal of the bells tolling the arrival of early middle age was impossible not to hear. Nor the sound of the new kids on the block.

Coming on strong and leading the new seventies pack of rockers was Bruce Springsteen, whose music was filled with the high-powered energy of straight-out rock 'n' roll layered with Dylanesque lyrics and a facade that resembled what might happen if Bob Dylan and Elvis Presley had got caught in the fly machine. Springsteen was sexual and off-the-street tough, hard, with songs filled with sweaty love. His music, new and nerve-hitting, could not have been more different from Paul's. And, finally, there was the Eagles, the group that, with "Hotel California," had beaten out both Paul and Artie at the Grammys for Song of the Year. This country-tinged song managed to be both cynical and romantic and to stay far removed from the social conflicts and vulnerable sensitivities of the Simon & Garfunkel songbook.

All of which made even it more difficult for Paul to decide what to do now. If anything. For the next five years, except for the very rare occasion, he kept his distance from the business while he tried to figure it all out.

Getting married again in the midst of it all didn't help.

Where Have You Gone, Mr. Simon?

F OR MOST OF 1976, PAUL STAYED UNDER THE MEDIA RADAR, making few public appearances and releasing little new music. He made a brief appearance on David Sanborn's jazzy, eponymous album in which he got together again with Phoebe Snow to record "Smile," and that November he agreed to host another episode of *Saturday Night Live*, at the behest of both Lorne Michaels and Chevy Chase, with whom he had continued to make the rounds of singles bars.

By now the weekend comedy show was a certified hit, rescuing Saturday night on NBC from the dustbin of reruns and old movies by offering a legitimate live comedy show that attracted huge numbers and made Michaels a power player.

Earlier that summer, Michaels came up with what he thought was a brilliantly funny idea. He wanted to bring the Beatles back together to appear as the show's musical guests the week of Thanksgiving, by publicly offering them $3,000 to perform three songs. As it happened, John was living in New York, George and Paul happened to be in the city that weekend, and Paul and Linda McCartney happened to be visiting John and Yoko Ono at the Dakota on Saturday night, April 24, when the offer was broadcast. John and Paul considered hopping into a cab and heading over to the NBC studios where the show was being broadcast live. However, they ultimately decided they were too tired and probably wouldn't be able to get there in time, and they let it go. (This was also the last time that John and Paul ever saw each other face to face.) About a month later, on the May 22 broadcast, Michaels upped the offer to $3,200 and agreed to throw in free hotel accommodations.

That November, however, George Harrison did agree to appear on the show, the same Thanksgiving week that Paul Simon was scheduled to host. Paul opened the show wearing a head-to-toe turkey outfit, something that was almost jarring to viewers who had come to know Paul as the singer who never so much as smiled. Here he was happily humiliating himself for the sake of a laugh, finishing off with an inspired performance of "Still Crazy after All These Years" in full-feather mode. It was a killer opening that matched the show's precredit sequence, in which George Harrison argued with Lorne Michaels and Chevy Chase that he, Harrison, should receive the whole $3,200 because he was the only Beatle to show up.

During the next musical set, Paul sang, in normal dress, "50 Ways to Leave Your Lover," and then, about an hour after a series of sketches, highlighted by Gilda Radner's brilliant, searing takeoff of Barbara Walters ("Baba Wawa"), Paul returned for yet another musical segment, and this time the audience in the studio (and presumably at home watching) went wild as he was joined by George Harrison. Harrison, always a victim of live-performance anxiety fears, stayed drunk for most of the week's rehearsals, while Michaels ate with him every night and tried his best to keep him as relaxed as possible.

Now, together, George and Paul performed a beautiful acoustic version of Harrison's "Here Comes the Sun," followed by an equally brilliant interpretation of Paul's "Homeward Bound," changing the sound, the feel, and the impact of both songs. This became one of the most magical moments of any episode in the show's storied live moments of unforgettable live TV.

Only it wasn't broadcast live at all, but completely prerecorded. "Here Comes the Sun" and "Homeward Bound" were actually taped earlier that week. "Here Comes the Sun" required three takes before both Simon and Harrison were happy with it. (Besides "Homeward Bound," in rehearsals they also did "Bye Bye Love," "Don't Let Me Wait Too Long," "Yesterday," "Bridge over Troubled Water," "Rock Island Line," and "Ride of the Valkyries." The entire performance later showed up on the Harrison audio bootleg *Living in the Underground*.) The opening segment, the $3,200 bit, was also prerecorded.

For all of his satisfaction playing with George Harrison, the thrill of the moment was overshadowed by the inescapable fact that he, Paul, was unable to write new songs he thought were any good, or at least as good as the ones he had written in the past. He was blocked and without a clue as to how to get past it. At least part of the reason, besides the shifting of the cultural sands, his divorce, his breakup with Artie, and the inevitability of growing older, as if that weren't enough, was his unhappiness with Columbia Records, which was in at least as much disarray has he was.

As early as 1973 the handwriting had started to show up on the subway walls for Clive Davis, as profits from record sales continued their overall post–Woodstock era downward spiral. It was due mostly to the rise of the West Coast sound, spearheaded by the Eagles and other seventies bands that chose to sign with the newer independent young-buck labels like David Geffen's Asylum. Geffen promised his acts a level of artistic freedom he said they could not get at any of the majors that made his upstart label quite appealing to some of the hottest stars of the day. Rock 'n' roll had become big business, and this was the decade where the inmates had decided they knew better how to run the asylum (hence Geffen's shrewd choice of name for his label).

Several of Columbia's best (and highest-earning) acts were tempted to leave after Bob Dylan bolted to Asylum, a move that sent shock waves through the industry. Everyone inside the business believed that while there might not have been a Dylan without Columbia Records in the sixties, likewise without Dylan there would not have been a Columbia Records in the seventies, at least not one that played a significant role in contemporary music. In that sense, although Dylan was not the label's biggest earner, the prestige factor he represented to the label was something no amount of money could buy. Dylan's defection was just one of a number of negative events for the label. Because of it, Columbia's continuing financial losses, and some serious personal problems Davis was having at the time, on May 29, 1973, at the age of forty-one, Clive was summarily fired from Columbia and told to leave the building immediately. On the way out the door, he was served with a civil complaint to the tune of $94,000 for expense account violations during his six-year tenure—1967 through 1973—as president of the label. (A year later he settled the civil suit; terms were not disclosed. In 1978 he was put in charge of Columbia Pictures' record division, a separate company, which he renamed Arista and eventually built into a powerhouse label.)

Davis's loss was nearly as devastating as Dylan's. Beginning with the Monterey Pop Festival and continuing with Santana, Janis Joplin, Billy Joel, Simon & Garfunkel, and Paul Simon and Art Garfunkel individually, Davis had made over the image and the sound of the label, for a while, into the sharpest edge of mainstream and progressive pop and rock.

After his firing, Davis was replaced briefly by Dylan discoverer John Hammond, whose power and influence at the label had long faded. Hammond proved either too old or too uninterested in the job, or too infirm, and was out (he would die from cancer only two years later). He replaced by lawyer Walter Yetnikoff, who had been the head of Columbia Records International. Yetnikoff's ascension, and Davis's and Hammond's departures, meant that the last vestige of the sixties-style progressive idealism and the special brand of artists it had brought to the label had come to an end; none of it boded well for Paul Simon.*

---

* Paul may have had intimations of Davis's Columbia Records mortality. According to Ben Fong-Torres, writing in *Rolling Stone*, the last time Paul saw Davis was during his last "singles" meeting at Columbia, during which Paul showed up unannounced and uninvited; he slammed a copy of *The Life of Krishna* on Davis's desk and left after telling him, "You need to read this book more than anyone I know."

With his contract coming to an end, and with no new material, Paul came up with the idea of recording an album with his friends, doing some of their songs along with one or two of his own (an idea ahead of its time; today it remains one of the mainstays of the recording business). He approached James Taylor, Billy Joel, and Bruce Springsteen, all of whom were open to talking it over, but in a phone conversation with Paul, Yetnikoff rejected the idea.

Mike Appel, Bruce Springsteen's first manager/publisher/producer, who had just come through a protracted legal battle with Springsteen over his future direction, was still friendly with Yetnikoff and remembers being in his office when the call from Paul came in. Paul had decided to personally communicate with Yetnikoff, hoping to get him to agree to his new album concept. Yetnikoff picked up the phone and gestured to Mike to wait and listen. After nodding his head up and down several times, Yetnikoff shouted into the receiver, *"NO! I DON'T WANT ANOTHER ALBUM OF ELIZABETHAN FOLK SONGS! AND FUCK YOU!"*

Paul settled for a 1977 *Paul Simon's Greatest Hits* package, a compromise that solved everything and nothing, as it supplied more immediate product but left unsettled the issue of a final, contract-fulfilling album of new songs. Yetnikoff was, to say the least, not a great admirer of Paul Simon's style of music, nor did he have any interest at all in being his friend or his mentor. Yetnikoff detested Davis's sixties style of with-it idealism and personal "I'm one of you" approach. For years, behind his back, Yetnikoff had been known to do a devastating impersonation of Davis's well-practiced not-from-the-neighborhood accent and pseudo-sophisticated physical hand gestures. To some, it was a display of obvious disdain, to others a clear sign of jealousy. According to Elliot Goldman, then head of CBS business affairs, "When Walter took that job, who was he? He was a lawyer who didn't have Clive's creative talent or Clive's polish. All of a sudden he has great notoriety because of his war on Warner Records."

It was a war begun by Yetknikoff, who had fired shots across the bow of Warner, the record label headed by Mo Ostin that was proving to be a formidable competitor to Columbia, and the other established majors as well, including Ahmet Ertegun's Atlantic and the venerable powerhouse Capitol, of Frank Sinatra, Beatles, and Beach Boys fame.

But it was Warner that most stuck in Yetknikoff's craw. The name Warner had always been associated primarily with movies, until Frank Sinatra started his own record label in 1960, called Reprise, that became so successful he sold it to Warner Music for a huge profit in 1963. So important was Reprise to Warner that it changed its name to Warner-Reprise. Mo Ostin was put in charge of the Reprise branch of the label, and former disc jockey Joe Smith was given the Warner part. Thus began the war of words and continued star-stealing between Warner and Columbia.

One of the first things Yetknikoff did as the new head of Columbia was to sign big acts away from Warner—"steal" was Ostin's term—among them James Taylor, with a hefty $1 million advance per album on top of a $2.5 million advance on signing, something Warner at the time simply couldn't match. Ostin, a soft-spoken but tough operator, then made it his business to exact revenge by stealing Paul Simon, the biggest rock name left on Columbia's roster.

Aware of rumors of Paul's willingness to defect to Warner, Yetnikoff vowed he would re-sign Simon, despite his personal dislike of him and his music, and the role Simon & Garfunkel had played in the label's glory years.

The acrimony between Paul and Yetnikoff got noticeably worse when Paul insisted, as he had with Davis, that he be allowed to sit in on the negotiations for his new contract. Paul said he needed to be a part of every aspect of these meetings, along with his trusted "guru," business manager and close friend Michael Tannen.

Yetnikoff flatly refused. Despite the fact that Columbia needed Paul to stay on the label, Yetnikoff simply could not bring himself to take orders from little Paulie Simon. "Walter hated his guts," recalled Debbie Federoff, Yetnikoff's secretary at the time. So much so that when Paul tried to attend a contract negotiation meeting between Yetnikoff and Tannen, Simon's arrival set off a three-way shouting match between Yetnikoff, Tannen, and Paul that resulted in Yetnikoff having Paul permanently barred from CBS's corporate "Black Rock" headquarters in midtown Manhattan. Before the actual meeting even began, Yetnikoff threw Paul out of his office and told him never to return "*Until you're dead!*" He then ordered security guards to escort

Paul from the building with instructions to never let him reenter the premises.

Paul then vowed to never record for the label again.

Paul began 1977 with an appearance at the inaugural ball for President Jimmy Carter, then an all-but-unknown peanut farmer governor from Georgia who had pulled off an upset victory in the first post-Watergate presidential election. Also there were Aretha Franklin, Leonard Bernstein, and Shirley MacLaine. After that, Paul's career took an unexpected but welcome turn as he was given another shot at the movies, this time from, of all people, Woody Allen.

The perversely brilliant Allen was directing and starring in what many still consider his best film, *Annie Hall*, a love-letter/showcase for his real-life girlfriend at the time, the tall, Waspy, elegant, and charming Diane Keaton. Allen's Jewish-rooted self-flagellation and neurotic guilt were at their peak of professional self-exploitation, and *Annie Hall* was a perfect vehicle for it. In the film, L.A.-phobic Alvy's (Allen) love of the ethnically rich Upper West Side New York is unmatched by anything and anybody, including Annie (Keaton), whom he loves precisely because of, or in spite of, her perfect Waspish ways. Allen brilliantly turned that conflict into a very funny, highly personal, and altogether entertaining film.

For the small part of Tony Lacey, an L.A. record producer of apparently unlimited power and narcissism, meant to illustrate part of what it was about the West Coast that he so abhorred, Allen wanted Paul Simon. And as if the film was not already fraught with the "doubling" aspects of real life—Allen's off-screen relationship with Keaton (who would soon leave him and take up with Warren Beatty)—there was the presence of Laurie Bird, Artie's real-life actress girlfriend, playing one of Lacey's girlfriends.

However, it was not Bird who caught Paul's eye, it was actress Shelley Duvall, cast (no less) as a rock critic. During filming, Duvall and Paul began an intense romance that continued on to New York City. She soon moved in with Paul and accompanied him when he, Artie, and Laurie attended the UK Britannia Awards to accept one for Simon & Garfunkel for Best International Non UK Album and Single Released between 1952 and 1977. For the occasion, Paul and Artie agreed to record a special one-off of "Bookends/Old

Friends." While together, Artie talked enthusiastically about his new album.

Afterward, Paul decided he wanted to go back to the studio and record one of two new songs he had recently written, "Slip Slidin' Away," and to do it with the hot country band the Oak Ridge Boys. Significantly, the Oak Ridge Boys had just left Columbia for MCA. Yetnikoff wasted no time in adding the two tracks to the upcoming compromise agreement *Greatest Hits* album. "Slip Slidin' Away" became the leadoff track on the album, followed by "Stranded in a Limousine," "Still Crazy after All These Years," "Have a Good Time," "Duncan," "Me and Julio Down by the Schoolyard," "Something So Right," "Kodachrome," "I Do It for Your Love," "50 Ways to Leave Your Lover," a new version of "American Tune" recorded by Paul and Phil Ramone and featuring Kathy Kienke and Richard Sortomme on violins, Janet Hamilton on cello, and Alfred Brown on viola, "Mother and Child Reunion," "Love Me Like a Rock," and "Take Me to the Mardi Gras." Yetnikoff, still smoldering at Paul, seriously threatened to call the album *Blatant Greatest Hits* but backed off shortly before it was released.

Annie Hall was released in 1977 to great acclaim and terrific box office. Allen was hailed as the next Charlie Chaplin (although he would have preferred being the next Ingmar Bergman). Paul's small but effective performance was received well, although some close to him wondered if it was too close to the real Paul, the singles-bar Mr. Cool who, along with Lorne Michaels, for whom he continued to make appearances on *Saturday Night Live*, gave annual "White" parties out in the Hamptons (everyone was required to wear white to the all-day bashes).

On December 7, 1977, Paul starred in his own network TV special, produced by Michaels, which seemed like nothing so much as an extended *SNL* skit, with several live performances interspersed throughout, backed by the Jessy Dixon Singers and a "surprise" drop-in visit by Artie. Also on the show were Lily Tomlin, Chevy Chase, and, in a no-dialogue appearance, Shelley Duvall. *The Paul Simon Special* was panned by the regular TV reviewers—one critic called it "about as funny as a pair of fallen arches." Later that year Paul and Michaels won Emmys for writing it, but the award did nothing to raise Paul's spirits about the show's dismal ratings and the fact that it was widely considered throughout the industry as an embarrassing failure.

The same week he won the Emmy, "Slip Slidin' Away," backed with "Something So Right," was released as a single and reached number five on the U.S. *Billboard* singles chart. Then, after their seesaw on-again, off-again romance, during which they were separated by distances both physical and emotional, Shelley Duval broke up with Paul, upon her return from a several-months-long stay in London to film Stanley Kubrick's 1980 *The Shining*, starring Jack Nicholson in the lead. Asked about the breakup, Duvall said:

> There was no special reason. It's just like in one of his songs. You like the window open, I like the window closed. Your basic incompatibility. I still love his music. I did before I met him, but I don't feel sad when I hear a Paul song. Why should I? I'm not in love with him anymore.

If Paul didn't seem that disturbed by Duvall's unemotional departure, it was probably because he thought she did him a favor, as he was already involved with someone else, an actress/writer/Hollywood princess he'd met in Los Angeles at the same time he'd met Duvall, while he was there filming *Annie Hall*.

Carrie Fisher, best known to millions of movie fans and to successive generations of George Lucas's *Star Wars* saga as Princess Leia, was the star-child of two of the biggest names of the fifties, pop crooner Eddie Fisher and all-American movie cutie Debbie Reynolds, the "Tammy" of the namesake series and one of the three principal dancers in Gene Kelly and Stanley Donen's 1952 movie *Singin' in the Rain*.

Paul was thirty-seven when they met, Fisher twenty-two. This fifteen-year age gap was just one of several key factors that ultimately proved insurmountable. Fisher was a California girl, the daughter of two major media stars, one a Jewish recording artist, Eddie Fisher, one decidedly not, the movie and nightclub star Debbie Reynolds. Paul was the product of a European-style upbringing, with parents who married once, to each other, and remained together their whole lives. Fisher, at a very early age, had gone through the trauma of her parents' very public divorce when her father left her mother to marry Elizabeth Taylor. Although too young to understand the details of all that was taking place around her, the emotional disturbance was real and left Fisher with some deep emotional scars. Her subsequent marriage to a Jewish, New York–born-and-bred pop singer might have, at least in part, been what psychiatrists refer to as a sort of acting out of a wished-for parent reunion, the kind of marriage that almost never works.

To further entwine the emotional strands, Fisher, the often self-described product of a broken mansion, dropped out of high school and followed in both her parents' footsteps and went into show business, where she forged a successful career as an actress, beginning with her hot-teenage spoiled-brat nymphet turn in Hal Ashby's steamy 1975 *Shampoo* (her only line of dialogue: "Wanna fuck?") and culminating in her 1977 iconic performance as Princess Leia. She also emerged as a witty, clever, self-deprecating, nobody's-fool writer.

Before her breakthrough in *Star Wars*, Fisher lived in London, to study at the Central School of Speech and Drama. For Fisher, the Brit experience was life-changing: "If it hadn't been for Central, I might have stayed a Hollywood kid, dressed in sequins and flinging mike cords for the rest of my life. I could have ended up in the [Las Vegas Hotel and casino] Tropicana Lounge." It was while at Central, in 1973, that she first auditioned for George Lucas, who was looking to make a film loosely based on the old Flash Gordon serials. He already had his "Flash," Harrison Ford (Han Solo), and his "Happy," Mark Hamill (here called Luke Skywalker), and in Fisher he found his version of Dale Arden (Princess Leia).

After the success of *Star Wars* Fisher moved to New York and shared an apartment with Griffin Dunne, then an aspiring film director waiting on tables to make ends meet. Dunne, who was just friends with Carrie, in turn introduced her to one of his friends, John Belushi, fresh from Chicago's Second City, who had been appearing since 1972 in the off-Broadway production of *Lemmings*, an improvisational skit show that was an outgrowth of the Second City, where Belushi had received his training as a comic actor. Through Belushi, she met Lorne Michaels. Along the way she had picked up a fondness for the drugs that at the time ran rampant through the Not Ready for Prime Time Players. Cocaine was the drug of choice that helped fuel the weekly deadline to produce ninety minutes of live comedy every Saturday night. Fisher quickly became close with Michael O'Donoghue, the so-called genius of the show, who was one of the quickest and sharpest improvisational conceptualizers around, and who fit in perfectly with the performance cast (he, too, occasionally performed), and for a while, he and Carrie were a couple. At one point they went to Ireland together, and, recalls Fisher, "I think we were actually the first people to do 'ludes and mead [*sic*]. I was shooting the *Star Wars* [sequels] and John and Danny [Belushi and Aykroyd] wanted to be in them as space creatures."

Soon, she was close with all three, and Lorne Michaels, and then, when Paul came into her life, she fell hard for him, and he for her.

I think I have a Jewish demeanor and a Protestant ethic. I think my extroversion is the Protestant manifestation, but emotionally I am Jewish, and I was always drawn to people who looked like I felt, a little upset, a little like an outcast, uncomfortable, ready to leave . . . I got involved with Paul fast. I met him in April and by the summer [of 1978] I was in Greece with him.

That same year, at Carrie's request, Paul went to Los Angeles to meet her dad, Eddie Fisher. Fisher played the loving father until, at one point, he took Paul aside and cautioned him that his daughter was a bit high-strung.

Paul would soon discover this was all too true. For Paul, whose previous "big" loves, Kathy and Peggy, were unknowns with no clear professional direction in their lives, playing the star of the relationship was a necessary part of his makeup; for Fisher, being the star was a natural force of inherited nature. Within months, their relationship had devolved into a form of competitive egotism—bickering, fighting, making up, then starting the cycle all over again until, in the spring of 1979, Fisher flew off to London to film *The Empire Strikes Back*, leaving Paul with nothing better to do than return at least some of the attention he had so expertly, if unconsciously, diverted with his pumping but frustrating love life, to his own still unresolved contract situation.

Playing that small part in *Annie Hall* had turned him into a huge admirer of Woody Allen, and infected him with a desire to make personal movies of his own. He had a film in mind he wanted to write and star in, filled with new songs he wanted to write for it. Paul's final decision to swtich labels came when he, via Tannen, presented the idea to Mo Ostin, who promptly offered Paul a $13 million guarantee to switch to Warner, assuring Paul that he would use his influence to get Warner's film division to make his movie.

When Yetnikoff heard about the deal, he refused to let Paul go, claiming he still had him under contract, but Tannen insisted that there was no way Paul would ever fulfill his remaining obligations to, or re-sign with, Columbia. Finally, Yetnikoff agreed to let Paul buy his way out of his remaining obligations to the label. According to Tannen, Yetknikoff's friend attorney Stanley Schlesinger, who represented CBS in the negotiations, claimed that Yetnikoff received $1.5 million from Paul to let him out of any further commitment to Columbia.

That ended Paul's storied fourteen-year association with Columbia Records and began his time at Warner, where he would record some of the greatest music of his career. But not before everything in life appeared to him to get even worse, if such a thing was possible. To his dismay, it was.

13

The Prince and the Princess and the Pony

PAUL NOW TURNED ALL HIS ENERGIES TO WRITING THE SCRIPT for the blatantly autobiographical movie he called *One-Trick Pony*, the title referring to someone who does only one thing well.

Paul's identification with Woody Allen was more than with just the obvious image of the Jewish schlub who is really a genius and somehow irresistible to beautiful women but too neurotic to love them. Like Allen, Paul had thought a lot in his early days in England of becoming a poet, or a satirist, and had even on more than one occasion tried to write a so-called serious novel, before giving up each time without being able to do it. He had also occasionally thought about doing a Broadway musical, but didn't have any idea how to adapt his style of music to the traditional sounds of the Great White Way.

True to his word, Mo Ostin had been able to convince Warner Brothers to back the film, which, in truth, had not been all that difficult to do. Knowing the fantastic sales numbers the soundtrack of *The Graduate* had earned for Columbia, the studio was eager to finance Paul's film, provided he give them a soundtrack album to go with it. Even if the film did not do well, Warner figured it would probably make back its entire investment from album sales alone.

Paul now immersed himself in both the writing of the script and the composing of the songs that, unlike those he had done for *The Graduate*, would be directly incorporated into the story. During this period he maintained his self-imposed near-isolation. He reemerged only to appear once on film in a cameo for Eric Idle and Neal Innes's brilliantly scathing satire on Beatlemania, *All You Need Is Cash*, popularly known as "The Rutles," broadcast on UK television in 1978. And, at the behest of Danny Goldberg, a popular record producer and executive on the same side of sociopolitical issues as Paul, he showed up in person for the final performance of the five nights of MUSE concerts held in New York City September 19 through 23, 1979, at Madison Square Garden and in Battery Park, which became popularly known as "No Nukes."

Paul performed rousing versions of "The Boxer" and "The Sound of Silence." However, possibly by his own design, he did not appear in the highly successful documentary movie directed by Goldberg, Anthony Potenza, and Julian Schlossberg, the resultant video, the "live" radio broadcast, or the album, which turned out to be one of his more prescient decisions at this point in his career.

The shows and accompanying media records of it featured, among others, Jackson Browne; Crosby, Stills and Nash; Tom Petty; James Taylor; and Carly Simon, all of whom were overshadowed by the shattering dramatic solo performance of Bruce Springsteen. At the height of his musical creativity and personal charisma, and yet, somehow, still a cult star, that night he unveiled for the first time anywhere his new song "The River" (from the forthcoming album of the same name), followed by a rollicking high-energy Detroit-hits medley with the E Street Band. No one could compete with Springsteen (then or now) for performances filled with high drama and blistering energy, and because of it everyone else at the concert looked, by comparison, a little less great. The other performances may have gotten stuck in the amber of late-seventies cause concerts, but Springsteen's performance remains contemporary, vivid, and unforgettable. Paul smartly decided to stay ashore for this tsunami.

By December 1979 Paul had finished his semiautobiographical screenplay—the character resembled a what-if-he-had-never-made-it version of himself—and took it directly to Warner, where it was decided by the Hollywood suit set that Paul's lack of acting experience would hurt the film if he played its central character himself, the aging, washed-up, loser boomer musician Jonah Levin. Yes, he had been in *Annie Hall*, and yes, he had done well, but in a small role. He had no real big-screen track record and therefore no proof he could carry a full-length film on his diminutive and inexperienced shoulders. Instead, they came up with idea of casting Gary Busey as Jonah, off his strong performance as Buddy Holly in Steve Rash's *The Buddy Holly Story* the year before, which had earned Busey a Best Actor Oscar nomination. (He lost to Jon Voight in Hal Ashby's *Coming Home*.) That Busey, a southern boy who lived on the edge, was nothing like the Jewish divorcé in *One-Trick Pony* didn't seem to bother the geniuses at Warner.

But Paul had final say in the casting of the film, and after he rejected Busey, Warner put up Richard Dreyfuss (who coincidentally had a one-line walk-on in *The Graduate* before he established himself in Hollywood). Dreyfuss had actually won an Academy Award for best actor two years earlier for his performance in Herbert Ross's 1977 film *The Goodbye Girl*. And, the Warner executives proudly boasted, he was Jewish and therefore perfectly suited to the role, but Paul rejected him, too, and all other names the studio proposed because, he insisted, the role was that of a musician and he didn't want anyone else lip-synching his songs and faking the look of his unique style of fingerpicking. No, Paul insisted, it was going to have to be him up there, acting, playing, and singing, or it would be nobody. To let the studio know he meant business, Paul went back to Mo Ostin, who in turn went to the movie executives and called a spade a spade, telling them if Paul didn't play the lead in his own film, there was a good chance he would never record anything for the record label. Not long after, the film, with Paul in the starring role, was fully green-lighted.

His desire to direct himself was something he could more easily be talked out of when the studio suggested Paul M. Young, who had recently directed *Rich Kids*, a film about two Manhattan boys whose authentic feel for the city's streets resonated strongly with Paul. Moreover, Young's style was low-key and he had no interest in turning the project into a "Paul Young" film. He was well aware of who the real auteur of this film was. Young was then set to direct.

In the film, Jonah is a rock star in his thirties who had one hit record ten years ago and nothing since, and is now reduced to opening for punk rock bands in small clubs. His marriage is breaking up, threatening the stability of his relationship with his son (who was the same age in the script as Harper was at the time), the only relationship he has been able to successfully maintain and the only one he is interested in still maintaining. At one point he finds himself on a sixties tribute show, alongside Tiny Tim and the Lovin' Spoonful, giving added depth to the changing times/left behind theme that runs through *One-Trick Pony*. During the show Jonah's sixties-style band is pushed off the stage to allow the more contemporary B-52s to come on, to the kind of cheering applause and enthusiasm that had never been there for him.

Jonah's wife, Marion, played by Blair Brown, who, perhaps not coincidentally, physically resembles Paul's first wife, Peggy, has been criticizing him, castrating him really, for not "growing up" and facing the truth about his own artistic failure. In one scene she tells him: "You've wanted to be Elvis Presley since you were thirteen years old. Well, it's not a goal you're likely to achieve . . . and he didn't do too well with it."

In another especially effective scene the band passes the time on a long bus ride by playing "rock 'n' roll deaths," naming those stars who have passed on, including Elvis. The band's preoccupation with death gives an added chill to their own existential lives as failed musicians.

By the end Jonah calls once more upon the spirit and ghost of Elvis that hangs over this quasi-homage by reciting Elvis's monologue from his classic version of Turk and Lou Handman's "Are You Lonesome Tonight" as a means of telling Marion that he still loves her. It is a touching, meaningful moment, one of the best and most interesting in the film, but it serves to defeat the hoped-for harder edge. In the end, Paul just didn't want to get that close to his own story. According to Paul, in the movie:

> I thought I would tell the story of my generation of musicians and I thought I would explore the crevices of my marriage but the closer I got, the further away I got. So whatever autobiographic bits are left in are just information that clings to the intestines as it passes through divorce. That's not exactly the metaphor I would choose for my marriage [to Peggy] but . . .

To help him prepare for his role in the film, at the suggestion of his old friend Charles Grodin, Paul enlisted the services of Mira Restova, the famous Method-driven teacher of no less a film legend than Montgomery Clift. At her urging, Paul temporarily relocated to Chicago to pick up the flavor of the city, including its famed broken-back "a" dialect, and to hang out in the small clubs where Jonah played every night. To put some distance between his own story and Jonah's, Paul had set the film in Chicago, which happened to be the home of the Second City, where most of the Not Ready for Prime Time Players had first gained attention as performers. In that way, the film was also a paean to his friend Lorne Michaels and the talented cast of TV players he had made famous (the film was actually shot in Cleveland, Warner's cinematic substitute for Chicago, where it was much cheaper to make).

Just before Paul left New York City to begin production, he met with Peggy, to try to ease her persistent fears that the film was going to be some kind of exposé of their marriage (which, in a sense, it was) and to assure her that the character of Marion was not really her. The level of his success at convincing her was probably not as high as either would have liked.

Similarly, Paul discussed the script with Artie, who had recently moved back from L.A. to the city, to get some input and perhaps to rekindle the memories and then the desire to share those great nights of their youth when they could easily spend hours talking and singing and never thinking about anything else. However, the more they discussed the film, the more Artie became convinced the movie was really about *him*, that Paul was trying to pump him for bits of information to make the script more real, and that its sole purpose was humiliation-by-film. No, Paul insisted, if it was about anybody besides himself it was Elvis Presley, the then recently deceased singer who had meant so much to both Paul and Artie (and whom Paul had seen in Presley's New York concert debut in 1972, when Paul was stunned by Elvis's highly affecting version of "Bridge over Troubled Water") and whose slow demise, which so clearly personified the death of fifties rock, had been especially excruciating for him to witness.

Like Peggy, Artie was not totally convinced by Paul's explanation.

Perhaps it was because of Artie's own faltering film career, something of a reversal from the days when they were growing apart while recording *Bridge over Troubled Water* and Artie was making *Catch-22*. Now, with his girlfriend, Laurie, Artie had moved back into a Manhattan penthouse, after particularly difficult professional ups and (mostly) downs for the both of them that had seriously affected their personal relationship. None of it had been helped by Artie's release of another new album, *Watermark*, intended to showcase himself as the new voice for Jimmy Webb, who had had a great run of hit singles with country singer Glen Campbell, the best of which was 1967's masterpiece (for both), "By the Time I Get to Phoenix." Like Artie's previous solo effort, *Watermark* was filled with a laundry list of the finest West Coast studio musicians, including Steven Bishop on guitar and vocals, David Crosby, and dozens of others, and was produced by Phil Ramone, with whom Paul had had much solo success.

However, in October 1977, despite a rush of reviews that declared that Artie had finally grown up and out of the protective shell of Simon & Garfunkel and that Webb was a far better collaborator for him, and despite a major forty-city tour, Artie's first in seven years, the album laid a big fat egg. So much so that Columbia quickly recalled it, deleted the first track, "Crying in My Sleep," a Webb-penned tune he had written especially for Artie, and replaced it with a track it had in the vaults featuring Artie, Paul, and James Taylor doing a version of

"What a Wonderful World," which Louis Armstrong had had a huge hit with a few years earlier. Remixed and rereleased in time for the tour, *Watermark* was saved by the single release of "What a Wonderful World," which reached number seventeen on the singles charts and stimulated sales of the album. The tour's final night, at Carnegie Hall, saw both Paul and Jimmy Webb come onstage. Paul and Artie did a blistering version of "My Little Town," and Artie closed, not with something from *Watermark*, but with a rousing version of "Bridge," which many who were there believe he never sang better than he did that night.

Meanwhile, Laurie's film career had seriously stalled, and relations between her and Artie became increasingly strained, possibly because of the professional jealousy that had managed to come between them just before taking *Watermark* on tour. Even worse, for Laurie, Artie had recently completed work on yet another major film, Nicholas Roeg's *Bad Timing: A Sensual Obsession*, a sexual thriller costarring the provocative Teresa Russell. Garfunkel hoped this was the picture that would revive his flagging film career.

But all of that hope disappeared on the evening of June 15, 1979, just before *Bad Timing* opened, when twenty-five-year-old Laurie Bird, whose last professional acting job was as Paul's girlfriend in *Annie Hall*, and whose youthful beauty and all-too-brief film career of just three movies would now earn her the title in some of the more ghoulish Hollywood circles as the female James Dean, committed suicide by drug overdose. She died in her and Artie's new apartment.

Artie was completely shattered by Laurie's death and immediately went into isolation, unable to see or talk to anyone about what had happened. Those closest to him thought he blamed himself because he had refused to marry her, something she apparently very much wanted, even more so when her career hit the skids. He was so grief-stricken he couldn't return to the apartment for several months, preferring the anonymity and isolation of an Upper East Side hotel that catered to those in the public eye who sought the privacy they occasionally needed. He wanted to be away from everyone, including Paul.

Having first been unable to talk to Artie meaningfully about his film, and then unable to comfort him in the immediate aftermath of Laurie's death, Paul reluctantly left for Cleveland, to work on *One-Trick Pony.* Filming actually began in September 1979 with an agreed-upon budget of six million dollars, which ballooned to seven million before filming was completed—not a great deal of money for a picture, but enough, Paul felt, to get the job done the way he wanted it.

However, before he could even begin to shoot his scenes, he was called away by Fisher, who wanted him with her for the June opening of *The Empire Strikes Back* in London, which everyone agreed was going to be *the* film event of the year. Dutifully, if not enthusiastically, Paul left his own movie behind, hopped on a flight, and arrived in London just in time for the gala premiere. If it was a demonstration of loyalty and support, it was also one of self-reassurance, as Paul knew that Fisher was going directly into production with *The Blues Brothers,* costarring her ex-lover, Dan Aykroyd. The morning after the London opening, Paul flew by himself back to Cleveland. After the one-month shoot, he returned to New York City to work with Phil Ramone on the production film's soundtrack.

As soon as he arrived in Manhattan, he called Artie to find out how he was coping. Not well. He was still in a state of depression over Laurie's suicide, overlaid with increasing anxiety about the upcoming release of *Bad Timing.* It had already opened in London to tepid reviews. On top of that, he was being sued by his ex-wife, who was pressuring him to renegotiate their divorce settlement.

Paul wanted to continue to try comfort Artie, but simply did not have enough time to do so. Warner was pressing for the single from the album in order to have it out prior to the movie's release. Working feverishly with Ramone in a small studio in midtown Manhattan's Hell's Kitchen, they managed to at least pull together "Late in the Evening," which was loosely based on Elvis Presley's superb version of "Mystery Train" and was filmed at the Aora Club in Cleveland during the making of the movie. For the B side they finished "Long Long Day," another track from the film.

To fill in the time before the movie's scheduled October opening, and to try to salvage his relationship with Fisher, who had in fact openly reignited her romance with Aykroyd while filming *The Blues Brothers,* Paul did a limited number of live shows, including one in

Philadelphia, where the always fiendishly funny Fisher showed up and joined him onstage for an ironically timed duet of "Bye Bye Love," and one in England, at the Hammersmith Odeon, the final show of the tour that, after his long hiatus, marked his official return to regularly scheduled public performance.

While in England, he was interviewed by Anne Nightingale on the BBC's *Whistle Test*, and became visibly exasperated when Nightingale opened an old but still sensitive wound when she asked how difficult it was for him to write songs without Garfunkel. When he corrected her by saying that Artie only sang with him and had nothing to do with the writing, an apparently skeptical Nightingale dug an even deeper hole for herself when she asked Paul if this was a well-known fact. Paul replied, "I guess everyone knows but you!" It was that kind of year for Paul.

Warner opened *One-Trick Pony* on October 3, 1980, as one of their "big" fall pictures. Most critics agreed that the music was great; what came in between wasn't. Built around a weak character, the film muddles along in callow kitchen-sink melodrama land before shifting gears and turning into a reclamation-of-ideals conflict centered on some master tapes that may or may not get released, the sort of drama that might be interesting only to someone in the music business. The assumption that the public cares as much about the process of music-making as about the music itself is the film's central and misguided assumption. Because of it, the film is altogether too insular, too vague, too precious, too trivial, and too whiny. Paul's worship of Woody Allen helped him capture Allen's signature ennui but not the part that makes it work on film—Allen's redemptive biting wit and his above-it-all-but-too-neurotic-to-enjoy-it conceit. In *One-Trick Pony* Jonah opens as a loser and ends as one, too, despite his (to him) triumphant taking back of his tapes. Because the victory is so so-what, it obscures the deeper, more important emotional story Paul was trying, and ultimately failed, to tell.

The film was a box-office loser, but the title song proved a big winner. Using Paul's penchant for street music that he had adapted so smartly in "Me and Julio" and "Mother and Child Reunion," and using the backup band he would later tour with (and who appeared in the film), consisting of the cream of the studio musician crop,

Paul and Richard Tee, Tony Levin, Eric Gayle, and Steve Gadd, the song cooked with a sophisticated rhythm and, for a Paul Simon lyric, was unusually simple and accessible. An immediate hit, it reached number six on the *Billboard* singles chart.

Artie's film opened the same day, and both films often played side by side in the same theater complexes (as they did at New York City's Gemini 1 and Gemini 2). Both films received only a limited release in the States, both received lukewarm (at best) reviews, and both did poorly at the box office. Several critics (correctly) dismissed *One-Trick Pony* as nothing more than an exercise in navel-gazing. In its review of the film's soundtrack album, *Rolling Stone* referred to *One-Trick Pony* as "that morose little art film," and the *New York Times* wrote about Artie's performance in *Bad Timing* that "he does a very credible job of conveying Alex's reserve but there is little in his performance to suggest a man in the grip of an obsession."

Both films disappeared quickly, and Paul slipped back into his own deepening depression. His troubled, seesaw relationship with Carrie Fisher was in trouble, and the return of Dan Aykroyd to her love life did nothing to help Paul's peace of mind. The failure of his film and his love-life problems led him directly into the open arms and leather chair of the nearest available psychiatrist.

The time had finally come, he realized, to get his head examined.

14

Saturday in the Park with Paul and Artie . . . and Carrie

I N 1980, WHEN *ONE-TRICK PONY* CAME OUT TO MIXED RE-
views and the soundtrack album didn't do nearly as well as I'd
hoped, it was a period of great depression for me. I was im-
mobilized. And it was about that time I came under the influence
of a man named Rod Gorney, who's a teacher and a psychiatrist
in Los Angeles. I heard about him from a friend and called him
from New York." Thus began one of the strangest episodes of Paul's
career.

So urgent was Paul's need to talk to Dr. Gorney that whenever he
went to see him, he would go directly from the Los Angeles airport to
the doctor's home. There he would begin his sessions by laying out
the major contradiction of his life; he was young, healthy, famous,
talented, and wealthy—and depressed to the point where he feared

169

he might no longer be able keep it together. Eventually, working with Dr. Gorney, Paul was able to cite the failure of the entire *One-Trick Pony* experience as one of the symptoms, rather than the cause, of his darkening state of mind. He was also able to compartmentalize his long and difficult battle with Yetnikoff and CBS, after realizing that the head of CBS had not really been involved in some sort of evil conspiracy to damage his career after all. And finally, after several sessions, he felt ready to focus on something more fundamental to his faltering sense of well-being—his complicated, and largely unsatisfying, relationship with Carrie Fisher.

The doctor theorized early on that Paul's issue was not creativity but self-worth (and the relationship between the two), that Paul's ego had been beaten up pretty badly by his professional failures and his unsatisfying personal relationships with both Artie and Carrie. The question came down to relevance. Paul had taken all his personal insecurities and turned them into aspects of his strictly professional dilemma. Just as Jonah wonders about it in the film, so Paul was questioning his own ability to remain relevant in a world whose taste for rock 'n' roll had shifted from Simon & Garfunkel to the B-52s.

After one of their sessions, Dr. Gorney pointed out that there was a guitar in the corner of the room and asked Paul if he would like to borrow it and try to compose some songs. Paul said he would, but that it sometimes took months for him to write even a single song. Just try to start one, the doctor suggested. Paul took it home with him to his new apartment at the storied San Remo on the West Side, overlooking Central Park, and put down a few lines of a song called "Allergies," which he got really excited about. Now Paul began working, every day, trying to find the thread from his older work that would lead him to create something new.

Artie had, meanwhile, begun his own method of self-help, in effect to try to sing his way out of his grief by reuniting with Jimmy Webb and the always dependable Roy Halee to record *Scissors Cut*, an album he dedicated to Laurie. It was released in October 1981, but despite generally good reviews—*Rolling Stone* called it "Art Garfunkel's finest solo album [to date]"—it failed to break into the American Top

100 chart listings (it made it as high as number fifty-two in England), sending Artie even deeper into his own downward spiral with feelings of guilt and worthlessness.

At about this time, Ron Delsener, then the most powerful concert promoter in New York City, who had carved out a niche for himself that had crowded out even Bill Graham as the number-one rock 'n' roll performance godfather of Manhattan, had begun talks with Gordon Davis, the parks commissioner of New York, about the possibility of putting on a free concert in Central Park.

The idea was to do something to help New York City. In the mid-to-late seventies the city was in serious economic decline. Rents were low, thanks to the huge number of apartments still protected under rent control, and that had led to a virtual halt in construction of new dwellings and improvements on old ones. Crime was high, drugs were everywhere, and corruption throughout the police force was rampant. Taking a walk in what had once been the jewel of the city, Central Park, was most New Yorkers' idea of the surest way to commit suicide.

The city's mayor, the jocular and endlessly self-promoting Ed Koch, decided Delsener's notion of a free concert in the park was the perfect way to boost the city's morale, as well as his own mayoralty, which was teetering from a third-term exposure of widespread citywide corruption that had all but rendered him powerless. Koch believed the goodwill of the free concert could go a long way toward polishing his own badly tarnished image.

With this nod of approval from City Hall, Delsener wasted no time in putting together a record-breaking audio and video rights deal with HBO that depended upon who would be the star of the show. Everyone on all sides agreed that that it had to be New York's own Simon & Garfunkel.

Delsener called Paul directly to prevail upon him to give something back to the city that had given him so much. Paul said he would do it if—and it was a big if—Delsener could help him get Artie to agree.

The promoter immediately began to put together the logistics of what would undoubtedly become the biggest musical event in the park's, maybe the city's, history. One of the first people Delsener called was Warren Hirsh, of Fiorucci and Hirsh Enterprises. Two years earlier, Hirsh had produced a successful James Taylor concert in the park, although nowhere near the scale of what Delsener was proposing. And the year before that Hirsh had been behind Elton John's concert in Central Park. His model had been a successful one—let the audience in for free and make back the costs, and then some, from sales of merchandise and broadcast rights. Doable, Hirsh told Delsener.

At first Delsener suggested to Paul that if he couldn't get Artie to do the whole show, Paul could bring him out for a song or two and finish with a rousing "Sound of Silence," but Paul quickly rejected that idea. He wasn't about to turn himself into the opening act for Simon & Garfunkel. The show would have to be a full-blown reunion of Simon & Garfunkel, or there would be no show, not with him anyway. At Delsener's urging, Paul placed the initial call to Artie. It took a while to track him down, as he was at the time walking his way through Switzerland (one of his more idiosyncratically restive hobbies was walking across countries). To Paul's surprise, Artie agreed to do the show.

Everything for Paul felt like it was beginning to click back into place. Whatever the reason, maybe his work with Dr. Gorney, his latest writing block had subsided, and he was composing again, every day, on the guitar and the piano, searching for ever more sophisticated stylings and chord progressions. Most of the new songs were, not surprisingly, about his relationship with Carrie. A romantic vision of love in all its imperfect glory was, as always, fertile writing turf for him, and his relationship with Carrie was thick with potential. She was bipolar, a major movie star, and a heavy drinker; he was a depression-prone rock star. And while the way they treated themselves and each other may have made him crazy, it also provided the fuel that sent his songwriting into overdrive.

That very summer they had gone for weeks without speaking, leaving Paul to wonder what she was up to and with whom. Plus, there was the endless snickering at parties and in the tabloids that he was her Eddie Fisher (the reference was at best mixed; he may have been her Eddie Fisher, but she was far more his Liz Taylor than his Debbie Reynolds).

However, for the Central Park concert, if everything else could be worked out, Paul knew he would wind up singing mostly old stuff. The show had already begun to take on a summary feel. And despite the grumblings of those who saw it as nothing more than a blatant attempt by two over-the-hill forty-year-olds to revive their flagging careers, Paul and Artie eagerly hit the rehearsal halls believing they had nothing left to prove to anybody.

At Paul's suggestion, Lorne Michaels was hired by the city to use his Broadway Video subsidiary company to work out the extremely difficult task of not just broadcasting the ninety-minute "live" broadcast over HBO, but re-editing it for future VHS sale (both versions were directed by Michael Lindsay-Hogg, whose rock 'n' roll credentials included the Beatles' 1970 feature *Let It Be*). A ninety-minute version of the concert was to be shown on HBO in February 1982. The rights for that broadcast went for a reported million dollars.

Eugene Lee was enlisted to construct the 160-foot "rooftop" stage to accommodate Paul's insistence on a full orchestra, at a building cost of more than three quarters of a million dollars. When both the city and HBO balked at the money for the set, Paul reportedly paid to have it built himself, and by doing so became the single largest investor in the show. He saw it as both personal payback to New York and a great investment. He was correct on both counts.

Paul and Artie rehearsed with Phil Ramone in the studio to help prepare for the live show and the LP that would capture it and with Roy Halee, who would engineer both. However, amidst all this creative energy, Paul and Artie quickly reverted to their familiar pattern, bickering like an old married couple trying to decide, and unable to agree, on how to celebrate an upcoming anniversary, until they began to question why they had wanted to get back together at all.

What may have set them off was the always touchy issue between the two about Paul's wanting to include a few of his newer songs, and several that he had written and recorded as solos, including "Late in the Evening," which he was convinced was his best in years. To do so, he needed a complete orchestra with horns, an idea that Artie insisted was a huge mistake. Despite the fact that he, too, had used lush arrangements and elaborate orchestrations on his albums, he steadfastly believed they should perform as they always had in the past, just two voices and one guitar. Impossible, Paul countered. Even if he wanted to play the whole set by himself, his injured finger was still too damaged. Artie then agreed to a backup guitarist. What, then, was the real difference between adding one piece and adding twenty-one pieces?

And they were off. In the end, out of persistence and because Artie didn't want to fight anymore, Paul put together the band he wanted.

As the September 19, 1981, show date got closer, a single ad appeared in each of the city's daily newspapers announcing the show, and that was all it took to set off Simon & Garfunkel fans into a frenzy. Demand for the free tickets was unprecedented. At dawn the morning of the show people started arriving at the Great Lawn trying to secure their place in front of the stage. By early evening more than a half million had gathered, and the free show turned into an event with a live audience larger than Woodstock.

By 8:15 the musicians Paul had hand-selected began to gather onstage, a roundup of the best studio musicians, many of whom had performed on both Paul's and Artie's solo albums, including David Brown (guitars), Pete Carr (guitars), Anthony Jackson (bass guitar), Richard Tee (keyboards, piano), Steve Gadd (drums, percussion), Grady Tate (drums, percussion), Rob Mounsey (synthesizer), John Gatchell (trumpet), John Eckert (trumpet), Dave Tofani (saxophones), and Gerry Niewood (saxophones). As the twilight began to deepen the city sky to steel blue, the brilliant arc of stage lights lit up and the avuncular Ed Koch strolled on stage. The audience cheered him, which he happily acknowledged, and for a moment it seemed as if he were under the impression that the purpose of the concert was for Simon & Garfunkel to introduce *him*. After milking the applause as long as he could, he said, simply, in his raspy voice, Bronx accent, and lower-lip lisp, "Ladies and gentlemen, Simon & Garfunkel!"

They trotted out from the wings like two kids, to thunderous applause, smiling and standing next to each other before, with mock exaggeration, they shook each other's hand. The crowd reaction intensified as Paul, guitar strapped on, and Artie for the first time in eleven years kicked open a concert together, using "Mrs. Robinson" as their entrée before seamlessly rolling into a terrific version of "Homeward Bound." "It's great to do a neighborhood concert," Paul cracked after the song ended, and the audience roared. "I hope you can all hear us," he added. He thanked the mayor, the police department, the fire department, and "the guys selling loose joints," before he began the guitar-solo introduction to a harmonically perfect version of "America." Paul's comment may have been prompted by a "spontaneous" yet well-publicized police drug bust at the Seventy-second Street Boat Basin earlier that day. Many in the audience took Paul's comments as the cue to light up (no drug arrests were made during the concert).

After their opening set, Paul exchanged his acoustic for an electric and performed a rousing "Me and Julio Down by the Schoolyard," which Art easily slipped into and behind, followed by another guitar change and a return to acoustic harmonizing for "Scarborough Fair" and "April Come She Will." They followed that with a nod to their Tom & Jerry days, a killer version of the Everly Brothers' "Wake Up Little Susie."

After an extended round of applause, Paul slipped on yet a different guitar and performed a beautiful solo version of "Still Crazy after All These Years," while Artie retreated into the side recesses of the stage, returning to join Paul on "American Tune"; Artie stayed for "Late in the Evening," then did a solo of his own, from *Scissors Cut*, "A Heart in New York," after which it was Paul's turn to solo again. "The Late, Great Johnny Ace" was his newest, which somehow melded the deaths of R&B's Johnny Ace whose classic "Pledging My Love" is one of doo-wop's foundational songs (Ace died playing Russian Roulette nearly three decades earlier) and John Lennon, murdered nine months earlier less than a mile away, gunned down by a crazed fan in front of the Dakota, where Lennon lived with his wife and baby. During Paul's performance a youngish man rushed the stage, shouting, "I have to talk to you!" Paul stopped playing and stepped back as the color drained from his face. Security guards immediately overwhelmed the man and dragged him off the stage. After a few more seconds of paralytic silence, Paul stepped back up to the mike and continued the song.

He never again sang that song live.*

Artie then returned and with Paul performed a mood-lifting, crunching version of "Kodachrome" that segued perfectly into Chuck Berry's "Maybelline." And, finally, Art performed a soaring "Bridge over Troubled Water" that stopped the show and brought everyone to their feet. For the final encore, they performed "The Boxer," with its strong and timely message of how, after changes upon changes, life remained more or less the same.

But the crowd simply wouldn't let the show end, and after several minutes of cheering and chanting, Paul and Artie returned yet again, this time to perform an exquisite acoustic version of "Old Friends/Bookends," "The 59th Street Bridge Song/Feelin' Groovy," and finally, the one song the crowd had waited for the entire evening, "The Sound of Silence." Still not satisfied, the audience cried for more, and after thanking the audience "from the bottom of our hearts," Paul cued in a reprise of "Late in the Evening" and invited the audience to sing along, after which Paul and Artie wrapped their arms around each other's shoulders, took deep bows, and left the stage as the audience cheered them into the night.

Despite its fabulous reception, neither Paul nor Artie were particularly happy with the show. According to Paul:

> Afterward, our first reaction was, I think, one of disappointment, Arthur's more than mine. He thought he didn't sing well. I didn't get what had happened, how big it was, until I went home, turned on the television and saw it all on the news, the people being interviewed, and later that night, on the front page of all the newspapers. Then I got it.

---

* On May 20, 1982, Paul was a guest on David Letterman's show. He performed the as-yet-unreleased "Citizen of the Planet" and a part of "The Late Great Johnny Ace." During the commercial break, Paul privately told Letterman he could never sing that song again. There is some speculation that Paul's mentioning of John Lennon was interpreted by the attacker as an attempt to commercialize on the late Beatle's name.

And so did everyone else. Suddenly, there was a huge demand for Simon & Garfunkel—live, on TV, on record, on tour. Two weeks after the February presentation on HBO, a double live album of the concert was released and shot into the Top Ten. Critic Stephen Holden rhapsodized over it in *Rolling Stone*, praising Dave Matthews's "scrupulous" arrangements, calling the song selection a summation of rock fatality "from doo-wop to the Dakota (even though 'The Late Great Johnny Ace was not included in the album')," the overall concept a beat-[generation]-inspired "phantasmagoria," and pointed out how heavily the presentation had been "improved" in the studio:

> The new album has magic to spare, some of it rough. Though labored over in the studio after the event, the tracks are far from 100% polished. It's actually refreshing. If *The Concert in Central Park* was Paul Simon's valentine to the Big Apple, it is Garfunkel's voice that really tugs at the heartstrings and sends the message home.

For his part, Paul didn't think it was an especially good recording, believing, as always, that Simon & Garfunkel music was better produced in a studio than performed live.

On the heels of the duo's sudden and hot return to the rock 'n' roll limelight, the British branch of CBS released *The Simon & Garfunkel Collection*, another compilation of several of the duo's biggest hits, which reached number four in England its first week. Despite the fact that Paul had already begun recording his new solo album on the West Coast, produced by L.A.-based Lenny Woronker and Russ Titelman, doing it out there to be able to spend more time with Carrie, he agreed, for the first time in eleven years, since the night in Forest Hills Stadium, to officially go back out on the road with Artie as Simon & Garfunkel.

It was not an easy decision for Paul to make and was likely influenced by Carrie's hitting near-bottom following the shocking March 5 drug-overdose death of John Belushi at the Chateau Marmont Hotel, the aftermath of which had led her to a brief romantic reconciliation with Dan Aykroyd. Paul wanted to stay on the West Coast to try to save whatever was left of his relationship with Fisher, but in the end the allure of the road and the first real chance to rekindle his friendship with Artie took precedence. On May 28, in Offenbach, Germany, Simon & Garfunkel kicked off their planned world tour with the first of fourteen major European concerts that would take them to Dortmund, Berlin, Copenhagen, Stockholm, Zurich, Rotterdam, Dublin, Paris, and London, followed by New Zealand. That leg of the tour lasted for the rest of 1982, and set them up for their largest North American tour yet. It began the following July in Akron, Ohio, and went through Pontiac, Michigan, up to Toronto, back down to Chicago, and on to Milwaukee; Minneapolis; Pittsburgh; East Rutherford, New Jersey; Baltimore; Foxboro, Massachusetts; Queens, New York; Laurel, Maryland; Atlanta; Houston; Dallas; Oakland; Vancouver, British Columbia; Los Angeles; San Diego; and Boulder, Colorado.

Everywhere they appeared, audience adulation was as enthusiastic as it had been in Central Park. They could have played another two years without a break, if they had wanted to. The only problem was that, as early as their London date at the famed Hippodrome, they realized all over again why they could no longer perform together. Their styles had become so divergent that they were barely able to rehearse the old songs before the old bickering returned with a vengeance, and they fought about everything. For the duration of the tour, they barely talked directly to each other.

Warner, meanwhile, was pushing them to extend the tour and release a Simon & Garfunkel studio album of new songs. The label had quickly released a single of "Wake Up Little Susie" from the Central Park concert and eventually the Central Park album (and video), which did far better than Paul's first Warner solo album, *Still Crazy after All These Years*. Aware that he was working on a new album, they encouraged him to make it with Artie, which Paul said he would consider.

Besides his troubles with Artie, Carrie, while still involved with Aykroyd, had made a film with Chevy Chase, Steve Rash's *Under the Rainbow*. During its making, she fell back into heavy drug usage. To get herself off the same dark path that had taken Belushi's life, she broke up with Aykroyd, tried to wean herself off her addictions to

LSD, Ecstasy, MDA, and Percodan, and moved back east to star in the Broadway production of *Agnes of God*.

During a break in the tour, Paul remained in New York City to be with her, and that's when Carrie told him she wanted to get married. One night not long after, Paul took himself to a Yankees game, sat alone, thought everything over, and decided before the bottom of the ninth he would try marriage a second time.

He and Carrie tied the knot five days later in his duplex overlooking Central Park West. The very small guest list included Carrie's parents, Debbie Reynolds and Eddie Fisher (who came with his mother and was seeing Debbie face to face for the first time since their screaming headline breakup; they were cordial and polite to each other), Carrie's brother, Paul's parents, his brother, Eddie, Lorne Michaels, Billy Joel and Christie Brinkley, Teri Garr, Robin Williams, Randy Newman, Charles Grodin, George Lucas, Kevin Kline, Paul's son Harper, and Artie and his companion for the evening, actress and movie director Penny Marshall, whom he had just started dating and who was also a close friend of Carrie's. Eddie Fisher gave the bride away during the traditional Jewish wedding.

Carrie and Paul reportedly had a blowout later that night, when they were finally alone. Amidst false rumors that they had gotten married because Carrie was pregnant, she accompanied Paul on the first few stops of the American tour, even coming onstage in Oakland, California, to thank everyone for joining them on her honeymoon. (Fisher did have an abortion due to an ectopic pregnancy during the marriage, but it remains unclear as to when she actually became pregnant.)

Meanwhile, as the tour went on, Artie's depression continued. He fretted about playing large impersonal outdoor arenas, such as Dodger Stadium in Los Angeles. He believed the intimacy of the Simon & Garfunkel sound was completely lost in such oversized venues. And neither he nor Paul was willing to sing some of the songs the audiences most wanted, like "Homeward Bound," which must have sounded to Artie like nothing so much a postadolescent reverie meant to be sung by a twenty-two-year-old. Alone. Singing it at forty years of age just didn't do it for him.

During another break in the tour, Paul took Carrie for a cruise down the Nile, followed by a visit to Kenya. It was on that trip that he made the decision that Artie would not appear on the new album after all, despite his having already recorded several vocal tracks for it. To be fair, Artie's own ambivalence and idiosyncrasies had played a major part in Paul's decision. He'd asked Artie to give up smoking pot and cigarettes at least during the recording period, to keep his voice sounding better. Artie said no. And he refused to learn the songs in the studio with Paul. Instead, he insisted on taking them with him to Europe and listening to them on a Sony Walkman while strolling alone through the side streets of the cities he had chosen to walk.

Talking to one reporter, Paul explained his decision this way: "I would be willing to do almost—that word is important—almost anything to make Art happy. I care about our friendship. The only thing I feel I won't do is change the essence of my work. That was the crux of our problem on this new album." Then, through an official spokesperson, Paul released the following statement: "Paul simply felt the material he wrote is so close to his own life that it had to be his own record. Art was hoping to be on the album, but I'm sure there will be other projects that they will work on together. They are still friends."

Paul's marriage to Carrie finally and totally collapsed in June 1983, several months after she completed shooting *The Return of the Jedi*, during which time it was heavily rumored in the press that she was having an affair with Harrison Ford.*

"Allergies," the first completed track on his new album, was released November 4, 1983, with Paul's vocal backed by a crackling Al Di Meola electric guitar solo. It was actually the song he had begun writing after visiting Dr. Gorney. It had evolved into a meditation on the difference between sense and sensibility, between thought and emotion, between knowledge and instinct, and the frequent incompatibility of the two. It failed to chart, and that did not bode well for the full album's upcoming release. In truth, its failure came as no surprise to the executives at Warner, who thought most of

---

* Paul and Carrie's divorce was finalized in April 1984.

the songs sounded too downbeat, emotionally isolated, and overly interior, and that they would have benefited from Artie's overlaid vocals. Even Mo Ostin thought it was not Paul's best work, or, at least, not the right album to release in the still-hot aftermath of the big Simon & Garfunkel comeback, but he officially announced its release with great enthusiasm. In the end, the only change he asked Paul to make was the title. Paul had originally wanted to call it *Think Too Much*, but, in deference to Ostin, changed it to the infinitely better *Hearts and Bones*.

The second single to be released was the new title track, a five-and-a-half minute chronicle of the demise of his relationship with and marriage to Carrie, with "two-and-a-half Wandering Jews" a clear reference to himself and (the half-Jewish) Fisher. In the album's liner notes, Paul called it one of his best songs, and said that "the arc of a love affair" was what the song was about.

Track 3 was "When Numbers Get Serious." Playful and diverting, it is simply about the exchange of telephone numbers.

Track 4, "Think Too Much," the original title track of the album, stands alone among Paul's work as the only song he recorded twice for one album. After deciding the first version was too up-tempo, he rerecorded a second version, which is this track. The song continues Paul's contemplation of the two sides of love—thought and emotion—shrouded in the failure of his second marriage.

Track 5, "Song about the Moon," was inspired by Sam Cooke's "Bring It on Home," using that song's chord structure. Interesting, offbeat, minor.

Track 6 was the original recorded version of "Think Too Much."

Track 7, "Train in the Distance," took a step back (and forward) and looks deeper into Paul's problems with marital intimacy by reflecting upon his first marriage, to Peggy. Paul had always been attracted to the sound of trains, and used it many times, especially in his early songs, as a metaphor about the distance of time and does so again here. "Train in the Distance" always gets a great reception when Paul performs it live, in a way that cooks the way the original recording doesn't. It is as if he found the song after it was frozen on the album. As a result it is among his most underrated songs and remains one of the buried gems on this album.

Track 8 was "Rene and Georgette Magritte with Their Dog after the War." Paul took the title from a caption of a photograph in an art book he had been studying. The song imagines the famed painter and his wife dancing to doo-wop songs; it is an image of two artists celebrating the more youthful and innocent times of their lives. It elaborates on the fantasy of an imagined dance between Paul and Fisher—two artists—at a time in their lives when everything between them was simpler, purer, and more loving.

Track 9, "Cars Are Cars," was filler.

Track 10 was the gorgeous "The Late Great Johnny Ace" that Paul had first performed live during the Central Park show. Here it is lush, complex, invigorating, sad, and moving, complete with a mournful string coda by Paul's friend, postmodern classicist Philip Glass. The song provided a fitting end to this sad and haunted album.

Rolling Stone gave *Hearts and Bones* four stars (out of five), and Stephen Holden, in a review for the *New York Times*, declared that the songwriting on the album "has a visionary beauty and eloquence that go beyond anything Mr. Simon has done before." Review after review said essentially the same thing, that it was Paul's best writing, enriched with a literate sense of lyrical beauty and infused with a musical history that struck at the heart of his doo-wop roots, and that it was a brave, even inspired, choice to make it a solo album rather than a Simon & Garfunkel one.

But audiences just didn't go for it. *Hearts and Bones* reached only number thirty-five on the album charts. With almost no airplay, in an era when FM rock stations were crowded with the newer and younger music of bands like R.E.M., Elvis Costello and the Attractions, and Michael Jackson, there was no way it could not be considered a flop, which made it two out of two for Paul at Warner, which had paid so dearly to bring him to the label.

As 1983 came to a close, Paul had a grim inventory to deal with. He had lost his wife, Carrie; his best friend, Artie; and, apparently, his audience. With his life and career in shambles and nowhere else to turn, after much contemplation followed by one burst of cosmic inspiration, he decided to make a final leap for redemption and, because of it, stumbled upon the most glorious of resurrections.

PART FOUR

Going to Graceland

15

Redemption's First Finale

THE IDEA TOOK SHAPE IN THE LAST DAYS OF 1983, AT PAUL'S home in Amagansett, Long Island. Following a small twelve-city solo acoustic tour to promote *Hearts and Bones*, he greeted the end of the old year and the arrival of the new one doing little else but staring for hours at the ocean waves, contemplating the darkest events of his recent past.

This is how he remembered his state of mind during that period:

It was a difficult time for me. . . . I had started to work on an album that became *Hearts and Bones*. Then I did the "Reunion Concert" with Art, and half-a-million people showed up and we decided to go out and do some concerts. Just a classic mistake. Then the album came out, that had been announced as a "Simon & Garfunkel" album, only as a solo album. I was exhausted, I didn't do anything to promote it, and it was a flop. In the midst of all of that, I got married to Carrie Fisher. What was I thinking? . . . all kinds of mistakes on top of mistakes on top of mistakes. So now I had a personal blow, a career setback, and the combination of the two put me into a tailspin.

It was a tailspin that would take another year for him to come out of, almost to the end of 1984, when he heard a recording of a new group whose sound electrified him.

I was building a house in Montauk [Long Island], and while I would drive out to the site, I would listen to this tape a friend had given me and I began to realize that I really liked that tape. After a couple of weeks of driving back and forth to the house, I began to wonder, what is this tape? It's my favorite tape now. I wonder who it is? And that's when things started to perk up.

Paul asked Warner Brothers to track down the band on the bootleg cassette that his friend guitarist Heidi Berg had given him. He had first met Berg when she was one of the players and coordinators of the *Saturday Night Live* house band and a member of the extended post-show party regular social entourage that grew out of it. The only thing he knew about the music was its unusual title—*Gumboots: Accordion Jive Hits, Volume II*—and he wanted to find out who the band was. Someone at Warner came back with the information that it was a South African vocal group called Ladysmith Black Mambazo, who specialized in what was called "Mbaqamba," or "township jive"; and that Ladysmith Black Mambazo had been founded in the sixties by Joseph Shabalala and was still in South Africa. ("Ladysmith" is the name of Shabalala's rural hometown; "Black" is a reference to oxen, the strongest of all farm animals; and "Mambazo" is the Zulu word for axe, representing the group's ability to "chop down" any singing rival who might challenge them).

Ladysmith Black Mambazo joined the regular cassette rotation in his car, which already included the Talking Heads' *Remain in Light*

Simon & Garfunkel dressed for the concert stage.

Simon and his then girlfriend, Shelly Duvall, at Studio 54, 1977.

George Harrison and Paul Simon during their historic appearance on *Saturday Night Live*, November 20, 1976.

A still from Paul's 1980 movie, *One-Trick Pony.*

Paul, with (left to right) Jon Bon Jovi, Billy Joel, and Elton John at a 1995 Rainforest Concert.

Art Garfunkel and Paul Simon promoting their upcoming 2003 reunion concert.

Paul Simon performs "Sweet Baby James" at the 2006 Musicares Person of the Year tribute.

Paul Simon, the night he received the Gershwin Prize for Popular Song, May 23, 2007.

Paul's return to performing, at the opening of the renovated Beacon Theater in New York City, February 13, 2009.

Paul with Ruben Blades, James Taylor, Bruce Springsteen, Dion, and Lou Reed at the Rock and Roll Hall of Fame 25th Anniversary, Madison Square Garden, October 2009.

Classic Simon & Garfunkel: Art and Paul reunite for a free concert on Central Park's Great Lawn before more than half a million fans, September 19, 1981.

Still classic: Art and Paul perform at the Rock and Roll Hall of Fame concert, Madison Square Garden, October 2009.

and the African-sounding *My Life in the Bush of Ghosts* by David Byrne and Brian Eno. Both of these were influenced by "high-life" music that he had first heard while visiting Africa in the sixties to work with Miriam Makeba and her husband Hugh Masakela, and again when he traveled to Kenya with Carrie. Now he wanted to dig deeper into the origins of this sound. He made plans to travel to Soweto to meet the members of Ladysmith Black Mambazo and possibly record with them. Paul asked Roy Halee to accompany him on the journey.

He was just about to leave for South Africa when he received a conference call from Quincy Jones, Michael Omaritan, and long-time music manager and social activist Ken Kragen. They wanted Paul to participate in a massive gathering of the cream of American musicians to record an original Michael Jackson/Lionel Richie composition, "We Are the World," a follow-up to the enormously successful British single "Do They Know It's Christmas," which featured thirty-six of the top Brit rock acts contributing their time and voices to a project intended to help the victims of the massive famine that had devastated Ethiopia. The entire concept had originated with Bob Geldof, the lead singer of the Boomtown Rats, who called this once-in-a-lifetime gathering "Band Aid."

Not long afterward, Michael Jackson, Lionel Richie, Ken Kragen, and Harry Belafonte decided to do an American version to aid the poor and the ravaged people throughout Africa. They called their project "USA for Africa," and hoped to feature in it more than a dozen of the biggest names in American music, including Jackson, Richie, and Belafonte. They already had firm commitments from Stevie Wonder, Diana Ross, Ray Charles, Willie Nelson, Bruce Springsteen, and Bob Dylan. Paul agreed to participate and postponed his trip to South Africa.

On the night of January 28, 1985, at 10:30 Pacific Coast time, after many of the same stars set to record the song and video had appeared on the live national telecast of the American Music Awards (which had begun at five to fit into East Coast prime-time TV schedules), they reconvened at the storied A&M Studios on La Brea Boulevard just south of Sunset Boulevard, once the film headquarters for Charlie Chaplin. Despite the unavoidably mythic proportion of the evening—selfless rock stars giving back, doing good, and so on, bolstered by stories of Bruce Springsteen driving himself into the parking lot in an old car with no chauffeur, the "Leave Your Egos at the Door" sign hung by Quincy Jones on the studio's front door, and the endless backslaps and overly emotive hugs that showed up on the hour-long MTV documentary—the night was not without displays of ego and self-centeredness. Prince, one of those who had made the commitment to be there, never showed up (rumors, never proved, claimed he had been offended by Bob Geldof's presence—Geldof was supervising the session and spoke prior to the recording about the conditions in Africa; Geldof had once called Prince a creep, and anyway Prince did not want to sing with so many people); Waylon Jennings stormed out of the session, the building, and some thought Los Angeles altogether when Stevie Wonder suggested one line of the song be sung by everybody at the same time in Swahili. As he left, Jennings shouted angrily back to Wonder that good ol' boys would never sing in Swahili. Later Michael Jackson quietly informed Wonder that Ethiopians did not speak in Swahili either, and the idea was subsequently dropped.

The single was rushed into release on March 7, 1985, in seven- and twelve-inch vinyl format, instantly went to number one on all pop charts, and stayed in that position for a month, moving more than twenty million units on its way to becoming the best-selling single-tune recording in the history of American popular music. Despite its worthy cause, however, not all the critics were in agreement about the quality of the song. Rock critic Greil Marcus dismissed the whole thing with a condescending, if indirect, jab at Jackson, calling it the equivalent of a Pepsi commercial. Nonetheless, the recording and its ancillary products raised nearly $65 million in relief aid, a milestone "event" that catapulted it into rock mythos, along the way accelerating Springsteen's already soaring thrust into superstardom on the heels of his career being "reborn" *in the USA*, and reinforcing the perception of Jackson's preternaturally weird but magnetic persona.

But as with the MUSE concerts, it did nothing for Paul except perhaps to further separate him from the current superstar mainstream, as he came off on both the short and long versions of the video looking, in comparison to such current eighties flashes as Cyndi

Lauper and such vital rock-star powerhouses as Springsteen, older, uncomfortable, unsure, and detached. Even the paranoid-looking Dylan seemed more comfortable.

Afterward Paul quietly requested that some of the proceeds be directed toward providing health care for poor children in New York City, and they were.

To show their appreciation for his help, Quincy Jones and Harry Belafonte agreed to help Paul work out the final details for his upcoming February trip to Soweto. By now he knew he had to carefully tiptoe around the long-standing United Nations Anti-Apartheid Committee, whose cultural boycott had effectively prevented other performers from playing to segregated audiences in South Africa. Hoping to avoid a Jane-Fonda-in-North-Vietnam type debacle, he wanted to keep as low a profile as possible, which is why he traveled with an entourage of one: Halee, whose T-shirt demeanor and jovial manner added to the everyman sensibility they hoped would allow them to slip past the sociopolitically correct media lions forever waiting for celebrities at the arrival gates of every politically incorrect airport.

It didn't work. From the moment Paul and Roy stepped onto South African soil, there was a groundswell of criticism for Paul's having made the trip. *Why hadn't he gone to Zimbabwe instead? Why wasn't he interested in exiled South African musicians? Was he a racist?* Paul's response to all of it was simple, honest, and direct. He said he was, essentially, not on any political mission, just a working musician in search of a good sound, and in order to get it, he had to go to where it was, not where people wanted it to be.

Having settled in Johannesburg, he and Halee went to the Ovation Studios to work with three groups of musicians—Tao Ea Matsekha, General M. D. Shirinda and the Gaza Sisters, and the Boyoyo Boys Band. For two weeks, the studios were filled with dozens of musicians, their wives and girlfriends carrying babies in their arms and parked on their hips while they chanted in the background, older children playing between the feet of all the musicians and relatives. In between sessions, South African musician Sipho Mabuse showed Paul and Halee the poorest sections of Soweto.

But the real action for him was in that studio, as day after day and night after night explosions of music came pulsing out of Ladysmith Black Mambazo and other talented and apparently happy bands of players he and Halee had managed to contact and gather together. If the privileged atmosphere of "We Are the World" had made him feel he was at least partly among the elite and the privileged of American rock 'n' roll, these singers and players made him feel just the opposite. These local musicians, who were not rich or world-famous, who sang only because they loved doing it, were just regular guys who happened to have the ability to sing and play like they were ringing a bell.

As Roy Halee recalled:

These were originally jams, ten or fifteen minutes, half an hour. Lo and behold, maybe a song would come out of that. The important thing for us to do there was to record these guys in a way that when we got to New York we could edit it.

The two weeks of sessions in Soweto resulted in a sweeping revitalization of Paul's musical energies. As he later put it, they "finished my disappointments and sorrows." Now he felt once more musically invincible, that nothing could bring him back down, not even his name being added to the UN blacklist for deliberately disregarding the boycott, or when the African National Congress voted to officially ban him, despite the fact that he had turned down an invitation to play a concert at "Sun City," a highly segregated South African resort for Africa's wealthy whites.

Instead, the African trip sharpened the focus of his intentions. He was not a political singer, or even a singer with causes, like early Dylan and middle-to-late Springsteen. He was not a fund-raiser or a protester. His only social relevance was as a singer-songwriter of rock 'n' roll; his only social protest of any lasting meaning had been Simon & Garfunkel's role in the over-the-counter cultural shift by the major label sounds away from their penchant for early fifties pap junk to mid-sixties pop rock. And, he now knew, it was that music that had, somehow, gotten away from him, that he was now searching for in South Africa. He had gone in search of his own music, looking for a way to move forward by going all the way back, into the heart of music's darkness in the hopes of once more ringing its brightest chimes.

Paul had six tracks of rough studio jams when he returned to New York City, music that would form the heart of his next album. Working with pen and pencil at the house in Long Island, he tried to put lyrics to the strands of music he had taken out of Africa, a slower process than he had anticipated, but eventually he had enough to begin to rerecord, overlaying and deepening the African cuts, playing some of them backward to enhance their sound, making up nonsense lyrics and sounds to fill in the rhythms, all the while trying to keep some sort of consistency that would make this a cohesive, thematic album rather than a series of individual ear-pleasing moments.

He eventually brought to the studio with him other musicians whose music he liked and who could help him refine and polish the sound he was searching for. He did one track with the up-and-coming East L.A. Mexican group Los Lobos, "All around the World or the Myth of the Fingerprints."* He recorded "That Was Your Mother" with Good Rockin' Dopsie and the Twisters. Later on he even brought in the Everly Brothers and Linda Ronstadt. All of what they did was good, but he was still looking for a unifying theme for this project.

What made this long and slow creative process possible was the fact that by now Warner Brothers couldn't have cared less about Paul, his project, or anything else he might be doing. As far as the corporate suits were concerned, he had proved a bad investment. After his first two albums on Warner bombed, the label more or less wrote him off, believing he was no longer worth any more of their time, attention, or money.

According to Paul, this was not necessarily a bad thing.

I had one big advantage being as cold as I was. Nobody is paying any attention to me [at the label]. I can do this all very

---

* Later on, Los Lobos accused Simon of a copyright violation for what they claimed was their song, which caused a major legal and personal rift between the band and Paul that has still not been completely resolved. As always in cases like this, the question of who contributed what is nearly impossible to untangle. According to Los Lobos's saxophone player Steve Berlin, Simon stole the song from Los Lobos and gave them no songwriting credit.

privately. Nobody will be checking in on how the tracks were going, can you send them to us, can we come to hear it, none of that.

As Roy Halee put it: "They thought that Roy Halee and Paul Simon were out of their minds, I know they thought we were both nuts."

Halee was right. Here is one Warner executive from the eighties talking about this period with Paul:

> He had come to us already a has-been, only no one seemed to want to admit it because all the executives at the time were baby boomers, children of the sixties, and to them Paul was and would always be a God. But he didn't sell records. Every time he went out, Columbia rereleased his old catalog, remixed and repackaged and they and him made all the money. Warner, at the time, had Prince, and he was the big deal at the label. He got all the attention and he had all the heat. He was sexy and a great stage performer, Paul wasn't. Prince was difficult, but he could afford to be difficult because he was selling records. And, of course, our biggest act was Madonna. She was the epitome of "now" in the eighties. The present and the future. Paul was, to the label's mind, stuck forever in the folk-music draught of the sixties. There was no way he could compete for the record-buying audience whose age range was, for the most part, fifteen- to twenty-three-year-olds. That's why no one cared when he went to Africa. He could have gone to the moon and it wouldn't have made any difference. Except he would have paid his own way.

Completing the album would take the rest of 1985, done in pieces in New York (April 1985), Los Angeles (May 1985), London (Abbey Road Studios, October 1985), and Louisiana (June 1985), with the tracks he had brought back from South Africa never far from reach. The ever-longer amount of time the album took to finish managed to cause yet another rift between him and Artie, who was at the same time recording a Christmas album with Jimmy Webb and had wanted to use Halee but couldn't because of his commitment to the African project. Artie, to say the least, was not happy with it.

Everywhere he traveled, Paul wrote, filling pages and pages of legal yellow pads with phrases that he knew he would use somewhere in the album to help connect the thematic dots. They were phrases made up of sounds, catchphrases, New York–centric symbols (like pizza), but they remained isolated jottings.

One phrase he especially liked and considered as the title for the second track on the album had potential as a theme. It was "driving through Wasteland." Starting with this allusion to T. S. Eliot's epic poem of life's bleak despair, all at once Paul hit upon the single sentence, or half a sentence, that pulled everything together. It was a simple but profound change. Not "driving through Wasteland." *Going to Graceland*.

That was it. Now he understood that the idea of a physical journey had been the right one to search for the roots of the music he loved best, but the spiritual direction was wrong. Not Africa. *Memphis*. The fourteen acres of land upon which Elvis's eighteen-room mansion formed the centerpiece, for which Elvis paid $102,500 in 1956, had become, since his death, a royal mortuary, a heavenly shrine to rock 'n' roll's ultimate angel of love, sex, youth, and rebellion. *That* was Mecca, and *that* where Paul wanted to spiritually deliver himself to rediscover and reinvigorate his own musical roots. He wanted to celebrate the joy and the rhythm and the rhyme and the sound, and the freedom that Elvis had delivered to him and to the world.

Now the album came together quickly, and upon its release its presence was quickly felt. *Graceland*, both the album and the single, did not just cue Paul's comeback; it became his moment of true musical greatness, taking its place alongside such signature Simon & Garfunkel songs as "Sound of Silence," "Bridge over Troubled Water," and "The Boxer." It was soulful, redemptive, toe-tapping, timeless, and *musical*, and the album, being a Paul Simon piece, was all at once celebratory and mournful and specific and ambiguous—suns shining like National guitars (a lyric that works even if one doesn't know that National is a brand of instrument), girls jumping on apartment trampolines in New York City, diamonds on the soles of shoes.

Graceland stood out even more because it was so utterly unlike anything else out there, on the radio, in concerts, or in clubs. By now rhythm and blues in America had chemically devolved into the half-life of disco, and Elvis was now Costello. The opening track of the album, "Boy in the Bubble," a combination of hope and dread, as Paul described it to David Fricke in *Rolling Stone* magazine, was an ironic, distanced look at the ups and downs of his own career, of the advantages to living "in a bubble," where the world can watch your every move, and the hard realization of being a public has-been when a new generation chooses its own heroes to "worship" on the pop charts. Intertwined with the driving percussive sounds he brought back from South Africa, and the familiar phrases that filled the pop tunes he had grown up with ("Don't cry, baby") the song played like an overture to a rock symphony—the unfolding of the map of the journey through the emotional heart, complete with marriages, divorces, children from a first marriage, fame, fortune, famine, nightmares, dreams, broken hearts, soldiering for fortune—that would eventually lead, as all rock 'n' roll roads must, finally and irrevocably to Graceland.

Although Paul would claim that both the album and the single were "my favorite record, my favorite song that I ever wrote, the best I ever did." *Graceland* had been quietly released by Warner Brothers on September 1, 1986, after all the supposedly "great" summer albums were already out and before the new fall records were ready for release. Much to the label's surprise, *Graceland* jumped onto *Billboard*'s Top Album chart at number three (number one in England and Australia) and looked as if it could stay there forever. It went platinum five times and eventually sold over fourteen million copies worldwide.

The first single released from the album, "You Can Call Me Al," was released early. Paul likely got the title from something he overheard at a party he had hosted, where he met the conductor and composer Pierre Boulez for the first time. As he was leaving, Boulez called Simon "Al," and the humor of the situation stuck with him. "You Can Call Me Al" (backed with "Gumboots") was released with an accompanying MTV-friendly video that costarred Paul and his good friend Chevy Chase. "Paul had a test pressing of the album and Lorne Michaels had a copy at his summer house," according to Chase.

> We all live out in Long Island in the East Hampton area and Lorne said, "Have you heard it?" I said, "I hadn't yet." He said "It's great." And Lorne played a couple of songs for me and then told me, "Paul's unhappy with this [first] video [Paul doing a monologue on *Saturday Night Live* shot through a TV monitor]. Why don't you do something?"

Out of that came the Paul Weis–directed, hilarious lip-synching, instrument-dragging, brass-instrument duet video that helped propel the song into the Top Ten on the *Billboard* charts, introducing Paul's new music and setting up the album's release. (The two subsequent singles, "The Boy in the Bubble" and "Graceland," failed to chart.)

On November 22, 1986, with the album still roaring, Paul made an appearance on *Saturday Night Live* in which he performed three new songs from the album, "Diamonds on the Soles of Her Shoes," "The Boy in the Bubble," and, despite his protestations against ever performing the song live again, "The Late Great Johnny Ace." Unexpected by all but Michaels and Paul, Art Garfunkel made one of his patented surprise appearances on the show during one of the nonmusical sketches in which Paul had agreed to appear.

The album's success went a long way toward righting some of the wrongs that Paul had endured for making that first trip to South Africa. In January 1987, the United Nations and the African National Congress finally officially removed Paul's name from their blacklists. A week later he won the British music industry's annual Best International Solo Artist Award.

That February, Paul attended the Twenty-ninth Annual Grammy Awards ceremony at the Shrine Auditorium in Los Angeles. *Graceland* had been nominated for 1986's Album of the Year, and during the show he performed a rousing version of "Diamonds on the Soles of Her Shoes." To no one's real surprise, *Graceland* beat out such formidable competition as Peter Gabriel's *So,* Janet Jackson's *Control,*

Barbra Streisand's *The Broadway Album*, and Steve Winwood's *Back in the High Life*.

When the winning album was named, a fit and youthful-looking Paul trotted up to the stage to accept his award from Whoopi Goldberg and Don Johnson. Holding the Grammy in his hands, he made a brief but powerful acceptance speech. After thanking everyone who had worked with him on the album, including the musicians who provided so much inspiration for it, he said, in part, that "South African artists and their countrymen live under one of the most oppressive regimes on the planet today and still they are able to produce music of great power and nuance." It was one more hail to the meaning and the power and the glory that was rock 'n' roll.

With this triumphant night's spectacular win, forty-five-year-old Paul Simon had completed one of the most phenomenal comebacks in the history of show business, and by doing so managed to redefine himself and his music not merely as an entertaining presence but a cultural force.

The *Graceland* world tour began in Europe on February 1, 1987, with a style and scope that recalled Dylan's legendary rambling "Rolling Thunder Revue" a decade earlier. Twenty-five friends and performers, including Ladysmith Black Mambazo, Miriam Makeba, and Hugh Masakela, traveled with Paul across three continents for the better part of two years. It was received well everywhere it played, but not totally without incident, as a curious combination of the taint of Paul Simon "racism" and the desire to hear Simon & Garfunkel "oldies" still managed to cling to the periphery of the event. Occasionally, in London and later on in the States, especially in college towns, demonstrators outside the arenas protested Paul's journey to South Africa. And there was one moment at London's Royal Albert Hall when Paul broke through the invisible wall he had always maintained between himself and his audiences. As soon as he finished singing "Graceland," someone from the audience shouted for him to do "The Sound of Silence," a suggestion that quickly turned into a cacophony of requests. Finally, holding one hand up, Paul said into the microphone, "I'm not a jukebox up here!"

The tour finally hit American shores on December 13, 1987, exploding into Madison Square Garden with an all-star New York–centric cast, as a benefit for Paul's favorite charity, the New York Children's Health Project. Appearing on the stage with Paul and Ladysmith Black Mambazo were Dion (DiMucci), Ruben Blades, Lou Reed, James Taylor, Chevy Chase (who performed "You Can Call Me Al" with Paul), Billy Joel, Grace Jones, Paul Schaeffer (and the World's Most Dangerous Band), Chaka Khan, Whoopi Goldberg, Lorne Michaels, Debbie Harry, Bill Cosby, and—Bruce Springsteen, who sang "Glory Days" with Paul and Billy Joel.

Fittingly, perhaps, the tour played its last show in Africa the following December, a triumphant finale held at the Rufaro Stadium in Harare, Zimbabwe.

When he returned home, even as the world continued to buy *Graceland*, and Warner continued to release singles from it, Paul already had his sights set on yet another continent to continue his quest for new musical inspiration.

And once again, he hoped the saints would look down upon him with grace and rhythm. And another hit album.

16

Saintly Rhythms

ARTIE HAD NEVER BEEN MUCH OF A FAN OF *GRACELAND*,
believing it was nothing more than an overblown novelty,
the South African sound worth maybe a song or two on
an album at most. He made no secret of his dislike for it, which
might have been made up of unequal parts individual taste, professional disappointment, and personal animosity for Paul's having not
included him in it. While Paul was traveling with his international
band for *Graceland* and being celebrated for it, Artie was either holed
up alone in his East Side apartment or traveling alone. He often took
ocean voyages via freighter, reading voraciously while enjoying the
anonymity and the solitude. Sometimes he drove across the country
by himself. Other times he simply preferred to walk.

Having neither the intensity nor the commitment that had fueled Paul's spiritual and creative pilgrimage to *Graceland*, whenever the muse made one of her visitations, Artie returned first to acting and then, eventually, to singing. In 1986 he appeared in another Mike Nichols film, *Good to Go*, which it was not; it opened and closed rather quickly and did nothing to propel either the actor's or the director's career. Artie's next album, *The Animals' Christmas*, was released that same year; it was not a blockbuster or a total bust—it sold about 110,000 copies—and failed to join the ranks of that year's sought-after annual holiday releases. Except for his last, brief "surprise" nonsinging appearance with Paul on *Saturday Night Live*, he remained aloof until sometime in 1987 when, it appeared, he had finally gotten over the professional trauma of the outsize success of *Graceland* and the personal trauma of Laurie Bird's suicide and was ready to move on to a new and very real emotional relationship.

Her name was Kathryn (Kim) Cernak, a onetime model and singer with the band Lime. Not long after they met and started dating, Artie returned to the studio and recorded a fresh collection of love songs. *Lefty* would take another year to finish and when it was released, it received fine reviews, but it failed to catch on with the public and quickly disappeared. The comparisons to *Graceland* did not help any. While Paul had stretched himself creatively and, by doing so, both found a new audience and regained his old one, with *Lefty* Artie had chosen to remain in the cloistered, dated world of the Same Old American Songbook, a sound and a body of work that, for someone who was not normally thought of as one of the pillars of the genre—a Frank Sinatra, a Tony Bennett, a Billie Holiday, or an Ella Fitzgerald—proved a tough sell (although years later Rod Stewart would have great success doing the same thing). The result was a further diminution of Artie's stature as a hitmaker at Columbia, where he had remained after Paul's move to Warner.

Instead of diving back into the musical waters, Artie decided to lick his professional wounds and repair his personal life. After finally resolving the long-standing divorce settlement dispute with his ex-wife, and ready once more to make an emotional commitment to a woman, in the fall of 1988 he and Cernak quietly tied the knot and, for the moment, Artie devoted himself to marriage rather than music.

Paul, meanwhile, continued to bask in *Graceland*'s golden glow. A year after the album won a Grammy for Album of the Year, the subsequent release of the "Graceland" single was nominated in 1987 for Record of the Year (the single had been released after the album had won the Grammy and technically qualified for the next year's awards). Up against Los Lobos' remake of "La Bamba," which they had recorded for the soundtrack of the film bio of Richie Valens, U2's great "I Still Haven't Found What I'm Looking For," Suzanne Vega's quirky "Luka," and Steve Winwood's "Back in the High Life," no one gave "Graceland" much of a chance, believing it was, at least when it came to winning Grammys, yesterday's news. Even though the album continued to do well, the single's late release had stalled at number eighty and, despite *Rolling Stone*'s having honored it as the 485th "Greatest Song of All Time," it still failed to register with the singles-buying crowd. Therefore, when "Graceland" won, it did so with added dramatic weight and solidified Paul's reinstatement as the most enduring, and biggest-selling, rock 'n' roll artist of his generation. (Even so, after the Grammy win, Warner rereleased the single, and it still didn't sell.)

Now, Warner was more eager than ever to get another album out of Paul, but when it became clear he didn't have anything new, they released a "Best of" compilation of his first two solo Warner albums, adding a few songs from his solo work at Columbia. Paul held the copyrights to all of his songs and that allowed him to negotiate for their rerelease on Warner, something Columbia had no objection to, as Paul's success kept selling Simon & Garfunkel albums, and whatever piece Columbia made from that was pure profit. However, *Negotiations and Love Songs, 1971–1976*, the title of the "Best of" album, taken directly from the lyrics to "Train in the Distance" that had originally appeared on *Hearts and Bones*, did poorly, peaking at number 110.

But this time no one at the label even thought about writing Paul off. They knew he was on the case, already on his way to South America to continue his quest to translate the world's music into his personal vernacular, the music he still called rock 'n' roll.

Rhythm of the Saints began, as had *Graceland*, by Paul's listening to tapes of indigenous foreign bands with irresistible rhythm sections, this time coming from Brazil, whose music had long appealed to him. Like R&B, Latino influences had played major roles in early rock 'n' roll. Many of New York's uptown doo-wop groups had roots that stemmed from their Puerto Rican origins, just as other groups were influenced by their African American heritage or their Italian American backgrounds.

Sometime in 1987 Paul traveled to Rio, taking along an entourage led by Roy Halee that included many of the same personnel he had worked with on the making of *Graceland*. There he replicated what he had done in South Africa—absorbed local sounds, recorded them, sat in and jammed with neighborhood players. Several of the musicians he worked closely with were new musicians and several were those he had worked with on *Graceland*, making *Rhythm of the Saints* part sequel, part extension, part exploration, and part revisitation.

Afro-Brazilian superstars Grupo Cultural Olodum, masters of the heavily percussive samba sound called "Batuque" or "Batucada," are behind the clarion Brazilian drums (recorded live in Pelourinho Square in Salvador) that opened the album's first track, "The Obvious Child." Grupo Cultural Olodum eventually toured with Paul behind *Rhythm*, and they opened and closed the show when they were on tour. Also among the dozens of Brazilian musicians included in the recording of the album were Brazilian singer-songwriter Milton Nascimento, who cowrote "Spirit Voices"; mandolin and *guitarra baiana* master Armandinho; Afro-Cuban drummer Francisco Aguabella; Puerto Rican–born drummer Giovanni Hidalgo; jazz percussionist and master of the berimbau Naná Vasconcelos; and jazz guitarist Rafael Rabels.

The musical styles on *The Rhythm of the Saints* were not exclusively Brazilian. Other major influences, mostly West, Central, and South African music, are quite distinctive. Cameroonian jazz composer Andre Manga plays bass, and *The Rhythm of the Saints* also highlights Simon's collaboration with Cameroonian guitarist Vincent Nguini, credited as cowriter on "The Coast," one of the album's more upbeat songs, which also features Ladysmith Black Mambazo. Malawi-born guitarist Ray Phiri, who, like Ladysmith, also appeared on *Graceland*, plays on much of this album as well. Famed trumpeter and world-beat bandleader Hugh Masekela, another *Graceland* alumnus, plays flugel-horn on one song. Ringo Starr contributes drums, and other musicians include U.S. saxophonist Michael Brecker, guitarist J. J. Cale, R&B keyboard player Greg Phillinganes, Simon regular percussionist Steve Gadd, guitarist and synth player Adrian Belew (yet another *Graceland* alumnus), and backing vocals by Charlotte Mbango.

Paul was in no hurry to release *The Rhythm of the Saints*. There was nothing left for him to prove to the public or to himself, no Garfunkel-less abyss for him to have to crawl out of. He had already made his great redemptive comeback and done it with dignity, distinction, and celebration. He had returned to the roots of the music he loved best, that inspired him the most, and, while doing so, had discovered the thrill of the process as much as the joy of the result. So he wanted to relax and enjoy this new journey, traveling several times back and forth from Brazil to New York, carefully compiling material as patiently and meticulously as a detective. He occasionally sat in on various friends' recordings, taking a taste of the action to keep his energies high and his hand in what his contemporaries were into.

In March 1988 he arranged and sang "Amazing Grace," a track laid down by Ladysmith Black Mambazo for their first Warner album, *Journey of Dreams*, which Paul had been instrumental in helping to make happen. In 1989 he produced, arranged, and sang vocals on "Rambler/Gambler," backed with "Whispering Bells," with his old friend from the sixties folk scene Joan Baez, for her album *Speaking of Dreams*. A few months later he sat in with fellow Brill Building alumnus Dion (DiMucci) on his New York–centric *Yo Frankie*, contributing a subtle but altogether brilliant touch singing on "Written on the Subway Walls/Little Star," Dion's homage to New York doo-wop-to-folk-rock styles; the song smartly borrowed from Simon & Garfunkel's "Sound of Silence," melding it with the Staten Island–based Elegants' graceful 1958 hit "Where Are You Little Star?" and the children's singsong "Twinkle Twinkle Little Star."

■ ■ ■

In January 1990 it was announced, to no one's great surprise, that Simon & Garfunkel were to be inducted into the Rock and Roll Hall of Fame. Created in 1983, the Hall had been the brainchild of the *Rolling Stone* magazine generation, led by Jann Wenner and Ahmet Ertegun of Atlantic Records. It was conceived as a place for boomers to honor their rock 'n' roll greats, with annual awards to be administered by an independent foundation. The concept was a good one, but the execution had run into several roadblocks, including the then controversial decision to build the museum in Cleveland, the so-called spiritual home of Alan Freed, considered by many to be either the Moses or the Godfather (or both) of rock 'n' roll (the fact that Cleveland put up $65 million in construction-site money didn't hurt its chances, although the annual induction ceremonies are always held at New York City's glamorous Waldorf-Astoria). The biggest initial objection to the hall seemed to be its overly warm embrace of the corporate mentality of a music and a lifestyle whose very existence had started out as the alternative. Rebellion, not financial reward, was the heartbeat of rock 'n' roll. Black-tie award dinners, fancy statuettes, and acceptance speeches sounded more like a product of the Academy of Motion Pictures. However, when performers like Bob Dylan showed up and made powerful and heartfelt speeches of thanks, and with the profuse coverage of *Rolling Stone* magazine, the annual awards dinners gradually became an established part of the "antiestablishment," to many a prestigious mark of achievement for a lifetime of great music; eligibility begins twenty-five years after an act's first professional recording.

On that Waldorf'd and tuxedo'd January night in 1990, Simon & Garfunkel were inducted along with other greats that included the late Bobby Darin, the Platters, the late Hank Ballard, the Four Seasons, the Four Tops, the Kinks, and the Who. For Paul and Artie the timing of this award was, to say the least, awkward, as the two were still barely speaking to each other. While preoccupied with the adventures of *Graceland* and *The Rhythm of the Saints*, Paul had kept his distance from Artie, and Artie had done the same with Paul.

Now, as they stood side by side before an audience of peers, Paul accepted his award first. It was presented to him by James Taylor, after which Paul wryly commented that the hall ought to open a separate wing for groups and duos whose members didn't get along with each other. "Now we can join all the other happy couples," he cracked, "like Ike and Tina Turner, the Everly Brothers, Mick and Keith, Paul and all the other Beatles." The audience laughed good-naturedly, appreciating the bit of self-deprecation.

When it was his turn, Artie, whose bank of hubris was not nearly as full, took a higher, if less jubilant tone, saying flatly into the microphone that Paul was "the person who most enriched my life by putting those songs through me."

Through him? Paul couldn't resist getting in the last word. "Arthur and I agree about almost nothing. But it's true, I have enriched his life quite a bit."

The audience giggled nervously as the tension between the two appeared ready to blow out the houselights, but a few minutes later they cheered wildly when Paul and Artie performed rousing versions of "Bridge over Troubled Water," "The Boxer," and, in a nod to their fifties doo-wop roots, the Spaniels' "Goodnight Sweetheart, Goodnight," which brought the house down.

Afterward, they did not speak to each other and left separately.

The next month, Paul attended Don Henley's annual Rainforest Foundation Fundraiser in Beverly Hills, California. During the performance portion of the show, Paul was invited onstage by Sting to perform together with Bruce Springsteen, Henley, Herbie Hancock, and Branford Marsalis.

In August he played at a benefit for the preservation of the Montauk Point Lighthouse, where he performed a killer version of "Sea Cruise," dueting with Billy Joel.

And that was it. There would be no more public appearances until the scheduled October 1990 release of *Rhythm of the Saints*, four years now after the 1986 release of *Graceland*.

The album debuted on *Billboard*'s Top 10 album chart, peaking at number four, one step lower than *Graceland*, which had made it to number three (both went to number one in the UK), and moved one million units in its first four weeks.

Rolling Stone gave it a four-star review, declaring:

> *The Rhythm of the Saints* extends [Simon's] reach not only further into the riches of world-beat music but further into the realm of the spiritual. . . . *The Rhythm of the Saints* . . . marries two distantly related world-beat forms into a vibrant, textured hybrid—the product of Simon's peerless studio craftsmanship.

It was all of that, for sure, but it was also something else, an almost too-vivid echo of *Graceland*. If there was anything about *Rhythm of the Saints* that disappointed, it was the self-consciousness of its concept, its restaging, as it were, of an original and highly explosive creative burst that somehow suggested nothing so much as a retro-greatness, a tired replay of a good thing. "The Obvious Child" (sign-of-the-times notable for not being released on vinyl), the only single of the three released to chart (the others being "Proof" and "Born at the Right Time"), failed to break into the Top 40.

Nonetheless, Paul put together a massive international tour behind *The Rhythm of the Saints,* one that was even more extensive than what he had done for *Graceland*, and played abroad for a year before finally arriving in the States for a massive end-of-tour celebration, a final night of Paul Simon and friends to be staged in, of all places, New York's Central Park.

The idea originated this time with Mayor David Dinkins, who had followed Ed Koch into New York City's top elected post. Now that the city was rebounding after a difficult period, Mayor Dinkins thought it might be a nice gift to the citizens who had been through so much over the past decade. While the tour was winding down, a team of lawyers, producers, PR specialists, Peter Parcher (Paul's attorney, who also served as one of the producers on the eventual television special), Warner Brothers executives, and representatives from Westwood One Radio were quickly assembled to see if the show could be put together in a matter of weeks. The key to the whole thing was the Parks Commission, which wasn't sure it was a good idea. Someone closely involved with the production remembered:

When they said okay, they wanted it to happen, everything else fell into place. It wasn't that easy to get everyone on the same page. Diana Ross had just done a concert in the park that had been something of a disaster because of the lightning storm that struck that night that raised the question of potential liabilities, and the presence of teenage thugs practicing "wilding," a form of gang-style mugging. That was the biggest obstacle. Someone from Paul's side reminded the city that a concert by him was always a peaceful event, and that seemed to convince the powers that not only could the show go on, but that he was the only one who should headline it.

Conception to presentation took a total of three months, all the time they had to get all the bureaucratic paperwork done, for HBO to clear the rights to broadcast it, for Warner to line up every performer's label to make sure they could participate, to plan security, everything.

Days before the show, Artie had picked up the phone and called Paul, who was receptive and gracious and invited Artie and his wife, Kim, and their son, James, to the estate on Long Island for a big family barbecue. At the house, Paul and Artie talked easily, with the others and then by themselves, but after a while it became clear that despite this latest gesture toward renewed friendship, Paul was not going to ask Artie to sing even one song together with him in Central Park.

Not long after that, Artie arranged his own schedule to make sure he would be out of the country when the event took place. Just as he was preparing to leave, a reporter from the *New York Times* called and asked him if it was true he wasn't going to make an appearance with Paul in Central Park. Yes, it was true, Artie told him. Why, the reporter asked. "I guess I'm not good enough to have been invited."

On August 15, 1991, to a thundering ovation, Paul walked onto the elevated platforms set up on the Great Lawn, where it was estimated that 750,000 New Yorkers had gathered this warm summer night to hail the return of their native son home (the "Woodstock"-like cover of the live album shows the vastness of the audience. From the other perspective, it was possible to look toward the stage and see all the way downtown to the tops of the World Trade Center towers in the background).*

Paul was psyched up and ready. After working his way through the best of *The Rhythm of the Saints* and *Graceland*, interspersed with some audience-pleasing Simon & Garfunkel hits that he performed solo, he finished the evening with a joyous five-set encore that included "Late in the Evening," "America," "The Boxer," "Cecilia," and, in spotlighted solo, a gorgeous, sophisticated fingerpick acoustic version of "The Sound of Silence." When he finished, he left the stage in triumph, to a cheering ovation that floated over the city like the sound of a million snare drums, and reverberated even louder throughout the world of rock 'n' roll.

---

* There were some who felt the show was too conscious an effort to duplicate the Simon & Garfunkel Central Park show of a decade earlier, and pointed to poor album sales as proof; the album released from it sold far fewer than the projected 500,000 units.

17

New Bohemian

B Y JANUARY 1992 FIFTY-YEAR-OLD PAUL SIMON HAD
finished his second world tour in four years. Now the absence of the crowds and the disappearance of the adulation
amplified the sound of the silence that permeated the house out in
Montauk. Whereas before the isolation had cocooned him within
the darkness of his own thoughts, now it seemed unnecessary. He
was back.

New York City became more acceptable to him as a place to go
to rather than flee from, and he began to spend more and more
time in the apartment on the West Side, renewing friendships and
recapturing the creative vitality of the streets. One day he opened
the mail and discovered that yet another remix of the old Simon &
Garfunkel songs had come out, this one released in England, where

the duo's popularity had never flagged. It was called *The Definitive Simon & Garfunkel*, whatever that meant, and was filled with the usual selection of the duo's finest. Every track was at least twenty-five years old. There was back, and then there was back.

Not long afterward, MTV approached Paul about doing an *Unplugged* segment for them, an episode of a series in which a rock legend performs acoustically and talks about each song before playing it. After thinking it over, Paul decided it was worth doing, and on March 4, 1992, he showed up at Kaufman Astoria Studios, appropriately enough in Queens, and performed twenty-one songs before a select live audience, from which ten would be chosen for the one-hour program.

In addition to Paul on vocals and guitar, there was a collection of musicians he had played with in the studio and on the road for many years, including Ray Phiri, Vincent Nguini, John Selolwane, Armand Sabal, Steve Gadd, Tony Cedras, Mingo Arauijo, Cyro Baptista, and Richard Tee. (This would be pianist Tee's last performance with Paul. On July 21, 1993, he died of prostate cancer, ending their long and fruitful association.) The music supervisor was Roy Halee.

Three months later, in June, MTV broadcast the show, which consisted of a well-balanced menu of Simon & Garfunkel and Paul Simon solo songs: "Born at the Right Time," "Me and Julio Down by the Schoolyard," "Graceland," "Still Crazy after All These Years," "Mrs. Robinson," "Bridge over Troubled Water," "Something So Right," "Boy in the Bubble," "Late in the Evening," and "Homeward Bound." Significantly, Simon & Garfunkel's signature, "The Sound of Silence," was not included, either in the taping or the final mix-down. Paul had wanted it that way. The emphasis here was to be on his singing and his guitar-playing. In a small TV studio, his acoustic stylings, especially, could be highlighted in a way that they could not on a live stage or in an arena. This was a good chance to flex a little, to pose, to remind the MTV generation who he was and why it should matter to them.

Plus, there were good ancillaries. In contrast to both the American and British seemingly endless rehashes of Simon & Garfunkel, here was a fresh set of Paul Simon performances for audiences that quickly went on sale in video and audio versions.

In the weeks and months that followed the "Unplugged" session, Paul gradually began to make himself more visible in the city, but with one big difference. He was no longer alone much of the time. His constant companion was now Edie Brickell.

He had first met Brickell back in 1990, while he was backstage at *Saturday Night Live*, and Edie Brickell and New Bohemians, a ska-influenced alt-rock group out of Dallas, happened to be the musical guest stars that night. Brickell's band was something of a throwback in the world of current popular music, and Paul was struck by how that made them stand out from the crowd, as much as he was by her fresh, good neo-hippie looks, her vocal abilities, and the song she and her band sang that night, "What I Am Is What I Am," from their 1988 debut album, *Shooting Rubber Bands at the Stars*. It sounded like something he might have written back in the day.

He had stood next to one of the cameras during the live telecast, and when the control room switched to another one, he playfully jumped in front of the inactive lens, at once distracting and attracting Brickell, who looked like the coolest girl in school and seemed to float above everything on a cushion of rhythm and rhyme, a rock 'n' roll anomaly in the iron-bra pop world of Madonna. As she later recalled, "He made me mess the song up when I looked at him . . . that's when we first laid eyes on each other."

They started dating shortly after that, and then, while Paul was off to Africa and South America and then immersed within the recording studio, Brickell toured with New Bohemians, mostly behind, of all people, Bob Dylan. "The New Bos," as they were often called, had caught Dylan's attention for the same reason they had caught Paul's, their musical prowess shaped in homage to the spirit of the sixties—folkie, acoustic, lyrically driven, and catchy—minus, presumably, the political overlay.

When both of them were finally free, Paul of his tours and Brickell of the band that broke up after one of its members was tragically shot to death, and they had the time and the desire to be together, on May 30, 1992, twenty-six-year-old Edie Brickell married fifty-year-old Paul Simon. The ceremony took place at Paul's Montauk estate. Six months later she gave birth to their first child, a boy they named Adrian.

The next year they performed together for the first time in public as a married couple at Willie Nelson's "Big Six-O" sixtieth birthday party, accompanying Willie on his classic version of Fred Rose's "Blue Eyes Cryin' in the Rain." Not long after, Paul settled full-time into his third attempt to unlock the secrets of domestic bliss, and it appeared that it would indeed be the charm, as married life and fatherhood seemed now to have succeeded in lifting him up and mellowing him out.

And then, as if by some cosmic cue, Artie, recently remarried and the father of a new child as well, returned to Paul's life. With new wives and children, which meant new lives really, and being older, less intense, and with little left to prove to each other or themselves, getting together as friends seemed easier than it had been in years.

In September 1993, following a successful release in England of *The Paul Simon Anthology* (and what may have been an unauthorized Italian edition of *Tom & Jerry—Their Greatest Hits*, consisting of virtually every track Paul and Artie had recorded prior to "The Sound of Silence"), Warner put out yet another remastered Paul Simon solo retrospective boxed set, *Paul Simon 1964–1993*. To celebrate its release and to promote it in order to feed fresh funds into his favorite charities, Paul agreed to a relatively brief four-month international tour. To the surprise of many, he invited Artie to come along with him for the whole ride. The invitation shocked no one more than Artie, who immediately and eagerly agreed to sing once more with Paul.

The shows kicked off with a month-long retrospective performed on a so-called legitimate Broadway stage, New York's glamorous Paramount Theatre, steps from the Brill Building and 1650, where so many years earlier, Paul had struggled to earn a living as a songwriter. Now he was a star on the fabled Great White Way. For the occasion Paul put together a band of the best of his regular backup musicians gathered from the various live and recording studio configurations he had played with through the years, consisting of established and up-and-coming musicians: Steve Gadd, Mike Brecker, Vincent Nguini, Armand Sabal-Lecoo, Tony Cedras, Ray Phiri, John Selolwane, Mingo Araujo, Chris Botti, Barney Rachabane, with Julie

Water on vocals. This cream-of-the-crop configuration stayed together for the entire tour, which included parts of Canada and a
finale stop in Tokyo. Invited to sit in for several concerts, depending
upon their availability, were Ladysmith Black Mambazo, the Mighty
Clouds of Joy, and Phoebe Snow. The shows' songs encompassed
Paul's entire career, and when appropriate, Garfunkel sang with
him.

It was this coordinated concert-style format, with "guest players"
coming to the mike, doing their thing and then retreating, that
further sparked an idea he had already had prior to the start of
the tour. To Paul, the interchanges among the terrific and diverse
range of singers and musicians were something as dramatic as they
were musical, the choreography a carefully staged musical contin-
uum that formed a type of concert theater. The idea of developing
that notion into a Broadway show for audiences who did not normally
attend either "musicals" or (so-called) rock concerts was something
he had been toying with for a while. His enthusiastic reception at
the Paramount Theatre, followed by his recent tour, with different
performers from night to night, depending on the availability of talented friends who wanted to sing one or two songs, made him believe
a formalized conception of it might actually work.

The notion had first taken shape back in 1992, after a chance
meeting Paul had had with West Indian–born poet and playwright
Derek Walcott at a social gathering, where the two had engaged in
conversation based on Paul's experiences with writing, recording,
and performing *Graceland*. As Simon later remembered:

> [D]uring those years, I met Derek Walcott. I was reading Derek
> Walcott's poetry when I was working on *The Rhythm of the Saints*.
> I sort of start work about ten in the morning, I work from about
> ten till three or four, and then I take a break somewhere in
> the middle of the day. But when I was taking my break instead
> of talking on the phone or reading the papers, I would read
> Derek's poetry, because I wanted to stay where I was [in my
> head], you know . . . in the Southern Hemisphere.
>
> Then a mutual friend told me that he was giving a reading
> at the 92nd Street Y, so I went up to meet him, and I invited

him down to the studio where I was working on the album, and we struck up a friendship. He was teaching at Boston U, and I spoke at a class . . . and I went up to Stratford to see his play *The Odyssey*, and so he knew that I was working on this musical [idea], and he was interested in musicals, in fact he was [at the time] writing a musical with Galt MacDermot, the guy who wrote *Hair*, [called] *Steel*, about steel drums. And then around the time that he won the Nobel, we said well maybe we should give this a try together and see how it works.

Walcott's play, based on Homer's epic poem, was about a physical journey that was, at the same time, a spiritual excursion. In it Paul saw some of the same themes he had tried to write about in *Graceland*, his own musical odyssey that was an imagined spritual journey to rock 'n' roll's symbolic temple. Paul was energized by Walcott's expertise in the symbolism of mysticism and its place in contemporary culture, and thrilled when the poet and playwright won the 1992 Nobel Prize for Literature. Walcott had long been active in noncommercial the-ater groups, was the author of more than twenty plays, and had a desire for commercial success that would allow him to straddle both sides of the creative fence—the purely artistic and the economically viable. Paul believed that a collaboration with Walcott would produce something meaningful and lasting; Walcott was a lot more than just another pretty voice.

It did not hurt that Walcott was, in turn, thoroughly charmed by *Graceland*.

When the eclectic 1994 tour ended, Paul turned his attention to producing his wife's first solo album, *Picture Perfect Morning*. With Roy Halee's help, he arranged several numbers and even played some acoustic guitar on it. All the while, though, he continued to think about the possibilities of his new concept. Every time he and Walcott got together, they talked about writing this street-smart, rock 'n' roll show for Broadway, and now Paul had a theme—the romance of, and ultimately the redemption from, street violence in the New York City of the fifties that he grew up in, when juvenile delinquency was rock 'n' roll's bad-boy older brother, after Elvis became the hot-button topic of the day.

> I began thinking about the Capeman story as the basis for a musical in 1989. . . . It felt like a very New York story with a great musical environment; it raised the possibility of examining changing musical styles as the story unfolded and moved back and forth between Puerto Rico and New York.
>
> Writing songs in a 50s style was very appealing to me, and so was writing songs in a Latin style, which was a significant and sort of exotic New York subculture to me when I was growing up. Since I was working at the time with Brazilian drums and West African guitars, it wasn't too much of a leap to begin thinking about music from Puerto Rico.

At times Paul's version of the moment of inspiration for *The Capeman* varied. In December 2007, he told *Entertainment Weekly*:

> I never thought [writing a Broadway show] would be interesting . . . until I was on tour with *Graceland*. I thought, well, here's Miriam Makeba and Hugh Masekela and Ladysmith Black Mambazo, and I sing, and then we sing duets, like different characters in a show—a show that didn't have a story, just a theme: South Africa. But I thought, If I saw this in a theatrical setting, I'd like it.

He now envisioned a musical built around the most infamous teenage killer in New York City's history, Salvador Agron, widely known, thanks in great measure to the hysterical front-page photo sensationalism fostered by the *New York Daily News*, "New York's Picture Newspaper," as "The Capeman."

To be sure, it was an idea that seemed, at first, to everyone related to the business of Broadway, a bizarre overreach for a rock star that would place him well beyond his comfort zone in an industry that had, until very recently, looked down on all things rock 'n' roll—*real* rock 'n' roll, that is, not the watered-down, lightened-up, overly choreographed, gaudily costumed versions of it that had

regularly appeared on Broadway after the 1992 surprise success of
a staging of the Who's *Tommy*, which in 1993 spawned Billy Joel's
and Twyla Tharp's *Movin' Out*, ABBA's 2001 *Mamma Mia* (following
an earlier opening on the West End), and Des McAnuff's 2005 *Jersey
Boys*, based on the music of the Four Seasons, written mostly by Bob
Gaudio and Bob Crewe. All of these shows, despite their potentially
gritty scenarios, were softened and prettified, and came off revealing
nothing so much as Broadway's difficulties in dealing with real rock
'n' roll. *Jersey Boys*, especially, was such an outrage to rock purists that
shortly after it opened, the usually affable Vin Scelsa, FM stalwart
and popular musicologist of the avowed counterculture wing of the
boomer generation, was prompted to dismiss it on the air as "the gay
Four Seasons."

Paul, of course, had no interest in using the Simon & Garfunkel
catalogue as a backdrop for dancers to swing across the stage and
leap into one another's arms to the ecstatic reception of $100-a-
ticket audiences. He was after something radically different from
anything he had done before. Writing for Broadway could be yet
another chance to experiment, to stretch, to grow as an artist.

With Walcott's help, Paul envisioned writing a real "book" show,
something like, but not overtly similar to, *West Side Story*, the Leonard
Bernstein/Arthur Laurent/Stephen Sondheim jazz and Broadway
ballad musical version of Shakespeare's *Romeo and Juliet*. When it
opened, it had outraged the late fifties Broadway set for even acknowledging a subject as distasteful as juvenile delinquency on the
Great White Way.

Now, more than thirty years after *West Side Story*'s controversial
arrival and subsequent ascension to Broadway's musical pantheon,
Paul was convinced that he and Walcott could write something even
better. He had no idea of the kind of resistance he was about to find
himself up against from the big-shot Broadway boys who ruled the
street like it was their exclusive atoll set in the middle of Manhattan;
apartheid would look like a fully integrated walk in the park.

As he and Walcott continued to work on *The Capeman*, the story
slowly took shape. It would be the literal and figurative journey of
the early life of crime of Salvatore Agron and chart the spiritual and
emotional path of his eventual redemption.

In real life, the Puerto Rican–born Agron, the stepson son of a Pentecostal Baptist, had been put into reform school at an early age, and by the time he was sixteen was the leader, or "the Prez" as he liked to be known, of an uptown Puerto Rican street gang called the Vampires, because of the blood-red lining of their uniform capes. The Vampires' street enemies were a rival gang known as the Norsemen. One night, looking for members of the Norsemen to rumble with, Agron and his fellow Vampires, among them one Tony Hernandez, who carried an umbrella with a sharpened tip, which led to his being known as the Umbrella Man, came upon two uptown college students, and in a confrontation Agron supposedly stabbed them both to death with a Mexican jagged dagger. There were numerous witnesses to the double murder, and Agron was quickly apprehended. The crime occurred at the height of the juvenile delinquency wave in New York City, and was tied, inevitably, to the rise of rhythm and blues and doo-wop rock 'n' roll; every government official, from the outraged governor Nelson Rockefeller to the city's fretful mayor Robert F. Wagner Jr., claimed to find a connection. The underlying flames of racism tied to Agron's capture, conviction, and incarceration were fanned until a firestorm of anti–Puerto Rican sentiment burned through the city. Against that backdrop, Agron was tried for murder.

The case was not just front-page news but became something of a cause célèbre among both liberals and conservatives when Agron became the youngest person ever to be sentenced to die in New York State's electric chair. At his sentencing, Agron enraged everyone when he shouted to the judge and the salivating press, "*I don't care if I burn! My mother could watch me!*"*

His incarceration in "the death house" continued for years, while those who were sympathetic to Agron's plight claimed that the poverty and deprivation he had experienced as a child made him as much a victim as a murderer. Agron's sentence spurred a national debate over capital punishment, and when no less a voice for sympathy than the revered Eleanor Roosevelt asked Rockefeller to consider

---

* Hernandez received a seven-to-fifteen-year sentence, later reduced through appeals and retrials to time served.

the social circumstances, the governor, who had long opposed inter-
vening but who always had an eye on making a run for the White
House and wanted to keep Mrs. Roosevelt's support, six days before
Agron's scheduled 1962 execution reluctantly commuted Agron's
sentence to twenty years.

During his long incarceration (which was later reduced again by
Governor Hugh Carey to allow Agron's transfer to a halfway house,
from which he briefly escaped, an element of his journey that became
integral to the show), Agron renounced violence, expressed regret
for his own actions, became a model prisoner, and participated in a
prison program of education and rehabilitation. He served his full
twenty years at Sing Sing and was finally released in 1979. Seven years
later, forgotten, alone, broke, and in ill health, Agron died in the
Bronx two days before his forty-third birthday.

And now Paul was determined to bring him back to life, eight
times a week.

18

The Singing Capeman

L IKE MANY NEW YORKERS, I REMEMBER THE CAPEMAN STORY
from my youth," Paul later wrote. "It was [the] summer between high school and college, and the story was all over the
papers and on TV. I remember thinking here was a kid my age—a
kid who had the look. Salvador Agron looked like a rock 'n' roll
hoodlum; he looked like the 1950s."

While working with Walcott, for the first time since those terrible
events Paul began to revisit the case and the times they took place
in, through various city newspaper archives. With the help of some
friends who were well connected to the police or in the newspaper
business, Paul was able to track down several people who had actually
known Agron in his gang-leader days.

He also immersed himself in the Latin-drenched doo-wop of the day. Urban Latin had always had something of the doo-wop sound in it, and during this time he listened mostly to the music of Willie Colon, Ruben Blades, and Fredy Omar, all of whom were part of a sub-culture within a subculture, a small niche that had developed within the New York–based music scene; at the same time he went to see all the Broadway musicals that were currently on the boards. Nothing much excited him about *Titanic* (Maury Yeston, composer), *The Life* (Cy Coleman), *Steel Pier* (Fred Kander, composer), *Play On!* (Tonya Pinkins), or *Jekyll and Hyde* (Christiane Noll), and with good reason. In the annals of Broadway musical history, they were all run-of-the-mill, overly derivative of all that had come before, and profoundly unimaginative as a contemplation of what might be. Except for a re-vival of the impossible-not-to-like *Guys and Dolls* by the irrepressible composer Frank Loesser, Paul felt he could do better, that he could write something more relevant than the tiresome story of a ship that had sunk nearly a hundred years ago, a glorification of street pros-titution that made it seem even more attractive and exciting than Gary Marshall's cartoonish 1990 *Pretty Woman*, and yet another ver-sion of an old Robert Louis Stevenson horror story where fright stole the spotlight and substituted for anything that suggested even the slightest emotional darkness.

And he spent a year searching for singers who could do real street-style a cappella, until by the spring of 1995 he was at last ready to begin casting the show that he now conceived to be performed in two acts, its story told without dialogue, entirely sung through a cycle of thirty-nine songs backed by a twenty-nine-piece orchestra and a large cast of forty-four mostly Puerto Rican actors and actresses; despite Walcott's continued involvement, there would be no spoken dialogue. This was in the fashion of the new so-called progressive Broadway musi-cal trend (which none of the above shows followed) set by a series of all-singing imports including *Evita* (London 1978, Broadway 1979; Andrew Lloyd Webber and Tim Rice) and *Les Miserables* (Paris 1980, Broadway 1987; Claude-Michel Schonberg, Alain Boublil, and Herbert Kretzmer). Interestingly, each had begun as an audio con-cept album before developing into staged presentations. Each was more or less based on true historical events but came smothered in dramatic license (which did not necessarily make them better). And each shared the notion of history-as-musical-as-sociopolitical-commentary that Paul envisioned for *The Capeman*.

The way he chose to do it was fine; the way he chose to talk about it was not, unwisely positioning himself as something of a Broadway savior rather than a novice trying to gain entry onto the turf of others. It was an attitude that many in the Broadway community found not merely irritating but impossibly arrogant. To Chris Willman of *Entertainment Weekly*, in response to why he thought what he was doing was any different from other so-called rock musicals, he said this:

> Theater music never absorbed [the energy] of rock and roll, [which] became the mainstream of popular music.... Whereas in its heyday, the '40s and '50s, it was the same composers writing for both the Top 40 and the stage.... I don't see that as a tragedy. The cream-of-the-crop writers of new generations didn't have any interest in [theater]. I'm sure Lennon and McCartney could have written a great musical if they wanted to. But why bother when you can have a satisfying experience making an album and then go on the road and—David Bowie is the first name that comes to mind—be as theatrical as you want?

For Paul, raising money for a show that to many seemed an unnecessary glorification of a cold-blooded killer, no matter how reformed, became even more difficult.

At a spring 1996 press conference to formally announce the show's going into production, Paul said that he hoped that he and Walcott had written a show that "would sweep you up and that examines the moral questions of forgiveness and the possibility of redemption." The only problem was, Broadway money people weren't impressed with forgiveness and redemption. They wanted gorgeous women, short skirts, lots of dancing, and hum-out-the-door show tunes. Eventually, Paul would have to literally put his money where his mouth was, and (it was reported) invest several million dollars of his own money to get the show mounted for a projected December 1997 opening.

The concept of *The Capeman* required two actors to play Agron, one the angry, unrepentant killer, and the other the older, reformed, enlightened prisoner. After numerous auditions, Paul settled on then-unknown-to-the-mainstream Puerto Rican–born salsa singer Marc Anthony to play the younger Agron. Anthony, in his early twenties, was a salsa singer whose diminutive physicality would easily allow him to pass for a teenager, and he possessed a fabulously full, yet authentic street-sounding voice that could fill a Broadway house. For the older Agron, Paul cast Panamanian-born salsa singer and actor Rubén Blades, who already had a considerable following among Latino audiences as a singer, and among American moviegoers, who most often saw him playing a thug. Ednita Nazario, another great singer and actress, the biggest-selling female recording artist ever to come out of Puerto Rico but largely unknown to the non-Latino population in the States and to Broadway audiences, was cast as Agron's mother, a role that required her to add years to her naturally youthful appearance.

When it came time to choose a director, Paul apparently did not recognize either the need or the importance of that role, or the power that came with it. As the composer, he felt he was at the top of the power chain, and that the director was, if anything, a relatively unimportant player, especially in a show that was all music and ultimately all about music.

Together with Walcott, he approved Susana Tubert to direct. She was Argentine, which pleased Paul, and a protégée of perhaps the most influential director on Broadway at the time, Harold Prince, which pleased Walcott. Tubert's résumé was impressive; she had directed several off-Broadway productions by Hispanic authors, and Prince was especially enthusiastic about her, which gave *The Capeman* a legitimacy among the Broadway set that it did not previously have.

Still, despite Tubert's strong credentials (or because of them), both Paul and Walcott were uneasy about handing over creative control to someone who had come relatively late to the concept of their show, and she was aware of that uneasiness the entire time she worked on *The Capeman*. "It was like [they feared] somebody was going to take the project away from them and destroy it," Tubert said later. In rehearsals, she said, the two men would work around her. "The insecurity level was so high on this project that the notion of a director collaborating with a creative team was very threatening."

Three months after she was hired, Tubert "left" *The Capeman.* When Paul was asked later what had happened, he said:

[A]ll the decisions were made in conjunction with Derek. And the first thing that he said to me was, believe me, Paul, you're not going to want an auteur director here, you're not going to want a director to come in and take our work and then reinterpret it and say, this is the way it is, he said it's going to drive you crazy . . . so I was trying to be very careful not to have someone who was going to come in and say, all right, I see this as a dream sequence. For a lot of the directors who are the most, you know, the biggest ones and the most famous ones, the way they work is they take a piece of work, they inhabit the piece of work, and then it comes out as their piece of work.

After Tubert's departure, Paul tried to take over more and more of the creative control of the show, something that did not please anybody else.

The first person that I chose to join the team was Bob Foley, who's a set designer, whose work I saw when he did *Carousel* in New York, and I thought it was brilliant. So I went to hire this guy. The people who were the producers at that time said no you can't hire the set designer, the director has to hire the set designer. I said well no I like this guy's work and I want to see him envision. They said, no, no, that's not your job, the director does that, and you're doing it backwards . . . then I chose Mark Morris as a choreographer, and they said no you can't do this, this is the director's job.

Eric Simonson, out of Chicago's famed Steppenwolf Theatre in Chicago, was the next director, handpicked by Paul. He had seen Simonson's 1992 production there of *Song of Jacob Zulu*, and he liked what he saw. After Tubert's departure, Simonson, who reportedly had lobbied hard for the job before Tubert had been hired, was now handed the reins of the production, charged with pulling it together, and told to do so without stepping on anyone's toes, meaning Paul's. In December 1997 he mounted the first act for producers and friends, the official first look for most of the investors and their friends and relatives. They weren't impressed.

Simonson was fired the next day. "*The Capeman* lives in a musical reality for Paul, and I don't think he knows what he wants in a theatrical reality," was Simonson's not-so-disguised attack on Paul for interfering with Simonson's view of what the show should look and sound like.

This time, Paul, probably taking the advice of his longtime friend and publicist Dan Klores, who was handling publicity for *The Capeman*, and who was also one of its producers, made no public comment about Simonson's departure. With the beginning of out-of-town tryouts imminent, the search intensified for director number three. Paul then agreed to promote Mark Morris, the show's choreographer, who had never directed anything on Broadway, either musical or a straight play, to become the show's next director, and the out-of-town tryouts were canceled. Rumors began to spread throughout the theatrical community that the show was now in danger of not opening at all.

Around this time Paul released a solo album of thirteen songs from the nearly thirty in the full score for *The Capeman*, which also featured, in relatively limited exposure, the voices of Anthony, Blades, and Nazario. However, there was no mistaking who was the star of the album. Bathed in doo-wop, Latino rhythms, and gorgeous lyrics, the album received rave reviews from rock critics and quickly charted. Its success put the Broadway wags on notice that despite their resistance to Paul's ways and his subject matter, he might just be able to pull it off.

In the *New York Times*, Stephen Holden, one of its resident arts critics, who had been a longtime champion of Paul's music while writing for *Rolling Stone* magazine, where he had never written a less-than-glowing review of either Paul's solo work or the Simon & Garfunkel songbook, wrote one of the few positive reactions to emanate from the Broadway establishment (which the *Times* was decidedly a part of). Holden wrote approvingly of Paul's having apparently

> forsworn the dense stream-of-consciousness lyric style and expansive world-music vocabulary of his last two albums, and has composed his version of show tunes. The album's 13 stripped-down songs, most of which adhere to 50s and early 60s rock-and-roll and Hispanic street styles, reveal Mr. Simon, who collaborated on the lyrics with Derek Walcott, as a superb storyteller in command of a rough streetwise vocabulary. Although Rubén Blades and Marc Anthony, the stars of the Broadway show, which opens in January, appear, this recording is really a solo project and not to be confused with an eventual original cast album.*

Rolling Stone itself, however, qualified its enthusiasm for the album, calling it "terrifically satisfying. [Even if] the sociopolitical aspects of the case occasionally lead Simon and Walcott to overreach in their lyrics, especially given the musical setting—'The politics of prison are a mirror of the street/The poor endure oppression, the police control the State' is a far cry from 'I just met a girl named Maria.' "

Once again, the Street wasn't amused by what it perceived as Paul's upstart behavior, even if at least part of the reason for the album's early release was to raise funds. It was considered traditional—and tradition mattered on Broadway—to release an "original cast album" *after* a show opened (and with all the songs and the entire cast), although that practice, like most on Broadway, had less to do with "tradition" than with economics. Cast albums were almost always money losers, unless they became "classics" like the scores of *My Fair Lady* and *South Pacific*. Only then would record companies invest in the expensive process of recording an entire score.†

---

* An original cast album was recorded but never released on CD. It is now available on iTunes as a download-only item.
† This has all changed post-*Capeman*, with the incorporation of record companies into entertainment conglomerates, and the production of shows developed from

When the album stalled at number forty-two on the charts, and the advance money for the anticipated January opening just a little more than a month away totaled less than five million dollars, everyone except Paul, who remained convinced the show was going to be huge, began to worry about its future. The problem that was becoming ever more apparent was that nobody, including Paul, had any idea what they were doing. Everyone was a rank amateur when it came to producing a Broadway show, including the producers, the director (who was also the choreographer), the composer, the lyricist, and the actors. At times the show was described in the watchdog press as an opera, as a fifties rock 'n' roll period piece, as an extended dance performance, as a formalized concert. It was, of course, all of these and none at the same time, and for a show that no one could describe, it became nearly impossible to build up significant advance sales.

As late as a month before its scheduled opening, Paul was still trying to describe what *The Capeman* was about, always hinting that much of the show's troubles came from its daring sociological themes rather than the general lack of experience of its creative team, cast, and crew: "It's an American story . . . what is shocking to some people is that Puerto Rican culture is part of America. The only thing different about this is that it's taking a culture that was marginalized and it's presenting it as something mainstream."

As optimistic as Paul remained, the show just couldn't get off the ground. Finally, that December, it fell to Dan Klores to make the best-spin announcement that the opening of *The Capeman* was going to be delayed a month (at least), because the show needed more rehearsals. Here is how the *New York Times* reported it:

After announcing this week that the Broadway opening of the Paul Simon musical *The Capeman* would be delayed for three weeks to Jan. 7, the producers were busily squelching

---

hit rock albums. In most cases, the albums to hit musicals are now seen as valuable ancillaries, funded by the production companies themselves prior to a show's opening.

rumors yesterday that the show was in trouble and that veteran
directors were being brought in to save it.... Dan Klores said
that the opening was being delayed only to provide time for
more rehearsal, the addition of at least one new song and other
tinkering. Broadway theater circles have been rife with rumors
in recent weeks about problems in the show.... He also denied
rumors that veteran directors like Mike Nichols or Nicholas
Hytner were coming in to work on the show.... Mr. Klores
said that the reason the musical was drawing such negative
attention was that the producers had decided to preview it in
New York, instead of first taking it to one or more other cities.
This was done, he said, purely for financial reasons, and it may
have been a mistake. Mr. Klores said that the producers had
no intention of replacing any member of the creative team,
including Mr. Morris.

However, on January 7, 1998, the day before the show was resched-
uled to open, it was postponed again, accompanied by yet another
announcement by Klores that Broadway veteran Jerry Zaks, a four-
time Tony-winning director (*House of Blue Leaves* in 1986, *Lend Me
a Tenor* in 1989, *Six Degrees of Separation* in 1991, and *Guys and Dolls*
in 1992), was being brought in to "help get the show into shape for
its [new] Jan. 29 opening." Klores tried to deny that this meant that
Morris was being replaced.

The show's director and choreographer, Mark Morris, will
remain in charge of the production and will attend all of Mr.
Zaks' sessions with the cast in coming weeks, Mr. Klores said
and he admitted that both Mike Nichols and Nicholas Hytner
had indeed been brought in to observe and offer suggestions
on how to improve [read save] the show.

The Capeman finally opened at the Marquis Theater on Broadway
the night of January 29, 1998, and the critics quickly and viciously
rejected it. Ben Brantley of the *New York Times* began his next-morning
review this way:

For those who regard theatergoing as blood sport, it promised to be the event of the season. A budget of $11 million; a world-famous composer new to the Broadway musical and openly contemptuous of its traditions; a protracted period of previews replete with tales of desperate last-minute revisions, a frenzied parade of advice-dispensing show doctors: *The Capeman*, Paul Simon's pop-operatic retelling of a street-gang murder in 1959, seemed to have all the elements that make theater-disaster cultists drool.

But it would take a hard-core sadist to derive pleasure from the sad, benumbed spectacle that finally opened last night at the Marquis Theater, three weeks behind schedule. Although it may be unparalleled in its wholesale squandering of illustrious talents, including those of the Nobel Prize–winning poet Derek Walcott (Mr. Simon's co-librettist and book writer) and the brilliant choreographer Mark Morris (the director of record), *The Capeman* is no fun even as a target. . . . It is certainly not a camp hoot, along the lines of such fabled flops as *Moose Murders* and *Carrie*. It's not even an intriguing "noble failure," the kind that causes you to scratch your head and think, "They came so close to getting it right." Instead, the show registers as one solemn, helplessly confused drone. It's like watching a mortally wounded animal. You're only sorry that it has to suffer and that there's nothing you can do about it. . . . But if the composer truly knows the heart of Salvador Agron, he has been unable to find the theatrical language for sharing that knowledge. *The Capeman* itself feels as flat as, and far less incendiary than, the blaze of headlines that illuminated its hero's tragic life.

It was a devastating review from Broadway's most powerful critic and it banged the final nail in the coffin of the troubled, if brilliantly conceived, project. A follow-up Sunday piece by the less remonstrative (and some believe more thoughtful) Vincent Canby in the *Times'* Arts and Leisure section praised the show's music but called the production incoherent.

After fifty-nine previews and sixty-eight regular performances played before half-empty houses, *The Capeman* closed on March 29, 1998, two months after it had opened. Its entire eleven-million-dollar investment was lost.

That spring *The Capeman* received three Tony Award nominations—Best Original Score: Paul Simon and Derek Walcott; Best Orchestrations: Stanley Silverman; Best Scenic Design: Bob Crowley. The awards were voted upon by the most powerful members of the Broadway establishment. *The Capeman* did not win anything.

In September 1998, a "tribute" album called *Broadway Sings the Best of Paul Simon* was released. Among the fifteen songs included that were sung by various Broadway performers was an Alet Oury cover of Paul's rather obscure "Red Rubber Ball," which had never been sung on Broadway by anybody. But nothing from *The Capeman*, not a single song, was included in the compilation.

Paul was devastated by *The Capeman*'s humiliating failure. His reaction was to once more close the door on the rest of the world and stay behind it for the rest of 1998 and part of 1999, licking his wounds and wondering, as he approached his sixtieth birthday, whether anybody out there would ever again be interested in anything he might ever do again.

Including himself.

PART FIVE

Making Plans for the Past with Simon and Garfunkel and Joe

19

Ladies and Gentlemen, Simon and Garfunkel

I T WASN'T UNTIL APRIL 25, 1999, MORE THAN A YEAR AFTER THE closing of *The Capeman*, that Paul made his official and, as it turned out, highly dramatic return to public view, with guitar in hand, ready to perform. The occasion was one Paul could not resist, a memorial by the New York Yankees for their legendary centerfielder Joe DiMaggio, whose passing a month earlier (on March 9) had marked the end of an era of classic New York baseball. During his storied tenure, the Yankee Clipper's team appeared in ten World Series and won nine of them, and in 1941, DiMaggio hit safely in fifty-six consecutive games, a record likely never to be broken.

Paul had been a lifelong Yankees fan, something that connected him to his youth, now more than ever a vital link to family, as his father's recent passing allowed the occasion, a melding of music and baseball, to take on a deeper and private sense of meaning and mourning. Both he and his father had worshipped DiMaggio, and Paul had paid homage to him and a generation's collective lost innocence when he sang in "Mrs. Robinson": "Where have you gone, Joe DiMaggio? A nation turns its lonely eyes to you . . . Joltin' Joe has left and gone away"—a tribute of sorts that, ironically, had angered the always insecure, and at times borderline paranoid, Yankee great. He was said to have loved fame but hated being in the invasive spotlight, was always suspicious of people making money off of his name, and hated any type of close scrutiny of his disastrous marriage to Marilyn Monroe. When he first heard his name in the lyrics to "Mrs. Robinson," he believed whoever wrote it must have thought he was dead and angrily told to a friend, "I haven't gone anywhere. I'm still here!"

With the not unexpected passing of the Yankees' Hall of Famer, a monument-unveiling memorial was quickly planned, and, despite DiMaggio's displeasure with the song, even after it was explained to him that the song was more reverential than mournful (a distinction it was said DiMaggio never believed or fully understood), Paul was asked to perform "Mrs. Robinson," from center field, on the very turf DiMaggio had played on for so many years. The appearance was supposed to be kept as quiet as possible, but word soon leaked that Paul was, indeed, going to make an appearance at the ceremony, and as the early spring sun lit up Yankee Stadium, the capacity crowd of 51,000 grew silent when, over the public address system, John Sterling, the radio voice of the New York Yankees, with typical flourish, introduced Paul:

Joe DiMaggio was immortalized in a 1968 song called "Mrs. Robinson." Ladies and gentlemen, please direct your attention to the area in center field. Here to pay a special tribute to Joe DiMaggio, is New York's own singer/songwriter/lifelong Yankee fan, Mr. Paul Simon!

The crowd exploded as Paul, wearing a Yankees cap, walked slowly to center field and sang a slightly slower-than-usual version of "Mrs. Robinson," accompanying only by himself with the song's familiar 1–6–2–5 acoustic fingerpick.

By June 1 Paul was ready to return to the road. As a warm-up, he did one unpublicized show at the Theater for the Living Arts in Philadelphia, with his regular touring band, which nonetheless produced a word-of-mouth sellout crowd. Five nights after that, an official press release announced that Paul would be touring for the next several months with—*Bob Dylan*. The show, dubbed "Paul/Bob '99" by fans and beat journals, was divided into two equal seventy-five-minute shows, with a post-intermission brief duet by the two legends, most of the time with Dylan opening and Paul closing.

The possibilities set the stage for the making of some historic rock 'n' roll. Here were two of the greatest voices of the sixties, both of whom had made the long run: Dylan, the rough and strong rural midwestern poet whose grandeur had engulfed not just the musical world but the literary one as well, and who had endured; in this incarnation he was a roadhouse rock warrior now embarking on a never-ending tour meant to put an end to the myth of the reclusive Voice-of-His-Generation-Bobness. And Paul Simon, the urban New York sweet street poet, influenced less by Woody Guthrie or Hank Williams than the Everlys, the Penguins, and the Crows; his lyrics were always more opaque than Dylan's, but also more easily listenable, with enough hooks to catch a boatload of fish and therefore more immediately top-ten appealing.

And now, Paul's idol/role model/obsession from the long-ago sixties—Paul had never forgotten Dylan's making fun of him at Gerde's—was not only ready, but also willing and able, to go on the road with him.

In his first media interview since the disastrous *Capeman*, Paul told *USA Today* how excited he was to be playing with Dylan:

> Lots of things about this appeal to me. . . . I like the idea of where we came from and what we evolved into. . . . I have no preconceived notions. I find him easy to be around and easy to work with. . . . I know lots of his songs and he knows a bunch of mine. We're looking to do some things acoustically together. I like "To Ramona" and he likes "Homeward Bound."

Dylan, also interviewed by the newspaper, sounded equally effusive even as the tongue in his cheek helped twist his words with a jagged, if sly condescension:

> I mean, Paul's written extraordinary songs, hasn't he? I consider him one of the pre-eminent songwriters of the times. Every song he does has got a vitality you don't find everywhere. . . . I've always liked "Only Living Boy from New York" [*sic*] and other songs from *Bridge Over Troubled Water*. When I played with the Grateful Dead, we were doing "Boy in the Bubble."

And almost as an afterthought, Paul added that he would play no new songs on the tour.

They performed like warhorses, forty-seven shows in eighty-five nights, from June 6 through September 21, sweeping across the United States, with one show in Vancouver, playing to capacity crowds at Madison Square Garden, the Hollywood Bowl, and, perhaps as a tribute to their shared idol Elvis Presley, a one-night sold-out stand in Las Vegas. Each show they sang one or two songs together following intermission, most often "The Sound of Silence," which they were never quite able to nail; it appeared that Dylan just couldn't remember the words to the song as Paul sang harmony and played guitar. Otherwise, the shows were serial killers, with Dylan and Paul, perhaps driven by each other's presence, performing some of the best sets of their touring careers. Paul took his core recording and touring band members with him—Nguini, Khumalo, Gadd, Haddad, Sheban, Campbell, Gorn, and Stewart.

By the tour's end Paul had liberated himself from the last vestiges of melancholia over *The Capeman* debacle. Then, as if on cue, in November 1999, Columbia Records issued yet another of its apparently never-ending, increasingly redundant, and totally unnecessary remixes of their Simon & Garfunkel catalogue, a twenty-song greatest hits set, *The Best of Simon & Garfunkel*, that its press release audaciously described as "the first compilation hits collection from the greatest pop duo of our time." The album included every Simon & Garfunkel single that had ever charted on *Billboard*, plus three B sides from those singles. The liner notes were written by no less a self-declared Simon & Garfunkel fan than Pulitzer Prize–winning journalist David Halberstam (the only reason to buy it).

On March 2, 2000, Paul made a rare nonsinging appearance at the Rock and Roll Hall of Fame's annual induction ceremony, held at New York's famed Waldorf-Astoria. He was excited about having the opportunity to introduce and induct one of his all-time favorite doo-wop groups, the legendary Moonglows, named by Alan Freed and fronted by Harvey Fuqua and Bobby Lester. The Moonglows' hits included the classic "Sincerely" (covered by the McGuire Sisters for white audiences), "Most of All," "In My Diary," and the truly astonishing "Ten Commandments of Love," one of the greatest pledge-my-love-to-thee records ever made.

At the microphone, Paul talked about what the music of the Moonglows meant to him. "It was a time when music could be heard as a divine gift. And in a world where nothing is perfect, the Moonglows' 'Sincerely' was perfect." With that he gestured to the stage, the lights went up, and the group performed a medley of their greatest hits.

Paul declined an invitation to play in the evening's traditional closing jam.

Two months later, as if in response to Columbia's Simon & Garfunkel latest reissue package, Warner released an album of Paul Simon's "Greatest Hits": *Shining Like a National Guitar*, a nineteen-song compilation that represented Paul's entire solo catalogue, including two songs from *The Capeman*.

That September Paul made an appearance at a Democratic Party fund-raiser held at New York's Radio City Music Hall, where he performed "Graceland," "Late in the Evening," "Bridge over Troubled Water," and "Teach Your Children," in which he was accompanied by Crosby Stills & Nash, Darlene Love, k.d. lang, Lenny Kravitz, Sheryl Crow, and Jon Bon Jovi.

A week later he joined José Feliciano onstage at Carnegie Hall, where together they performed "Homeward Bound," "The Boxer," and "Late in the Evening," after which Paul led the crowd in singing "Happy Birthday" to Feliciano.

And then, with no fanfare, on October 3, 2000, Paul released *You're the One*, his first new studio album of original songs in a decade, which he also produced and which was recorded and mixed by Andy Smith at the Hit Factory in New York City. *You're the One* was a decidedly low-key affair, the title borrowing its name from an old Vogues hit from the early sixties. "Darling Lorraine" borrowed its title from the 1959 hit by the Knockouts. Other highlights from the album were "Old," a tongue-in-cheek reaction to the anticipated reaction to this set of songs, which prompted just that reaction, and the title song "You're the One," a typically middle-aged, wonder-of-you song written for Lulu, his daughter with Edie Brickell. A lot of the album felt like the aural equivalent of a father pulling out a folded-up wallet of photos from his back pocket and dropping them open to show to strangers passing by, and about as interesting. Little of it sounded youthful, adventurous, or compelling—too much was rocking chair, too little was rock 'n' roll. It had the problem none of the sixties icons from Dylan on down had yet been able to conquer and likely never would: how to grow old gracefully in quarter time, without sounding lost-youth-obsessed, or suffering from a musically lethal dose of age-denial and self-delusion. The songs on *You're the One* were well-enough written and performed with Paul's customary grace and beauty, but they were nevertheless inexcusably dull.

When it failed to place on *Billboard*'s Top Twenty album list, to try to increase sales Paul made a rare appearance on *The Today Show* and then embarked on a limited world tour of Sweden, Germany, England, Italy, and France, which, due to a surprising (to Paul) and welcomed overwhelming demand quickly turned into a big world tour that eventually came back and rolled across America, highlighted by Paul's inviting his son Harper (by Peggy), now an aspiring musician in his own right, onstage every night to perform "The Boxer" with him.

While he was on tour, *You're the One* was nominated for a Grammy for Album of the Year, making Paul the only artist ever to be nominated for that award at least once in five consecutive decades. Aware of the milestone, he rearranged his tour schedule to be able to attend the ceremonies.

The awards were broadcast February 21, 2001, live on CBS, from the new Staples Center in Los Angeles, the home of the Los Angeles Lakers. It was hosted by Jon Stewart. Paul was among an eclectic group of performers who played during the event, including *NSYNC, Christina Aguilera, Destiny's Child featuring Beyoncé, Eminem & Elton John, Nnenna Freelon with Take 6, Faith Hill, Madonna, U2, Macy Gray, Brad Paisley, and Dolly Parton. Equally eclectic were the year's list of nominees, which showed just where popular music was that year and where it wasn't: Beck's *Midnite Vultures*, Eminem's *The Marshall Mathers LP* (the heavy favorite), Radiohead's *Kid A*, Steely Dan's *Two Against Nature*, and Paul's *You're the One*. The winner that night turned out to be Steely Dan, the act thought by many to be least likely to win, whose late-seventies jazz-rock duo had all but disappeared with the onset of the disco eighties and who had made an album that everyone thought had slipped through under the radar but, perhaps as a protest vote against the extremely talented but not easily likable Eminem, wound up stealing the Grammy and the show.

Afterward, a bemused Paul hung out at the Warner/Elektra/Atlantic tent, chatting with Mark McGrath, the melodic lead singer from the band Sugar Ray; the self-proclaimed white-trash-and-proud-of-it Kid Rock; and Lars Ulrich, the drummer for Metallica. The next day Paul resumed his tour across America, which would last for the rest of the year.

Early in 2001, Paul was notified that he had been voted into the Rock and Roll Hall of Fame as a solo performer, along with Aerosmith, Solomon Burke, the Flamingos, Michael Jackson, Queen, Steely Dan, and Richie Valens. At the induction ceremonies, on the night of March 19, 2001, held as always at the Waldorf-Astoria, Paul was introduced and inducted by Marc Anthony: "I am delighted to see Paul here tonight. After we did *The Capeman*, we were put into separate witness protection programs."

The good-natured quip was met with laughter and applause, which intensified into a standing ovation as Paul emerged from the side entrance and took the podium. When the applause faded, Paul ran through a ten-minute litany of his musical influences and inspirations that included the Penguins, the Moonglows, (the late, great)

Johnny Ace, and, of course, Elvis Presley. He said that Elvis's "Mystery Train" remained one of his all-time favorite recordings and that he had spent a career trying to recapture that sound. After a pause and a deep breath, he singled out Artie, to thank him for sharing the "amazing days" of their early success, adding that the sound of their voices blending together was how he imagined the songs he wrote should sound, and that he regretted the ending of their friendship. "I hope that one day before we die, we will make peace with each other."

The audience broke into wild applause, which Paul turned into laughter when he quickly added, "No rush."

He then thanked Phil Ramone, who had first introduced him to his longtime keyboardist (the late) Richard Tee and drummer Steve Gadd, sighing that they had been like brothers to him. He also expressed his appreciation to Steve Shehan, Jamey Haddad, Mark Stewart, and Vincent Nguini for playing on the new album and having made *You're the One* "one of the most rewarding creative experiences of my career."

Then, after a dramatic pause, Paul choked a little as he spoke softly into the microphone and thanked his father for having been his greatest teacher, and God for the talent he had given Paul to live out the rock 'n' roll dream that started that night so long ago when he was only twelve years old and first heard "Gee" by the Crows on New York's *Make-Believe Ballroom* radio show.

Paul, one month shy of sixty years old, settled down in the city with Edie and their three young children, Adrian, Lulu, and Gabriel, to relax and regroup after his long, productive, and rewarding career, with no plans to perform again in the foreseeable future. Unfortunately, none of that would be possible after the morning of September 11, 2001, when New York City became the target of a terrorist act of war. Ten days later, on September 21, at Madison Square Garden and broadcast live all over the world, Paul sang a mournful solo version of "Bridge over Troubled Water."

Two more years passed, during which time Paul occasionally returned to Europe for a few one-off solo concerts. Then, in 2003, Paul and Artie caught everybody by surprise when they announced they were reuniting for one more world tour. Shortly before it began, they were interviewed on NPR, where host Scott Simon asked Artie why he had agreed to get back together with Paul. "Why not," Artie answered. "We both sing, we harmonize, and we have a history of doing it well together." Paul was a little more forthcoming:

> The reason we came back after ten years of not even being in contact, we hadn't sung together for so long. And there were so many requests for us to tour together that it became something that had a logic to it. This fall, we decided to go back out on tour. . . . It's a nice way to officially say good-bye.

On October 20, 2003, appropriately enough in Cleveland, Ohio, the official home of the Rock and Roll Hall of Fame, Simon & Garfunkel kicked off their "Old Friends" tour, which took them around the world and ended nine months later with an outdoor event at the Coliseum in Rome, Italy.

Three years later, on October 9, 2006, six years after *You're the One*, Paul, with sixteen Grammys under his belt, released his "long-awaited" (the record company's description) tenth solo album, *Surprise*, a collection of original songs, produced by rock avant-gardist Brian Eno.* Most of the album, which had a mordant tone, was said to be inspired by the September 11 terrorist attacks and the wars in Iraq and Afghanistan that followed. Typically, Paul took his time preparing it. The album's other major theme was more personal, Paul's turning sixty (which he did in 2001, the year of the attacks) and the issue of relevance in the short-attention span of rock 'n' roll.

> Once you go away for a bit, you wonder who people think you are. If they don't know what you're up to, they just go by your history. I'm so often described as this person that went

---

* Eno is Brian Peter George St. John le Baptiste de la Salle, an English vocalist, composer, and record producer, who founded Roxy Music in the early eighties. Eno also produced albums for U2 (under the group name Passengers) and the Talking Heads.

to other cultures, which is true, but I never thought of it that way. I suspect people are thinking, "What culture did you go to?" But this record is straight-ahead American.

Surprise was a commercial hit, reaching number fourteen in the *Billboard* Top 200 and number four in the UK. Most critics also praised the album, and many of them called it a real "comeback" for the artist. Stephen Thomas Erlewine from *All Music Guide* took note of Simon's effort to blend his classic folk sound with Eno's electronic textures, and wrote that "Simon doesn't achieve his comeback by reconnecting with the sound and spirit of his classic work; he has achieved it by being as restless and ambitious as he was at his popular and creative peak, which makes *Surprise* all the more remarkable." The album was supported with the successful Surprise Tour.

Surprise was recorded in Eno's studio in London, and in Nashville; it was another collection of easy, relaxed tunes, some dealing with fatherhood, some with the environment. According to Paul, "Working with Brian Eno opens the door to a world of sonic possibilities, plus he's just a great guy to hang with in the studio, or for that matter in life. I had a really good time." Among its best tracks were the Oscar-nominated "Father and Daughter," from the animated film *The Wild Thornberrys*, "Outrageous," and "How Can You Live in the Northeast," which Paul had actually written years earlier and pulled out of the trunk to fill out *Surprise*. The album had a decidedly easy-listening jazz overlay, in which the presence of Herbie Hancock and Bill Frisell can be heard.

Christian Hoard, writing in *Rolling Stone*, gave the album a generous three and a half stars, mostly for the energizing presence of Eno, and then went on to gently skewer the aging Simon's efforts at remaining middle-aged and relevant:

Despite the album's shiny surface, Simon sounds like Simon . . . with the same pained wiseass spirit that made him poet laureate of New York alienation in the early Seventies . . . *Surprise*'s mellow introspection ends up just being sleepy on slow burners like "I Don't Believe". . . that almost keeps you wishing the Eno-Simon collaboration had happened thirty years ago.

Between June and November 2006 Paul did a brief twenty-seven-performance tour that stretched across the United States, up into Canada, and across the pond to Europe.

On the evening of May 23, 2007, Paul traveled to Washington, D.C., to accept the first Gershwin Prize for Popular Song, created by the Library of Congress to "recognize, celebrate, and encourage musical creativity, the wellspring of its vast musical collections." It was named after one of America's greatest songwriters, a pillar of what has come to be known as "The Great American Songbook." Broadcast (at a later date) by PBS, it became a career-summation night, with many of Paul's friends showing up to celebrate and perform, a glittering list that included Shawn Colvin (who had recorded one of the better covers of "Kathy's Song"), Alison Krauss, Lyle Lovett, James Taylor, Philip Glass, the Dixie Hummingbirds, and Ladysmith Black Mambazo. And at the end, there was Artie, out of place and perfectly in place, dueting with Paul on "Bridge over Troubled Water."

Like all broadcast award shows, it fell somewhere between genuine and ingenuous; tribute and riveting and redundant. Still, Paul looked gracious and seemed genuinely moved by it all, a perfectly fitting way for a sixty-five- year-old rock 'n' roll singer suffering from chronic tinnitus to take his final bow.

And for a while it appeared that's the way it would be. Except for an occasional appearance for charity or other worthy causes, such as the concert to benefit the victims of Hurricane Katrina, it seemed he had chosen to end his long professional run. He even left his beloved Upper West Side apartment in New York City for a sprawling family home in New Canaan, Connecticut, that had retirement written all over it.

But in the end, the restless desire to make music got the better of him, and he became actively involved with his son Harper's long-awaited eponymous debut album, helping out with the production, playing on one or two songs, and cowriting three (and arranging for a few longtime friends and associates to play on it, including Charlie McCoy, Lloyd Green, and Mike Leech). Also participating were Inara George, Lowell George's daughter, and Sean Lennon.

And then, in February 2008, Paul agreed to be interviewed before a live audience at New York's 92nd Street Y by former U.S. poet laureate Billy Collins. After running through a series of questions (too often interrupted by Collins's competitive I-know-more-about-rock-'n'-roll than you do), Paul finally picked up the acoustic guitar that had been sitting next to him like a second silent guest and played a simple fingerpick version of "Slip Slidin' Away," and the magic was back in full view.

That night led to a Q and A at the Barnes and Noble bookstore in New York's Chelsea section of Manhattan to help promote the publication of a book of Paul's lyrics. An overflow crowd showed up and filled the three levels of the store, eager to catch even a glimpse of him. During the interview Paul was unusually frank about his artistic choices as a way of approaching what his music had always been about.

A lot of the sounds and rhythms that I use and fell in love with are from very early on. Some of them are actually in my DNA . . . fourths, intervals of fourths are in a lot of music, Indian music, Celtic music, there must be something about [it]. The fifths also. We hear them, we love them . . . there are certain sounds that are deeply ingrained in us and we love them. When I find them, I always go to them. I'll use them again and again. I'm always putting the sound of a certain vocal group on all my records. It's usually me singing with myself and making the sounds, the sound of Gospel quartets, you can hear it in back-up groups like the Crickets . . . it's a very prominent bass and a falsetto and a tenor in there. I love that sound and I use it all the time. That sound has gone away, I never hear it in pop music anymore, I guess you can say it's dated but I don't care. I don't think about dated . . . certain sounds are very emotional, and if you can find those sounds and you have something to say, the listener is open and drawn to the sound and will then listen to the words and absorb what you have to say. But people won't listen to a sound, or a rhythm they don't like.

The interview, conducted by Katherine Lanfer, moved Paul ever closer to a formal return to full-scale performing.

In April 2008, Paul played a month-long three-part retrospective of his entire musical career at the Brooklyn Academy of Music, the highlight of which was a concert version of *The Capeman*. The sold-out shows proved the hottest ticket that spring in New York City, prompting talk of a full revival of the Broadway show. It was more than a rumor. Oskar Eustis, the head of the Public Theater, began planning to bring the show back in the same concert form it had played at BAM, eliminating the Walcott book, keeping only the songs, and using Paul onstage to perform his score as he had on the soundtrack album, with Marc Anthony returning to sing the part of the young Agron.

Paul then agreed to play two nights at New York's Beacon Theatre the following February. The occasion was aptly ironic. The Beacon, an Upper West Side institution, had recently undergone a major refurbishment that restored it to its onetime place of glory.

The opening night of the sold-out shows, with no less a rock luminary than Paul McCartney sitting in one of the new boxes, Paul ran through the songs that made up the soundtrack of his life, including a hefty section of *The Capeman*, which tore the place apart. And for an encore, to everyone's delight and no one's real surprise, Paul brought out Artie, to an overwhelming rush of applause and cheers, and when the crowd died down, together they performed a beautiful set made up of "The Sound of Silence," "The Boxer," and "Old Friends/Bookends."

The response was more thunderous than at the start. Even the normally reticent McCartney rose to his feet, two fists over his head to show his approval of this simple journey back to the shared days of their sixties youth, when Beatlemania ruled the world and Simon & Garfunkel sang their songs of love and played the game.

In 2009 Harper's album was ready for release, and sixty-eight-year-old Paul watched his thirty-seven-year-old son get ready to enter the industrial world of music. "Tennessee," one of the songs Paul cowrote for the album, which was released the following year on the Vagrant label, was described by Ben Greenman in the *New Yorker* (November 2, 2009) as having a "twinkling pedal-steel"-based sound that makes it a lighter cousin to "Graceland."

For Harper everything lay ahead. Paul knew it would not be easy. Siblings and offspring of famous rock acts did not have a great success rate (Sean Lennon and Jakob Dylan quickly come to mind). And there was the question of direction. No one knew anymore how to become a star without a unified radio wave as music's primary promoter, or widely available retail outlets for CDs. In truth, "product in the bag" sales were now beside the point in the music industry. Personal appearances in ever-larger venues seemed the only way to go, but to fill those venues a musician had to have a following, and in order to gain a substantial following, one had to have sales. With the decline of rock 'n' roll as the safely rebellious rite of passage it had been in Paul's prime, for Harper there seemed no clear path to follow. In truth, Harper did not sound as much like his father as the PR hacks were already proclaiming. Artistically he was closer to the lyrically clever, rhythmically strong, and sweet-voiced Brett Dennen.

With Harper out on his own, Paul quietly decided to go back on the road with Artie for yet one more round of their by-now-familiar "farewell concerts." Why not? as Artie was so fond of saying. Why not sing "Bye Bye Love" for the umpteenth time to screaming fans shouting for one last encore of "The Sound of Silence"? Frank Sinatra had his old familiar songs right up until the end, a performance of a performance, singing his familiar charts of songs about the endgame, the bitterness, the booze, the three o'clock in the morning look back on all the days of his life. Even if Simon & Garfunkel's songs were about the beginning and not the end, even if they were all about young love (both successful and failed), about dreams and desires and longing and hope, in the end it would still now have to be for their boomer audience, bald and wide and semiretired, who resisted moving forward by loving to look back and were always eager to jump into the one-night-stand time machine with them. And really, was it so bad? If it had once been a lifestyle for Paul and Artie, it was now a living. Everybody had a right to live, even if, for the AARP generation, the action was mostly in their memories of yesterday rather than their dreams of tomorrow.

And so it went. Awards. Reunions. Reissues. Awards. Reunions. Reissues. The Rock and Roll Hall of Fame's 25th Anniversary. More awards. More reunions. More reissues. More shows. More interviews. Like an MP3 set on perpetual replay, Simon & Garfunkel could keep saying good-bye for the last time forever.

For Paul, sixty years on, he was still not finished delivering his generation from the days of old. A sold-out revival of *The Capeman* played in Central Park for three nights in the summer of 2010 to the possibility of a full Broadway revival. Soon enough, Joltin' Joe would be waiting for him at home to pat him on the back for touching all four.

But not quite yet.

ACKNOWLEDGMENTS

In 1970 I suffered a debilitating accident that put me in a hospital for three months and left me wondering whether I would ever be able to make a full recovery and return to my normal life, such as it was. Still several years away from breaking into mainstream (that is, paying) publishing, and trying to figure out how to get there, my life was interrupted by, well, by an unexpected twist along that fabled highway of life, and I woke up to find myself in a private room in an East Side hospital of New York City, facing a long, slow, and at times painful recovery.

I had long hair and a full beard in those days, could not tell the difference between, and couldn't have cared less, what brand of anything I wore, had little money and no possessions of any real worth besides a brand-new BA in my back pocket that didn't seem to mean a whole lot to me or to anyone else, especially publishers, when I tried to interest them in my writing. I hadn't as yet come to terms with myself and for all the romantic dribs and drabs I managed to write down, calling it poetry, film criticism, or letters to myself, I was, in truth, drifting in my youthful city-boy way; I had been a somewhat successful child actor but had seen the last days of it after spending several seasons in summer-stock companies learning why I didn't want to do that for the rest of my life. Meanwhile, I moved easily, if not so gracefully, from lover to lover, believing I was emotionally invincible and enjoying living out my own personal Superman complex, when it all came crashing down in front, behind, around, and on top of me that cold and horrible January day.

By the grace of God and the city—both easily possible for me to believe in back then—because of the neighborhood I lived in at the time, the Upper East Side, in a small studio about a block from Bloomingdale's (where I spent many an afternoon wandering, telling myself people-watching was a great writing exercise but really killing time and avoiding actually writing), after the accident I was admitted to the hospital and put in a private room, despite not having any money or insurance, if you can believe it, and received great personal care my entire time there.

In the days after my condition stabilized, I told a friend who came to visit that all I wanted was the small green radio I kept beside my bed in my apartment to be brought to the hospital. At night, when the hallways grew deathly silent, and the nursing staff took their places at their stations, I would soft-click that radio on and listen to WNEW-FM, New York's "hip" rock station of the day, until I fell fitfully into sleep. One night, in the darkness, "Bridge over Troubled Water" came on, and even though I had heard the song countless times before, this time as I lay there, I felt like it was the first time I had ever *really* heard it. I was riveted. Art Garfunkel's voice and Paul Simon's playing and words were like hands that came through that small speaker to hold and comfort me in my time of need. "So long silver girl" sounded to me like a beautiful, if sad, farewell to my former life, and with it everything and everyone I had loved. I turned off the radio and thought about that song for the rest of the night, about its beauty and sadness and hope and grace. I finally cried, overwhelmed all over again. The next morning, I knew I was somehow going to pull through. I knew I was going to make it.

I was one of those tough, loner city kids who had grown up on rock 'n' roll, whose best friends were Alan Freed, Murray the K, Scott Muni, Symphony Sid, Alan Fredericks, Bob-a-loo, and on cold school day mornings, Herb Oscar Anderson. I had watched my older brother's tough-guy friends, the ones with no sleeves on their T-shirts to show off their baseball biceps, who had the best-looking girlfriends in the world, and who worked tough, going-nowhere day jobs, get together every Friday night on the street corner where we lived, form a circle of four, and make the most deliriously beautiful music imaginable, using their voices as instruments to fill the night, and my young and impressionable sponge of a life, with song.

I made the shift in the early sixties from doo-wop to the Village after the first time I heard the voice of Bob Dylan on the radio. Not long after that I met Phil Ochs, who would become my dear friend and first great teacher of writing. Rock 'n' roll (and to us sixties kids, folk music and, a little later, folk rock, fit naturally under that umbrella) took on an even more urgent place in my life as the war in Vietnam became, to my generation, the real-life bogeyman coming to take us away into the darkness of America's and our own worst nightmare. Music became my generation's underground news, our defense, our salvation, our security blanket, and our aphrodisiac, the essence of our pride and courage, the soundtrack to our love-making, the reassurance and encouragement for our rebellions. But despite all that I tried to do to avoid the draft, I surely would have wound up in uniform, one of the white boots forced to march in a yellow land, if not for the accident that got me out of the draft and nearly removed me from the realm of the living.

When I was finally released from the hospital, one of the first things I did was to revisit all the Simon & Garfunkel albums. I was amazed at how much better they had gotten while stacked up silently sitting against the wall of my small East Side apartment. After that, I stayed closer in touch with their music, liking some of it, not all, but enough to move them into my private pantheon.

Years later, one day in 1986, while I was living in Norfolk, Virginia, now a writer-in-residence with three books published (my first about Phil Ochs, following his crazy shocking death) and a career that had been stopped short by an inexplicable writer's block that had already lasted three years, I was driving along when suddenly I had to pull the car over to the side of Route 64 because what was coming out of the radio made it impossible for me to listen and drive at the same time. I was hearing Paul Simon's "Graceland" for the first time, and it did for me what it did for so many, and I'm sure for Paul: it reminded me of who I really was, who I really wanted to be, and it allowed me to measure the difference between what I had become and what I wanted to become, and that day I set out on my own redemptive journey to close that gap. So there it was again, the power of rock 'n' roll; and there he was again, Paul Simon, reminding me once more of all that was really important to me in my life and all that wasn't and shouldn't be. Like so many people who wanted to do something, to be somebody, to strive for Method true expression, I had been distracted, like Dorothy, off the yellow brick road on the way to Oz, by those inviting, yet deadly, poppy fields. For me, the poppy field represented a personal and professional complacency (not drugs), and "Graceland" was like a slap in the face by a beautiful girl that can be taken as either a correction or a caress, or both, but cannot be ignored. The song, and Paul's singing of it, was strong enough to wake me from the short nap that had turned into a long sleep. The next day I did my first good writing in years.

I enjoy writing about the lives of those who have made a difference, in my life and in the world that we (they and I) share. I am a native New Yorker, an outer-borough kid (from the Bronx, where Dion and the Earls were my first hometown rock 'n' roll heroes). I learned to play the guitar from Phil Ochs and, years later, even studied at Eddie Simon's Guitar School (where I learned a lot). I have always believed that to better understand the work of an artist, it is necessary to try to understand the lives they lead. In the end, there is a convergence, a moment when you realize that the work is the life, and the life is the work. I hope you've enjoyed reading this look at Paul Simon's life as much as I've enjoyed writing it.

There are a lot of people who helped me, and I want to thank some of them here. As is the case when the subject one writes about is still living, it is always problematical to express one's public appreciation. Where those who helped do not want an accredited thank-you, I readily comply. Many (but not all) are friends. They include the great, legendary Lou Christie; Al Contrera of the Classics; and Meredith Rutledge, who assisted me at the Rock and Roll Hall of Fame, mostly by filling in names, dates, songs sung on certain occasions, and so on. Many years ago I had the pleasure of meeting and working with Chris Charlesworth, a great rock writer who works for the British publishing house that first put out that country's edition of my first book, *Death of a Rebel.* I traveled to London to reconnect with Charles, and he supplied me with valuable information and great insight. Mike Appel was also helpful in trying to explain the business of music to me all over again as he had when we wrote *Down Thunder Road* in the early 1990s. For me he has been a great friend and someone who never fails to come through. One of my dearest friends from my teen years is Michael Nussbaum, who grew up in Queens and remembers well Paul and Artie when they were kids in school, along with several of their classmates. Michael happily shared those memories with me, in addition to pointing me in the direction of others who could help. David Herwitz did some great research for me and helped in compiling the discography. I wish to credit Paul Maclauchlan for his remarkable compilation of Paul Simon's recordings and concerts.

When one takes on a project like this, it is not uncommon to come across, or be given, rare clips, outtakes, live footage—all sorts of materials that prove extremely helpful. I was fortunate to be given a copy of the Simon & Garfunkel television special *Songs of America,* which I watched over and over. I found it to be eye-opening and fascinating, a time capsule from the sixties that really should be seen by the public again, if for no other reason than to show younger lovers of popular music what the mind-set was back then, beyond Woodstock, Monterey Pop, and Bob Dylan in *Don't Look Back.* These events and the documentary films that capture their essence are priceless social and artistic artifacts of a time long gone by. I think *Songs of America* is good enough, with its revealing blend of rock-star narcissism and youthful, idealized social responsibility, to be right up there with them. People tend not to remember how overtly political much of popular music was back then, including many of the songs of Simon & Garfunkel that reached beyond "Seven O'Clock News/Silent Night." Rock 'n' roll really did begin before the very talented Lady Gaga.

Thanks to my editor, Stephen Power, and the good people at Wiley, including John Simko and Ellen Wright, who helped on the production end. After having written for so long about the movies, my other great artistic passion, it is great to return to my first love, rock 'n' roll.

And to my wonderfully faithful readers, I thank you all, and know that soon we shall all meet again, just a little further on up the road.

PAUL SIMON DISCOGRAPHY

The following is a list of recordings for which Paul Simon was a performer or a composer. Bootlegs, covers by other performers, and songs and albums for which Paul acted as the producer only are not included. Unless otherwise noted, all listings are for U.S. releases and all Tom & Jerry recordings are by Simon & Garfunkel.

1957

45 RPM: "Hey, Schoolgirl"/"Dancin' Wild"
>   Recorded as Tom & Jerry (Jerry Landis/Paul Simon, Tom Graph/Art Garfunkel)

1958/1959

45 RPM: "True or False"/"Teenage Fool"
>   Paul Simon recording as "True Taylor"

45 RPM: "Our Song"/"Two Teenagers"
>   Tom & Jerry

45 RPM: "That's My Story"/"(Pretty Baby) Don't Say Goodbye"
>   Tom & Jerry

ALBUM: *Tom & Jerry*
>   1. "Hey, Schoolgirl"
>   2. "Our Song"
>   3. "That's My Story"
>   4. "Teenage Fool"
>   5. "Tia-Juana Blues"

6. "Dancin' Wild"
7. "Don't Say Goodbye"
8. "Two Teenagers"
9. "True or False"
10. "Simon Says"

1959

45 RPM: "Anna Belle"/"Loneliness"
Tom & Jerry

45 RPM: "Baby Talk"/"I'm Gonna Get Married"
Tom & Jerry

45 RPM: "Just a Boy"/"Shy"
Paul Simon recording as Jerry Landis.

45 RPM: "All Through the Night"
The Mystics; Paul Simon lead vocal, writer, and arranger.

45 RPM: "Don't Tell the Stars"
The Mystics; Paul Simon lead vocal.

1961

45 RPM: "I'm Lonely" [aka "I'm Lonesome"]/"I Wish I Weren't in Love"
Paul Simon recording as Jerry Landis

45 RPM: "Play Me a Sad Song"/"It Means a Lot to Them"
Paul Simon recording as Jerry Landis.

45 RPM: "I'll Drown in My Tears"/"The French Twist"
Tom & Jerry

45 RPM: "Motorcycle"/"I Don't Believe Them"
Tico and the Triumphs; produced, arranged, and written by Paul Simon; Paul Simon as Jerry Landis, Mickey Borack as Tico.

1962

45 RPM: "Surrender, Please Surrender"/"Fighting Mad"
Tom & Jerry

45 RPM: "Express Train"/"Wildflower"
Tico and the Triumphs

45 RPM: "Get Up and Do the Wobble"/"Cry, Little Boy, Cry"
　　Tico and the Triumphs

45 RPM: "Love Teen-Ranger"/"Lisa"
　　Jerry Landis

45 RPM: "Cards of Love"/"Noise"
　　Tico and the Triumphs

45 RPM: "Tick Tock"/"Please Don't Tell Her"
　　Paul Simon and Les Levine, backed up by Tico and the Triumphs

1963

45 RPM: "I'm Lonesome"/"Looking at You"
　　Tom & Jerry

45 RPM: "Carlos Dominguez"/"He Was My Brother"
　　Paul Simon recording as Paul Kane

1964

ALBUM: *Wednesday Morning, 3 A.M.*
　　1. "You Can Tell the World" (B. Gibson/H. Camp)
　　2. "Last Night I Had the Strangest Dream" (Ed McCurdy)
　　3. "Bleecker Street"
　　4. "Sparrow"
　　5. "Benedictus" (traditional, arranged & adapted by Paul
　　　　Simon and Art Garfunkel)
　　6. "The Sounds of Silence"
　　7. "He Was My Brother" (P. Kane)
　　8. "Peggy-O" aka "Pretty Peggy-O" (traditional)
　　9. "Go Tell It on the Mountain" (traditional)
　　10. "The Sun Is Burning" (Ian Campbell)
　　11. "The Times They Are a-Changin' " (Bob Dylan)
　　12. "Wednesday Morning, 3 A.M."
Simon & Garfunkel; all original songs except where indicated
otherwise; produced by Tom Wilson. Rereleased in 1990 as part
of the box set *Simon & Garfunkel Collected Works* on LP and CD.
Released again as a single CD in 2001 with bonus tracks.

ALBUM: *Carlos Dominguez*

Paul Simon recording as Paul Kane; released in the United Kingdom.

45 RPM: "He Was My Brother"/"Carlos Dominguez"

Paul Simon recording as Jerry Landis.

ALBUM: *Golden Goodies: Volume 17*

Multi-artist compilation; track #2 (of 12 tracks) is "Hey, Schoolgirl" by Tom & Jerry.

1965

45 RPM: "Red Rubber Ball"

The Cyrkle; co-written by Paul Simon.

Album: The Paul Simon Song Book

1. "I Am a Rock"
2. "Leaves That Are Green"
3. "A Church Is Burning"
4. "April Come She Will"
5. "The Sound of Silence"
6. "A Most Peculiar Man"
7. "He Was My Brother"
8. "Kathy's Song"
9. "The Side of a Hill"
10. "A Simple Desultory Philippic"
11. "Flowers Never Bend with Rainfall"
12. "Patterns"

Paul Simon; produced by Stanley West and Reginald Warburton. Rereleased as part of the 2004 CD box set *Paul Simon: Collected Works.*

45 RPM: "The Sound of Silence"/"We've Got a Groovy Thing Going"

Simon & Garfunkel

45 RPM: "I Am a Rock"/"Leaves That Are Green"

Simon & Garfunkel; released in UK only.

1966

ALBUM: *Come the Day*

The Seekers; two songs co-written by Paul Simon and Bruce Woodley:

1. "Red Rubber Ball"
2. "I Wish You Could Be Here"

ALBUM: *Sounds of Silence*
1. "The Sounds of Silence"
2. "Leaves That Are Green"
3. "Blessed"
4. "Kathy's Song"
5. "Somewhere They Can't Find Me" (rewrite of "Wednesday Morning 3, A.M.")
6. "Angie" aka "Anji" (written by B. Jansch, mislabeled on the cover as Davy Graham).
7. "Richard Cory"
8. "A Most Peculiar Man"
9. "April Come She Will"
10. "We've Got a Groovy Thing Goin'"
11. "I Am a Rock"

Simon & Garfunkel; produced by Bob Johnston. Rereleased as part of the box set *Simon & Garfunkel Collected Works*, 2001.

45 RPM: "Someday, One Day"
The Seekers; written by Paul Simon and Bruce Woodley; released in UK only.

45 RPM: "Leaves That Are Green"/"Homeward Bound"
Simon & Garfunkel

45 RPM: "That's My Story"/"Tia-Juana Blues"
Simon & Garfunkel (rerelease of Tom & Jerry version)

45 RPM: "I Am a Rock"/"Flowers Never Bend with the Rainfall
Simon & Garfunkel

45 RPM: "The Dangling Conversation"/"The Big Bright Green Pleasure Machine"
Simon & Garfunkel

ALBUM: *What's Happening*
Various artists; includes "Loneliness," credited to Simon & Garfunkel but actually a Jerry Landis track.

ALBUM: *Parsley, Sage, Rosemary and Thyme*
1. "Scarborough Fair/Canticle"

2. "Patterns"

3. "Cloudy"

4. "Homeward Bound"

5. "The Big Bright Green Pleasure Machine"

6. "The 59th Street Bridge Song (Feelin' Groovy)"

7. "The Dangling Conversation"

8. "Flowers Never Bend with the Rainfall"

9. "A Simple Desultory Philippic (Or How I was Robert McNamara'd into Submission)

10. "For Emily, whenever I May Find Her"

11. "A Poem on the Underground Wall"

12. "7 O'Clock News/Silent Night"

Simon & Garfunkel; produced by Bob Johnston. Rereleased on CD as part of the box set *Simon & Garfunkel Collected Works*, 2001.

45 RPM: "A Hazy Shade of Winter"/"For Emily, whenever I May Find Her"

Simon & Garfunkel

1967

ALBUM: *Simon & Garfunkel*

1. "Hey, School Girl"

2. "Our Song"

3. "That's My Story"

4. "Teen Age Fool"

5. "Tia-Juana Blues"

6. "Dancin' Wild"

7. "Don't Say Goodbye"

8. "Two Teen Agers"

9. "True or False"

10. "Simon Says"

Simon & Garfunkel recording as Tom & Jerry; produced by Sid Prosen.

45 RPM: "Having You Around"/"You Don't Know Where Your Interest Lies"

Dana Valery; Paul sings.

45 RPM: "At the Zoo"/"The 59th Street Bridge Song (Feeling Groovy)"

Simon & Garfunkel; "At the Zoo" is a slightly different version than the one that eventually appears on *Bookends*.

45 RPM: "Fakin' It"/"You Don't Know Where Your Interest Lies"

Simon & Garfunkel; "Fakin' It" is a slightly different version than the one that eventually appears on *Bookends*. "You Don't Know Where Your Interest Lies" is the only Simon & Garfunkel song that does not appear on any of their original albums. It shows up for the first time, in stereo, on the *Old Friends* box set.

45 RPM: "Scarborough Fair/Canticle"/"April, Come She Will"

Simon & Garfunkel

ALBUM: *A Very Merry Christmas*

Various artists; Simon & Garfunkel appear on track #4, "The Star Carol," which was also included on *Old Friends*.

1968

ALBUM: *The Live Adventures of Al Kooper & Mike*

Paul added harmony vocals to "The 59th Street Bridge Song (Feelin' Groovy)" in the studio.

1969

45 RPM: "The Boxer"/"Baby Driver"

Simon & Garfunkel; the mono mix of "Baby Driver" is slightly different from the version that appears on *Bridge over Troubled Water*.

1970

ALBUM: *Bridge over Troubled Water*

1. "Bridge over Troubled Water"
2. "El Condor Pasa"
3. "Cecilia"
4. "Keep the Customer Satisfied"
5. "So Long, Frank Lloyd Wright"
6. "The Boxer"
7. "Baby Driver"
8. "The Only Living Boy in New York"
9. "Why Don't You Write Me"

    10. "Bye Bye Love"

    11. "Song for the Asking"

Simon & Garfunkel; produced by Roy Halee, Paul Simon, Art Garfunkel; rereleased as part of the box set *Simon & Garfunkel Collected Works*, 2001.

45 RPM: "Bridge over Troubled Water"/"Keep the Customer Satisfied" Simon & Garfunkel

1972

ALBUM: *Paul Simon*

    1. "Mother and Child Reunion"

    2. "Duncan"

    3. "Everything Put Together Falls Apart"

    4. "Run That Body Down"

    5. "Armistice Day"

    6. "Me and Julio Down by the Schoolyard"

    7. "Peace Like a River"

    8. "Papa Hobo"

    9. "Hobo's Blues"

    10. "Paranoia Blues"

    11. "Congratulations"

Produced by Paul Simon and Ray Halee; reissued with bonus tracks in 2004 as part of the box set *Paul Simon Collected Works*.

45 RPM: "Mother and Child Reunion"/"Paranoia Blues"

45 RPM: "Me and Julio Down by the Schoolyard"/"Congratulations"

ALBUM: *Simon & Garfunkel's Greatest Hits*

    1. "Mrs. Robinson"

    2. "For Emily, whenever I May Find Her"

    3. "The Boxer"

    4. "The 59th Street Bridge Song (Feelin' Groovy)"

    5. "The Sound of Silence"

    6. "I Am a Rock"

    7. "Scarborough Fair/Canticle"

    8. "Homeward Bound"

    9. "Bridge over Troubled Water"

    10. "America"

11. "Kathy's Song"

12. "El Condor Pasa"

13. "Bookends"

45 RPM: "Duncan"/"Run That Body Down"

1973

ALBUM: *There Goes Rhymin' Simon*

    1. "Kodachrome"

    2. "Tenderness"

    3. "Take Me to the Mardi Gras"

    4. "Something So Right"

    5. "One Man's Ceiling Is Another Man's Floor"

    6. "American Tune"

    7. "Was a Sunny Day"

    8. "Learn How to Fall"

    9. "Saint Judy's Comet"

  10. "Love Me Like a Rock"

Paul Simon; produced by Paul Simon; rereleased as part of the box set *Paul Simon Collected Works*, 2004.

45 RPM: "Take Me to the Mardi Gras"/"Kodachrome"
Released in UK only.

45 RPM: "Kodachrome"/"Tenderness"

45 RPM: "Loves Me Like a Rock"/"Learn How to Fall"

45 RPM: "American Tune"/"One Man's Ceiling Is Another Man's Floor"

ALBUM: *That's Enough for Me*

Peter Yarrow; "Groundhog" single from the album written by Paul Simon. Originally intended for but not included on *Bridge over Troubled Water*.

1974

ALBUM: *Live Rhymin'*

    1. "Me and Julio Down by the Schoolyard"

    2. "Homeward Bound"

    3. "American Tune"

    4. "El Condor Pasa (If I Could)"

    5. "Duncan"

    6. "The Boxer"

    7. "Mother and Child Reunion"

    8. "The Sound of Silence"

    9. "Jesus Is the Answer"

  10. "Bridge over Troubled Water"

  11. "Loves Me Like a Rock"

  12. "America"

Produced by Phil Ramone; rereleased as part of the box set *Paul Simon Collected Works*.

45 RPM: "The Sound of Silence"/"Mother and Child Reunion"

1975

45 RPM: "Gone at Last"/"Take Me to the Mardi Gras"
Phoebe Snow duets with Paul Simon on "Gone at Last."

45 RPM: "My Little Town"/"Rag Doll"/"You're Kind"
"My Little Town," Simon & Garfunkel; "Rag Doll," Art Garfunkel; "You're Kind," Paul Simon.

ALBUM: *Still Crazy after All These Years*

    1. "Still Crazy after All These Years"

    2. "My Little Town" (Simon & Garfunkel)

    3. "I Do It for Your Love"

    4. "50 Ways to Leave Your Lover"

    5. "Night Game"

    6. "Gone at Last" (duet with Phoebe Snow)

    7. "Some Folks' Lives Roll Easy"

    8. "Have a Good Time"

    9. "You're Kind"

  10. "Silent Eyes"

Paul Simon; produced by Paul Simon and Phil Ramone.

45 RPM: "50 Ways to Leave Your Lover"/"Some Folks' Lives Roll Easy"

1976

ALBUM: *Sanborn*
David Sanborn; Paul Simon wrote the lyrics for "Smile" and sings on the track with Phoebe Snow.

45 RPM: "Still Crazy after All These Years"/"I Do It for Your Love"
"I Do It for Your Love" is the London version.

1977

45 RPM: "Slip Slidin' Away"/"Something So Right"
The Oak Ridge Boys appear with Paul Simon on "Slip Slidin'
Away."

ALBUM: *Greatest Hits, etc.*
1. "Slip Slidin' Away"
2. "Stranded in a Limousine"
3. "Still Crazy after All These Years"
4. "Have a Good Time"
5. "Duncan"
6. "Me and Julio Down by the Schoolyard"
7. "Something So Right"
8. "Kodachrome"
9. "I Do It for Your Love"
10. "50 Ways to Leave Your Lover"
11. "American Tune"
12. "Mother and Child Reunion"
13. "Loves Me Like a Rock"
14. "Take Me to the Mardi Gras"
Produced by Paul Simon.

45 RPM (UK): "Stranded in a Limousine"/"Have a Good Time"

1978

45 RPM: "Wonderful World"/"Wooden Planes"
Paul Simon, Art Garfunkel, James Taylor; also appears on Art
Garfunkel's *Watermark*.

45 RPM: "Stranded in a Limousine"/"Have a Good Time"

1980

ALBUM: *One-Trick Pony*
1. "Late in the Evening"
2. "That's Why God Made the Movies"
3. "One-Trick Pony"

4. "How the Heart Approaches What It Yearns"

5. "Oh, Marion"

6. "Ace in the Hole"

7. "Nobody"

8. "Jonah"

9. "God Bless the Absentee"

10. "Long, Long Day"

Paul Simon; produced by Paul Simon and Phil Ramone; remastered and rereleased in 2004 with bonus tracks.

45 RPM: "One-Trick Pony"/"Long, Long Day"

1981

45 RPM: "Oh, Marion"/"God Bless the Absentee"

ALBUM: *Scissors Cut*

Art Garfunkel; Paul sings on "In Cars," written by Jimmy Webb.

ALBUM: *Dreaming of a White Christmas*

Compilation album; Simon & Garfunkel sing "The Star Carol."

ALBUM: *The Simon & Garfunkel Collection*

1. "I Am a Rock"

2. "Homeward Bound"

3. "America"

4. "59th Street Bridge Song"

5. "Wednesday Morning, 3 A.M."

6. "El Condor Pasa"

7. "At the Zoo"

8. "Scarborough Fair/Canticle"

9. "The Boxer"

10. "Sound of Silence"

11. "Mrs. Robinson"

12. "Keep the Customer Satisfied"

13. "Song for the Asking"

14. "Hazy Shade of Winter"

15. "Cecelia"

16. "Old Friends/Bookends Theme"

17. "Bridge over Troubled Water"

Compilation album; various producers; released in UK only.

ALBUM: *Paul Simon Collected Works*

> Paul Simon; five-LP set that contains original versions of *The Paul Simon Songbook* (only U.S. release of this UK LP), *Paul Simon, There Goes Rhymin' Simon, Live Rhymin'*, and *Still Crazy after All These Years*.

ALBUM: *Simon & Garfunkel Collected Works*

> Five-LP set that contains the original versions of *Wednesday Morning, 3 A.M.; Sounds of Silence; Parsley, Sage, Rosemary and Thyme; Bookends;* and *Bridge over Troubled Water;* rereleased on CD in 1990.

ALBUM: *Tom & Jerry Meet Tico & the Triumphs*

> 1. "Hey, Schoolgirl"
> 2. "Dancin' Wild"
> 3. "That's My Story"
> 4. "True or False"
> 5. "Our Song"
> 6. "Two Teen-Agers"
> 7. "Don't Say Goodbye"
> 8. "Teenage Fool"
> 9. "Baby Talk"
> 10. "Fightin' Mad"
> 11. "Motorcycle"
> 12. "I Don't Believe Them"
> 13. "Wild Flower"
> 14. "Express Train"
> 15. "Get Up and Do the Wobble"
> 16. "Cry Little Boy Cry"
> 17. "The Lone Teen Ranger"
> 18. "Lisa"
> 19. "Noise"
> 20. "Cares of Love"

> Tom & Jerry (side one), Tico and the Triumphs (side two); released in Europe only.

1982

ALBUM: *The Concert in Central Park*

> 1. "Mrs. Robinson"

2. "Homeward Bound"

3. "America"

4. "Me and Julio Down by the Schoolyard"

5. "Scarborough Fair"

6. "April Come She Will"

7. "Wake Up Little Susie"

8. "Still Crazy after All These Years"

9. "American Tune"

10. "Late in the Evening"

11. "Slip Slidin' Away"

12. "A Heart in New York"

13. "Kodachrome"/"Maybelline"

14. "Bridge over Troubled Water"

15. "50 Ways to Leave Your Lover"

16. "The Boxer"

17. "Old Friends"

18. "The 59th Street Bridge Song"

19. "The Sound of Silence"

Simon & Garfunkel; produced by Paul Simon, Roy Halee, Phil Ramone.

45 RPM: "Wake Up Little Suzie"/"Me and Julio Down by the Schoolyard"

From *The Concert in Central Park*

1983

ALBUM: *Trouble in Paradise*

Randy Newman; Paul sings on "The Blues."

45 RPM: "The Blues"/"The Same Girl"

Randy Newman; Paul sings on "The Blues."

45 RPM "Allergies"/"Think Too Much"

ALBUM: *Hearts and Bones*

1. "Allergies"

2. "Hearts and Bones"

3. "When Numbers Get Serious"

4. "Think Too Much" (b)

5. "Song about the Moon"

6. "Think Too Much" (a)

7. "Train in the Distance"

8. "Rene and Georgette Magritte with Their Dog after the War"

9. "Cars Are Cars"

10. "The Late Great Johnny Ace"

Produced by Paul Simon, Russ Titelman, Roy Halee, Lenny Waronker; rereleased in 2004 with bonus tracks.

1984

45 RPM: "Think Too Much" (a)/"Song about the Moon"

1985

45 RPM: "We Are the World"/"Grace"
Paul sings on "We Are the World."

ALBUM: *USA for Africa*
Includes 45 RPM "We Are the World"

ALBUM: *Songs from Liquid Days*
Philip Glass; Paul wrote the lyrics to "Changing Opinion."

45 RPM: "You Used to Call Me"
Terrance Simien and Paul Simon

45 RPM: "You Can Call Me Al"/"Gumboots"

ALBUM: *Graceland*

1. "The Boy in the Bubble"

2. "Graceland"

3. "I Know What I Know"

4. "Gumboots"

5. "Diamonds on the Soles of Her Shoes"

6. "You Can Call Me Al"

7. "Under African Skies"

8. "Homeless"

9. "Crazy Love"

10. "That Was Your Mother"

11. "All around the World or the Myth of Fingerprints"

Produced by Paul Simon.

45 RPM: "Graceland"/"Hearts and Bones"

ALBUM: *Shaka Zulu*

>Ladysmith Black Mambazo; produced by Paul Simon; released in South Africa only.

1987

45 RPM: "The Boy in the Bubble"/"Crazy Love Vol. 2"

45 RPM: Diamonds on the Soles of Her Shoes"/"All around the World or the Myth of Fingerprints"

45 RPM: "Under African Skies"/"I Know What I Know"

>Linda Ronstadt sings with Paul on "Under African Skies."

ALBUM: *Yauraté*

>Milton Nascimento; Paul Simon sings on "Dream Merchant" ("O Vendor De Sonhos") and did the vocal arrangements for the album; released in Brazil only.

1988

ALBUM: *Journey of Dreams*

>Ladysmith Black Mambazo; produced by Paul Simon. Paul does vocals on and arranged "Amazing Grace."

ALBUM: *Negotiations and Love Songs, 1971–1986*

>1. "Mother and Child Reunion"
>2. "Me and Julio Down by the Schoolyard"
>3. "Something So Right"
>4. "St. Judy's Comet"
>5. "Love Me Like a Rock"
>6. "Kodachrome"
>7. "Have a Good Time"
>8. "50 Ways to Leave Your Lover"
>9. "Still Crazy after All These Years"
>10. "Late in the Evening"
>11. "Slip Slidin' Away"
>12. "Hearts and Bones"
>13. "Train in the Distance"
>14. "Rene and Georgette Magritte with Their Dog after the War"
>15. "Diamonds on the Soles of Her Shoes"

16. "You Can Call Me Al"

17. "Graceland"

Produced by Paul Simon, Roy Halee, Phil Ramone.

1989

ALBUM: *Yo Frankie*

Dion; Paul Simon sings on "Written on the Subway Wall/Little Star."

1990

U.S. BOX SET: *Simon & Garfunkel Collected Works*

Rerelease of 1981 five-LP set on three CDs

ALBUM CD: *Nobody's Child—Romanian Angel Appeal*

Various artists; Paul Simon and George Harrison's performance of "Homeward Bound" from *Saturday Night Live*, November 20, 1976.

ALBUM CD: *The Rhythm of the Saints*

1. "The Obvious Child"

2. "Can't Run But"

3. "The Coast"

4. "Proof"

5. "Further to Fly"

6. "She Moves On"

7. "Born at the Right Time"

8. "The Cool, Cool River"

9. "Spirit Voices"

10. "The Rhythm of the Saints"

Produced by Paul Simon.

45 RPM: "The Obvious Child" (single mix)/"The Rhythm of the Saints"

CASSETTE: "The Obvious Child" (single mix)/"The Rhythm of the Saints"

1990

SINGLE CD: "The Obvious Child"/"The Rhythm of the Saints"/"You Can Call Me Al"/"The Boy in the Bubble"

CD: *Paul Simon and Friends*

> Paul Simon, Neil Sedaka, Tony Orlando, Johnny Rivers, Frankie Valli, and Tommy Edwards; the artists do not appear together. These are reissues, including three songs by Paul Simon as Jerry Landis: "Play Me a Sad Song"/"It Means a Lot to Them"/ "Flame." Released in UK only.

1991

SINGLE CD: "Proof"

> one-sided, single-song CD

ALBUM/CD: *Paul Simon's Concert in the Park*

1. "The Obvious Child"
2. "The Boy in the Bubble"
3. "She Moves On"
4. "Kodachrome"
5. "Born at the Right Time"
6. "Train in the Distance"
7. "Me and Julio Down by the Schoolyard"
8. "I Know What I Know"
9. "The Cool, Cool River"
10. "Bridge over Troubled Water"
11. "Proof"
12. "The Coast"
13. "Graceland"
14. "You Can Call Me Al"
15. "Still Crazy after All These Years"
16. "Loves Me Like a Rock"
17. "Diamonds on the Soles of Her Shoes"
18. "Hearts and Bones"
19. "Late in the Evening"
20. "America"
21. "The Boxer"
22. "Cecilia"
23. "The Sound of Silence"

Produced by Paul Simon.

CD BOX SET: *The Collection*

> Produced by Ian Hoblyn; released in Japan only.

CD #1: *Born at the Right Time—The Best of Paul Simon*
1. "Mother and Child Reunion"
2. "Duncan"
3. "Me and Julio Down by the Schoolyard"
4. "Take Me to the Mardi Gars"
5. "Kodachrome"
6. "American Tune"
7. "Gone at Last"
8. "50 Ways to Leave Your Lover"
9. "Still Crazy after All These Years"
10. "Slip Slidin' Away"
11. "Late in the Evening"
12. "Jonah"
13. "Hearts and Bones"
14. "The Boy in the Bubble"
15. "Graceland"
16. "You Can Call Me Al"
17. "The Obvious Child"
18. "Born at the Right Time"

CD #2: *Graceland: The African Concert*
1. "Township Jive"
2. "The Boy in the Bubble"
3. "Gumboots"
4. "Whispering Bells"
5. "CrazyLove, Volume II"
6. "I Know What I Know"
7. "Under African Skies"
8. "Homeless"
9. "Graceland"
10. "You Can Call Me Al"
11. "Diamonds on the Soles of Her Shoes"

CD #3: *Interview with Paul Simon*

CD: *The Definitive Simon & Garfunkel*
1. "Wednesday Morning, 3 A.M."
2. "The Sound of Silence"
3. "Homeward Bound"

4. "Kathy's Song"

5. "I Am a Rock"

6. "For Emily, whenever I May Find Her"

7. "Scarborough Fair/Canticle"

8. "The 59th Street Bridge Song/Feelin' Groovy)"

9. "7 O'Clock News"/"Silent Night"

10. "A Hazy Shade of Winter"

11. "El Condor Pasa"

12. "Mrs. Robinson"

13. "America"

14. "At the Zoo"

15. "Old Friends"

16. "Bookends Theme"

17. "Cecilia"

18. "The Boxer"

19. "Bridge over Troubled Water"

20. "Song for the Asking"

Simon & Garfunkel; released in UK only.

1992

ALBUM/CD: *Dreaming of a White Christmas*
Various artists; Simon & Garfunkel sing "The Star Carol."

1993

ALBUM/CD: *Across the Borderline*
Willie Nelson; Paul Simon plays guitar on "American Tune" and "Graceland."

CD: *Tom & Jerry—Their Greatest Hits Vol. 2*

1. "Looking at You"

2. "Hey, Schoolgirl"

3. "Lighthouse Point"

4. "That Forever Kind of Love"

5. "Back Seat Driver"

6. "True or False"

7. "Fighting Mad"

8. "Anna Belle"

9. "Surrender, Please Surrender"

10. "Loneliness"

11. "I'm Lonesome"

12. "Dancin' Wild"

13. "Don't Say Goodbye"

14. "Motorcycle"

15. "Noise"

16. "Sleepy Sleepy Baby"

17. "Bingo"

18. "Dreams Can Come True"

19. "Lisa"

20. "Cards of Love"

21. "I Don't Believe Them"

22. "Tia-Juana Blues"

Simon & Garfunkel as Tom & Jerry, and various post–Tom & Jerry solo and duo recordings; released in Italy only.

CD BOX SET: *Paul Simon Anthology*

CD #1

1. "The Sound of Silence"

2. "Cecilia"

3. "El Condor Pasa"

4. "The Boxer"

5. "Mrs. Robinson"

6. "Bridge over Troubled Water"

7. "Me and Julio Down by the Schoolyard"

8. "Peace Like a River"

9. "Mother and Child Reunion"

10. "American Tune"

11. "Loves Me Like a Rock"

12. "Kodachrome"

13. "Gone at Last"

14. "Still Crazy after All These Years"

15. "Something So Right"

16. "50 Ways to Leave Your Lover"

17. "Slip Slidin' Away"

18. "Late in the Evening"

19. "Hearts and Bones"

20. "Rene and Georgette Magritte with Their Dog after
the War"

CD #2

1. "The Boy in the Bubble"

2. "Graceland"

3. "Under African Skies"

4. "That Was Your Mother"

5. "Diamonds on the Soles of Her Shoes"

6. "You Can Call Me Al"

7. "Homeless"

8. "Spirit Voices"

9. "Obvious Child"

10. "Can't Run But"

11. "Thelma"

12. "Further to Fly"

13. "She Moves On"

14. "Born at the Right Time"

15. "Cool Cool River"

16. "The Sound of Silence"

CD BOX SET: *1964/1993—Paul Simon*

Produced by Paul Simon.

CD #1

1. "Leaves That Are Green"

2. "The Sound of Silence"

3. "Kathy's Song"

4. "America"

5. "Cecilia"

6. "El Condor Pasa"

7. "The Boxer"

8. "Mrs. Robinson"

9. "Bridge over Troubled Water" (guitar demo)

10. "Bridge over Troubled Water"

11. "The Breakup"

12. "Hey, Schoolgirl"

13. "My Little Town"

14. "Me and Julio Down by the Schoolyard"

15. "Peace Like a River"
16. "Mother and Child Reunion"
17. "Congratulations"
18. "Duncan"
19. "American Tune"

CD #2

1. "Loves Me Like a Rock"
2. "Tenderness"
3. "Kodachrome"
4. "Gone at Last"
5. "Take Me to the Mardi Gras"
6. "St. Judy's Comet"
7. "Something So Right
8. "Still Crazy after All These Years'
9. "Have a Good Time"
10. "Jonah"
11. "How the Heart Approaches What It Yearns"
12. "50 Ways to Leave Your Lover"
13. "Slip Slidin' Away"
14. "Late in the Evening"
15. "Hearts and Bones"
16. "Rene and Georgette Magritte with Their Dog after the War"
17. "The Late Great Johnny Ace"

CD #3

1. "The Boy in the Bubble"
2. "Graceland"
3. "Under African Skies"
4. "That Was Your Mother"
5. "Diamonds on the Soles of Her Shoes"
6. "You Can Call Me Al"
7. "Homeless"
8. "Spirit Voices"
9. "The Obvious Child"
10. "Can't Run But"
11. "Thelma" (from *Rhythm of the Saints* sessions)

12. "Further to Fly"
13. "She Moves On"
14. "Born at the Right Time"
15. "The Cool, Cool River"
16. "The Sound of Silence"

1994

CD: *Picture Perfect Morning*

Edie Brickell; produced by Paul Simon and Roy Halee; Paul Simon plays acoustic guitar on "Green," "When the Lights Go Down," and "Picture Perfect Morning."

CD: *Earthrise*

Various artists; live performances from several Rainforest Benefits; Paul Simon sings "Under African Skies."

CD: *The Unplugged Collection, Volume One*

Various artists; Paul sings "Graceland."

1995

SINGLE CD: "Something So Right"

Annie Lennox; Paul Simon plays guitar and adds vocals; released in UK only.

CD: *Medusa*

Annie Lennox; Paul Simon sings and plays guitar on "Something So Right."

1996

CD: *Go Cat Go*

Carl Perkins; "Rockabilly Music" written by Paul Simon and Carl Perkins; produced and mixed by Paul Simon.

"Don't Stop the Music," Paul Simon, percussion; Harper Simon (Paul's son), guitar.

"A Mile Out of Memphis" produced and mixed by Paul Simon; Paul Simon vocals and guitar; Harper Simon, lead guitar.

CD: *Graceland*

Enhanced original CD for CD-ROM; videos and interviews with many of the people involved with the album and the tour.

1997

CD: *Carnival!*

> The Rainforest Foundation; various artists; Paul Simon sings "Ten Years."

CD BOX SET: *Old Friends*

> Simon & Garfunkel; compilation producer: Bob Irwin.

CD #1

1. "Bleecker Street" (demo version)
2. "The Sound of Silence"
3. "The Sun Is Burning"
4. "Wednesday Morning, 3 A.M."
5. "He Was My Brother"
6. "Sparrow"
7. "Peggy-O"
8. "Benedictus"
9. "Somewhere They Can't Find Me"
10. "We've Got a Groovy Thing Goin'"
11. "Leaves That Are Green"
12. "Richard Cory"
13. "I Am a Rock"
14. "The Sound of Silence" (single remix version)
15. "Homeward Bound"
16. "Blues Run the Game" (previously unreleased)
17. "Kathy's Song"
18. "April Come She Will"
19. "Flowers Never Bend with the Rainfall"

CD #2

1. "Patterns"
2. "Cloudy"
3. "The Dangling Conversation"
4. "Scarborough Fair/Canticle"
5. "The 59th Street Bridge Song (Feelin' Groovy)"
6. "For Emily, whenever I May Find Her"
7. "7 O'Clock News/Silent Night"
8. "A Hazy Shade of Winter"

9. "At the Zoo"

10. "A Poem on the Underground Wall"

11. "Red Rubber Ball"

12. "Blessed"

13. "Anji"

14. "A Church Is Burning"

15. "Fakin' It"

16. "Save the Life of My Child"

17. "America"

18. "You Don't Know Where Your Interest Lies"

19. "Punky's Dilemma"

20. "Comfort and Joy" (previously unreleased)

21. "Star Carol" (previously unreleased)

CD #3

1. "Mrs. Robinson"

2. "Old Friends/Bookends Theme"

3. "Overs"

4. "A Most Peculiar Man"

5. "Bye, Bye Love"

6. "The Boxer"

7. "Baby Driver"

8. "Why Don't You Write Me"

9. "Feuilles –O" (demo)

10. "Keep the Customer Satisfied"

11. "So Long, Frank Lloyd Wright"

12. "Song for the Asking"

13. "Cecilia"

14. "El Condor Pasa"

15. "Bridge over Troubled Water"

16. "The Only Living Boy in New York"

17. "Hey, Schoolgirl/Black Slacks"

18. "That Silver Haired Daddy of Mine"

19. "My Little Town"

CD: *The Bridge School Concerts Volume One*

Various artists; Simon & Garfunkel perform "America."

1998

CD: *Songs from* The Capeman
    1. "Adios Hermanos"
    2. "Born in Puerto Rico"
    3. "Satin Summer Nights"
    4. "Bernadette"
    5. "The Vampires"
    6. "Quality"
    7. "Can I Forgive Him"
    8. "Sunday Afternoon"
    9. "Killer Wants to Go to College"
   10. "Time Is an Ocean"
   11. "Virgil"
   12. "Killer Wants to Go to College #2"
   13. "Trailways Bus"

Produced by Roy Halee; all songs written and sung by Paul Simon. The original cast album, including all thirty-nine songs, was released as a download June 27, 2006, and is available only as a download from iTunes.

CD: *Walgreens Holiday Favorites Christmas Collection Volume One*
Rerelease; Simon & Garfunkel perform "The Star Carol."

1999

CD: *Saturday Night Live: The Musical Performances*
Various artists; Paul Simon sings "Diamonds on the Soles of Her Shoes."

CD: *The Best of Simon & Garfunkel*
    1. "The Sound of Silence"
    2. "Homeward Bound"
    3. "I Am a Rock"
    4. "The Dangling Conversation"
    5. "Scarborough Fair/Canticle"
    6. "The 59th Street Bridge Song (Feelin' Groovy)"
    7. "A Hazy Shade of Winter"
    8. "At the Zoo"
    9. "Fakin' It (mono version, first time on CD)

10. "Mrs. Robinson"
11. "Old Friends"/"Bookends"
12. "The Boxer"
13. "Bridge over Troubled Water"
14. "Cecilia"
15. "The Only Living Boy in New York"
16. "Song for the Asking"
17. "El Condor Pasa (If I Could)"
18. "For Emily, whenever I May Find Her"
19. "America"
20. "My Little Town"

2000

CD: *Paul Simon—Greatest Hits—Shining Like a National Guitar*

1. "Graceland"
2. "You Can Call Me Al"
3. "Mother and Child Reunion"
4. "The Cool Cool River"
5. "50 Ways to Leave Your Lover"
6. "The Obvious Child"
7. "The Boy in the Bubble"
8. "Rene and Georgette Magritte with Their Dog after the War"
9. "Late in the Evening"
10. "Bernadette"
11. "Slip Slidin' Away"
12. "Take Me to the Madi Gras"
13. "Diamonds on the Soles of Her Shoes"
14. "Still Crazy after All These Years"
15. "Kodachrome"
16. "Loves Me Like a Rock"
17. "Me and Julio Down by the Schoolyard"
18. "Hearts and Bones"
19. "Trailways Bus"

CD: *You're the One*

1. "That's Where I Belong"
2. "Darling Lorraine"

3. "Old"

4. "You're the One"

5. "The Teacher"

6. "Look at That"

7. "Senorita with a Necklace of Tears"

8. "Love"

9. "Pigs, Sheep & Wolves"

10. "Hurricane Eye"

11. "Quiet"

Produced by Paul Simon.

2001

CD: *Simon & Garfunkel: The Columbia Studio Recordings 1964–1970*

Remixed and expanded versions of the five original Simon & Garfunkel Columbia albums:

Wednesday Morning, 3 A.M.

"Bleecker Street," demo version

"He Was My Brother," demo version

"The Sun Is Burning," demo version

Sounds of Silence

"The Blues Run the Game," outtake

"Barbriallen," demo version

"Rose of Aberdeen," demo version

"Roving Gambler," demo version

Parsley, Sage, Rosemary and Thyme

"Patterns," demo version

"A Poem on the Underground Wall," demo version

Bookends

"You Don't Know Where Your Interest Lies," single version

"Old Friends," demo version

Bridge over Troubled Water

"Feuilles-O," unreleased demo version

"Bridge over Troubled Water," demo version

CD: *America: A Tribute to Heroes*

Various artists; Paul performs a live version of "Bridge over Troubled Water."

CD: *Live from New York City, 1967*

    1. "He Was My Brother"

    2. "Leaves That Are Green"

    3. "Sparrow"

    4. "Homeward Bound"

    5. "You Don't Know Where Your Interest Lies"

    6. "A Most Peculiar Man"

    7. "The 59th Street Bridge Song (Feelin' Groovy)"

    8. "The Dangling Conversation"

    9. "Richard Cory"

    10. "A Hazy Shade of Winter"

    11. "Benedictus"

    12. "Blessed"

    13. "A Poem on the Underground Wall"

    14. "Anji"

    15. "I Am a Rock"

    16. "The Sound of Silence"

    17. "For Emily, whenever I May Find Her"

    18. "A Church Is Burning"

    19. "Wednesday Morning, 3 A.M."

Simon & Garfunkel; produced by Paul Simon, Art Garfunkel, Roy Halee, Bob Irwin; recorded at Lincoln Center, January 1967.

CD: *The Paul Simon Collection—I'm On My Way, Don't Know Where I'm Goin'*

    1. "Mother and Child Reunion"

    2. "Me and Julio Down by the Schoolyard"

    3. "Kodachrome"

    4. "Something So Right"

    5. "Loves Me Like a Rock"

    6. "50 Ways to Leave Your Lover"

    7. "Still Crazy after All These Years"

    8. "Late in the Evening"

    9. "Slip Slidin' Away"

    10. "Hearts and Bones"

    11. "Diamonds on the Soles of Her Shoes" (single version)

    12. "The Boy in the Bubble" (single version)

    13. "Graceland"

14. "You Can Call Me Al"

15. "Spirit Voices"

16. "The Cool, Cool River"

17. "Adios Hermanos"

18. "Love"

19. "Hurricane Eye"

20. "American Tune" (live, New York City, 1973)

21. "Duncan" (live, London, 1973)

22. "The Coast" (live, New York City, 2002)

23. "Mrs. Robinson" (live, New York City, 1999)

24. "Bridge over Troubled Water" (live, New Orleans, 2001)

Two-CD set; the first has nineteen previously released songs, and the second has five previously unreleased live recordings.

CD: *Before the Fame*

1. "Dream Alone"

2. "Teenage Fool"

3. "Beat Love"

4. "I Love You (Oh Yes I Do)"

5. "Just a Boy"

6. "Play Me a Sad Song"

7. "It Means a Lot to Them"

8. "Flame"

9. "Shy"

10. "Lone Teen Ranger"

11. "Two Teenagers"

12. "Hey, Schoolgirl"

13. "That's My Story"

14. "Don't Say Goodbye"

15. "Our Song"

Compilation of early Simon & Garfunkel/Tom & Jerry recordings

2004

CD: *Paul Simon Songbook*

U.S. release of original UK LP released in May 1965; contains two tracks not on the original: "I Am a Rock" and "A Church Is Burning."

CD: *Graceland*

Remastered rerelease; includes "Diamonds on the Soles of Her Shoes," unreleased version, and an earlier version of "All around the World or the Myth of Fingerprints."

CD: *Old Friends Live on Stage*

1. "Old Friends"/"Bookends"
2. "A Hazy Shade of Winter"
3. "I Am a Rock"
4. "America"
5. "At the Zoo"
6. "Baby Driver"
7. "Kathy's Song"
8. "Tom & Jerry Story" (spoken)
9. "Hey, Schoolgirl"
10. "The Everly Brothers Intro" (spoken)
11. "Bye Bye Love" (with the Everly Brothers)
12. "Scarborough Fair"
13. "Homeward Bound"
14. "The Sound of Silence"
15. "Mrs. Robinson"
16. "Slip Slidin' Away"
17. "El Condor Pasa"
18. "The Only Living Boy in New York"
19. "American Tune"
20. "My Little Town"
21. "Bridge over Troubled Water"
22. "Cecilia"
23. "The Boxer"
24. "Leaves That Are Green"
25. "Citizen of the Planet"

Simon & Garfunkel

CD: *Paul Simon*

Remastered; bonus tracks: "Me and Julio Down by the School Yard," demo, San Francisco 1971; "Duncan," demo, San Francisco; "Paranoia Blues," unreleased version.

CD: *There Goes Rhymin' Simon*

> Remastered; bonus tracks: "Let Me Live in Your City," previously unreleased work in progress; "Take Me to the Mardi Gras," acoustic version; "American Tune," unfinished demo; "Love Me Like a Rock," acoustic demo.

CD: *Still Crazy after All These Years*

> Remastered; bonus tracks: "Slip Slidin' Away," demo version; "Gone at Last," original demo version.

CD: *One-Trick Pony*

> Remastered; bonus tracks: "Soft Parachustes," unreleased soundtrack recording; "All Because of You," outtake; "Spiritual Highway," unreleased soundtrack version.

CD: *Hearts and Bones*

> Remastered; bonus tracks: "Shelter of Your Arms," work in progress; "Train in the Distance," original acoustic version; "Rene and Georgette Magritte with Their Dog after the War," original acoustic version; "The Late Great Johnny Ace," original acoustic version.

2005

CD: *You're the One*

> Remastered; bonus tracks: "That's Where I Belong," remastered live version; "Old," remastered live version; "Hurricane Eye," remastered live version.

CD: *Rhythm of the Saints*

> Remastered; bonus tracks: "Born at the Right Time," original acoustic demo; "Thelma," outtake; "The Coast," previously unreleased; "Spirit Voices," previously unreleased.

2006

CD: *Surprise*

> 1. "How Can You Live in the Northeast"
> 2. "Everything about It Is a Love Song"
> 3. "Outrageous"
> 4. "Sure Don't Feel Like Love"
> 5. "Wartime Prayers"
> 6. "Beautiful"

7. "I Don't Believe"
8. "Another Galaxy"
9. "Once Upon a Time There Was an Ocean"
10. "That's Me"
11. "Father and Daughter"

Paul Simon; produced by Paul Simon in collaboration with Brian Eno.

NOTES

Chapter 1   Two Princes from Queens

10   *"He used to play there"*   Simon, quoted by Anthony DeCurtis, *In Other Words*, 119.

10   *"I was seven or eight"*   Laura Jackson, *Paul Simon*, 6.

11   *"Once talking to my parents"*   Jon Landau, *Rolling Stone*, July 20, 1972.

12   *"That's nice, Paul."*   Joseph Morella and Patricia Barey, *Simon and Garfunkel*, 5.

12   *"Left-handed people"*   Ibid., 4.

13   *"I used to walk home"*   Jesse Colin Young, quoted in Robbie Wolliver, *Bringing It All Back Home*, 130.

13   *"Artie was the most famous"*   Paul Simon, from an interview he gave to *Playboy* magazine, conducted by Tony Schwartz, March 18, 1984.

13   *"My clear recollection"*   Joe Smith, *Off the Record*, 281–282.

15   *"New York became a pool"*   Ibid., 282.

15   *"The main thing about playing"*   Simon, *Playboy* interview.

16   *"We started singing doo-wop"*   Paul Simon, NPR (National Public Radio), *All Things Considered*, June 4, 2004.

16   *Once he had the song*   From an interview Paul Simon gave at Barnes and Noble bookstore, Twenty-third Street and Union Square, November 13, 2008.

16   *"in one of those booths"*   Morella and Barey, *Simon and Garfunkel*, 15.

17   *"I was playing occasional gigs"*   Al Kooper and Ben Edmonds, *Backstage Passes*, 50.

17   *"Being short"*   Morella and Barey, *Simon and Garfunkel*, 10–11.

18   *His shortness wasn't the only problem*   From an interview Paul did with Ed Bradley on *Sixty Minutes*, January 30, 1994, in which he discussed the beginning of the cultural divide, citing "Earth Angel" as the linchpin song.

19   *like busting out of jail*   Bob Dylan, quoted by Douglas Brinkley, "Bob Dylan's America," *Rolling Stone*, May 14, 2009.

23   *"This was a memorable experience"*   Simon, Barnes and Noble interview.

24   *They returned to New York*   Jackson, *Paul Simon*, 26.

24   *"It was all over my head"*   Art Garfunkel, *Sixty Minutes* interview.

Chapter 2   Paul's Mystic Journey

26   *"fodder for eunuchs"* Paul Simon, interviewed by *Record World*, April 1966.

28   *"Carole would play piano"* Bruce Pollock, *Hipper Than Our Kids*, 18–19.

29   *"We were all set to do"* Al Contrera, interview with author, June 15, 2009.

33   *The rest of the Village was filled* Background for the history of Greenwich Village and interviews with Mike Porco, in Robbie Wolliver, *Bringing It All Back Home*, throughout, and Marc Eliot, *Death of a Rebel*, throughout.

Chapter 3   "Kathy's Song"

36   *"Rock and roll got very bad"* Simon, quoted in Patrick Humphries, *The Boy in the Bubble*, 15.

37   *"The first night"* Garfunkel, quoted in Joseph Morella and Patricia Barey, *Simon and Garfunkel*, 28.

43   *"Dylan and the Beatles and Stones"* Simon, quoted in Anthony DeCurtis, *In Other Words*, 124–125. Simon & Garfunkel performed several shows for European TV in 1966. A few video recordings of various shows still float through the vast rock 'n' roll bootleg archives. Most likely this comment is from a show they did in June 1966 called *Twin*.

43   *"the inability of people"* Art Garfunkel, Morella and Barey, 32.

45   *"It's Simon & Garfunkel"* Adler, quoted in Morella and Barey, 35.

45   *"I thought they must be"* Ian Whitcomb, *Rock Odyssey*, 152.

45   *"I remember Simon & Garfunkel"* Louis Bass, quoted in Robbie Wolliver, *Bringing It All Back Home*, 128.

45   *"Simon & Garfunkel were uptown guys"* Robert Shelton, *No Direction Home*. It is not clear whether this quote actually appeared in the *Times*. Morella and Barey quote it without attribution but suggest he wrote this or something similar to it for the *Times*.

46   *"Dylan and I were at Folk City"* Shelton, 251.

47   *"When [Simon and Garfunkel] first showed up"* Dave Van Ronk and Elijah Wald, *The Mayor of MacDougal Street*, 180. Prior to his passing, Van Ronk was also interviewed by this author for background on the village scene, August 14, 1977.

48   *"All of us war babies"* Kenney Jones, interview with author, May 28, 2005.

Chapter 4   The Calm before the Storm

54   *"This young American"* Les Lowe, quoted in Victoria Kingston, *Simon and Garfunkel*, 29.

55   *"I had a very strong liking"* Paul Simon, quoted in Jeffrey Pepper Rodgers, *Rock Troubadours*, 8–9.

58   *"To be twenty-two"* Paul Simon to David Hepworth in 1986, quoted in Patrick Humphries, *The Boy in the Bubble*, 32.

Chapter 5   The Sounds of Simon

65   *"[Paul] was horrified"* Al Stewart, quoted in Patrick Humphries, *The Boy in the Bubble*, 41.

66   *"I had come back"* Paul Simon, *Playboy* interview, February 1984.

67   *"I met Roy"* Lou Christie, interview with author, July 2009.

68   *"According to Artie"* Paul Simon, *Twin,* June 1996.
69   *"it says far more about"* Robert Christgau, *Any Old Way You Choose It,* 67.
70   *"I didn't want to be Dylan"* Anthony DeCurtis, *In Other Words,* 124.
72   *"Simon & Garfunkel had a peculiar"* Paul Simon, quoted by Jon Landau, in a *Rolling Stone* interview, July 20, 1972.
73   *"It was never my song"* Carthy, quoted in Humphries, *The Boy in the Bubble,* 36–37.

Chapter 6   A Gathering of the Tribes

79   *a chance to try LSD* According to Victoria Kingston, in *Simon and Garfunkel,* 71–72, after being offered the acid tabs, Paul, who had never taken LSD before, later said that "I pretended it was fortunate . . . because [I said]I always take acid after breakfast and I didn't have any for tomorrow." He saved the tablets (from that weekend) and eventually took them in New York, on the night the Arab-Israeli war began, the same night that Muhammad Ali lost his title. . . . "I thought, I'd try this now."

81   *At Monterey, as part of the* In his autobiography, *Papa John,* John Phillips recalled running into Paul Simon backstage, hanging out with Jimi Hendrix. Phillips asked Paul what that was like. Paul said, "He's amazing, an unbelievable player." "You and Hendrix jamming. That must have been a trip," Phillips said. "What were you playing?" "Not lead," Paul said, deadpan.

Chapter 7   The Graduate

88   *As Nichols later remembered* All quotes from Mike Nichols are from an appearance he made to discuss *The Graduate* at the Lincoln Center Film Society, New York City, March10, 2010.

89   *"When I heard about the project"* Clive Davis, *Clive: Inside the Record Business,* 250.
90   *"Paul had been working"* Art Garfunkel, quoted by Josh Greenfeld, "The Two Most Eligible Jewish Bachelors Never to Become Doctors," *New York Times,* October 13, 1968.

92   *"Are you sure"* Clive Davis, *Clive: Inside the Record Business,* 250–251.
92   *"There just isn't enough"* Ed Kleban, quoted in ibid.
92   *"Look," Paul said.* Paul Simon, ibid.
94   *"I'm going to start"* Paul, to Artie, related by Artie to Pete Fornatale, *Simon & Garfunkel's* Bookends, 86.
95   *"I was learning on the job"* John Simon to Pete Fornatale, ibid., 86–87.
95   *the full version of "Mrs. Robinson"* There have been a surprising number of covers for what is essentially a novelty song. The Lemonheads had a hit version of it in the early nineties. Frank Sinatra covered it in 1969 on his album *My Way* (replacing "Jesus" with "Jilly"), Billy Paul recorded a swing version, and Booker T & the MG's did an instrumental "soul" version. The James Taylor Quartet did it jazz-funk style, the folk-punk band Andrew Jackson Jihad based their song "People II: The Reckoning" on the song, and Bon Jovi recorded the song live and included it as a bonus disk on their *These Days* album. The Dutch band the Nits wrote a continuation of the romance between Mrs. Robinson and Benjamin, with new lyrics and music that Paul Simon refused to grant permission for. Nonetheless, "Mrs. Robinson" appeared on their 1998 album *Alankomaat* and was released as a single in the Netherlands. The alternative

band CAKE did a cover, as did the punk band Pennywise. Most recently, the Indigo Girls did a version to accompany the *Desperate Housewives* television series.

96   "Bookends *was our first*"   Paul Simon, *Playboy* interview, February 18, 1984.

97   "*a kind of snapshot album*"   *The* Rolling Stone *Record Review Guide*, 352. Dave Marsh wrote the passage and rated the Simon & Garfunkel albums in the guide, giving *Bookends* four out of five possible stars. (*Simon & Garfunkel's Greatest Hits* later received their only five-star.)

Chapter 8   A Time It Was

99   "*I don't like to waste time*"   Paul Simon, quoted in Josh Greenfield, *New York Times*, October 13, 1968.

99   "*about being a poet*"   Ibid.

99   "*Mostly Paul and I*"   Art Garfunkel, quoted in ibid.

104   "*I was reading the Bible*"   Paul Simon, *Playboy* interview, February 1984.

105   "*He couldn't hear it*"   Jon Landau, *Rolling Stone*, July 20, 1972.

106   "*If you're going to get an hour*"   Charles Grodin, quoted by Victoria Kingston, in her book, *Simon & Garfunkel: The Definitive Biography*. Some of the information regarding the TV special in this chapter is from Kingston.

107   "*So we said,*"   Kingston, 104.

107   *The show began with*   The content of the film as described is from the author's viewing.

111   "*At that point*"   Landau, *Rolling Stone*, July 20, 1972.

111   "*I was ready*"   Kingston, 95

111   "*At this point*"   Paul, quoted by Jon Landau, *Rolling Stone*, 1972.

114   "*Peggy made me feel*"   Ibid.

114   "*Before others find out*"   Clive Davis, *Clive: Inside the Record Business*, 257.

Chapter 9   So Long, Frank Lloyd Wright

118   "*Tannen quickly became Paul Simon's guru.*"   Mike Appel, interview with author, March 2009. Appel would know. He was Bruce Springsteen's first manager/publisher/producer until the two had a falling-out in 1975. Springsteen was prevented by the courts from recording until the dispute was settled. During this time, Simon became friendly with one of the few journalists he would talk to on the record, Jon Landau, then a rock critic for a number of small publications before joining *Rolling Stone* magazine. Landau also met and came to know Tannen quite well. When Appel was being replaced by Landau (the essence of the dispute between Appel and Springsteen), and Springsteen was broke, Landau put Springsteen in touch with Tannen, who helped to get him back on his feet. According to Tannen, "[while working for Paul Simon] I wasn't [acting as a] lawyer, but more like an outside agent." Appel concurs, suggesting that Tannen was responsible for "hundreds" of foreign publishing deals for Simon. Eventually, when the Appel/Springsteen affair settled, Tannen continued to work closely with Landau, now Springsteen's manager, and Peter Parcher, Springsteen's new attorney, hired at the urging of Tannen. Tannen's quote is from Fred Goodman, *The Mansion on the Hill*, 293, as is some of the background for this note.

118   "*when Simon & Garfunkel hit it big*"   Goodman, *Mansion on the Hill*, 293.

118   *"I'm really curious"*   George Harrison, quoted by Paul Simon in Landau.
120   *"When I met Paul"*   Phil Ramone, quoted in Ted Fox, *In the Groove*, 251.
122   *"Paul Simon's long and manicky"*   Landau's review for *Rolling Stone* magazine appeared on March 2, 1972.
122   *called it "disappointing"*   *High Fidelity*, March 1972.
124   *"I'd run into him"*   Chris Charlesworth, interview with author, May 2009.

Chapter 10   On Top and Alone

127   *"About three bars into the first song"*   Art Garfunkel, quoted in Joseph Morella and Patricia Barey, *Simon and Garfunkel*, 136.
129   *"Artie continued to equivocate"*   Clive Davis, *Clive: Inside the Record Business*, 257.
130   There Goes Rhymin' Simon   Some of the detail and supplementary information about *There Goes Rhymin' Simon* are from unpublished material by Chris Charlesworth, and a subsequent extensive interview with Charlesworth by the author. Chris Charlesworth, *The Complete Guide to the Music of Paul Simon and Simon & Garfunkel*.
131   *"Kodachrome" is about nothing*   Paul Simon, Barnes and Noble interview, December 5, 2008.

Chapter 11   Still Crazy

136   *"My wife attacked the tinsel"*   Art Garfunkel, quoted in Victoria Kingston, *Simon and Garfunkel*, 163.
137   *"I had liked that she could be critical"*   Paul Simon, quoted in Joseph Morella and Patricia Barey, *Simon & Garfunkel*, 148–149.
137   *"Everything I did was put down"*   Ibid.
139   *"Graham used to sing"*   Art Garfunkel, interview with Stuart Grundy, BBC, 1975.
140   *"I was very much attracted"*   Ibid.
141   *it took another nine months*   Phil Ramone, quoted in Kingston, *Simon and Garfunkel*, 165.
142   *according to Paul's brother Eddie*   Ibid., 169.
142   *"a sort of cruel song"*   Paul Simon, quoted in Chris Charlesworth, *The Complete Guide to the Music of Paul Simon and Simon & Garfunkel*.
144   *"We knew that Paul"*   Lorne Michaels, quoted in Laura Jackson, *Paul Simon*, 150–151.
145   *"that folk-singing wimp"*   Ibid., 151. The person who made the comment is not named.
145   *The eighteenth annual Grammy ceremonies*   Paul also won for Best Male Vocalist for *Still Crazy after All These Years*. Simon & Garfunkel were nominated for Best Vocal Performance by a Group for "My Little Town" but lost to the Eagles, for "Lyin' Eyes." So, technically, Garfunkel could claim that, if not the entire album, at least one song from *Breakaway* was at least included in the nominations that year for a Grammy.

Chapter 12   Where Have You Gone, Mr. Simon?

151   "NO . . . I DON'T WANT"   Walter Yetnikoff, quoted by Mike Appel, interview with author, June 15, 2009.

151   *"When Walter took that job,"*   Elliot Goldman, then CBS Business Affairs head, quoted in Fredric Dannen, *Hit Men*, 120.

152   *"Walter hated his guts,"*   Debbie Federoff, quoted in ibid., 123.

152   "Until you're dead!"   Yetnikoff, quoted in ibid., 124.

154   *"about as funny as"*   Laura Jackson, *Paul Simon*, 156.

155   *"There was no special reason."*   Shelley Duvall, quoted in Joseph Morella and Patricia Barey, *Simon and Garfunkel*. Paul made no public comment about the split with Duvall.

156   *"If it hadn't been for Central,"*   Carrie Fisher, quoted in ibid., 187.

157   *"I think we were actually the first"*   Fisher, quoted in Tom Shales and James Andrew Miller, *Live from New York*, 134.

157   *"I think I have"*   Fisher, quoted in Morella and Barey, *Simon and Garfunkel*, 188.

Chapter 13   The Prince and the Princess and the Pony

163   *"I thought I would"*   Paul Simon, quoted in Victoria Kingston, *Simon and Garfunkel*, 201.

168   *"that morose little art film"*   Steven Holden, *Rolling Stone*, October 16, 1980.

Chapter 14   Saturday in the Park with Paul and Artie . . . and Carrie

169   *"In 1980, when* One Trick Pony"   *Playboy* interview, February 1984.

170   *"Art Garfunkel's finest"*   Stephen Holden, *Rolling Stone*, October 15, 1981.

176   *"Afterward, our first reaction was"*   Paul Simon, quoted in Victoria Kingston, *Simon and Garfunkel*, 241.

177   *"The new album"*   Holden, *Rolling Stone*, November 24, 1983.

180   *"I would be willing"*   *Playboy* interview.

Chapter 15   Redemption's First Finale

185   *"It was a difficult time for me"*   Paul Simon, in *Paul Simon—Graceland*, DVD, Warner Brothers.

186   *"I was building"*   Ibid.

190   *"finished my disappointments and sorrows"*   Ibid.

191   *"I had one big advantage"*   Ibid.

192   *"They thought that Roy"*   Ibid.

192   *"He had come to us"*   This comment is from a Warner executive who wishes to remain anonymous.

194   *"You Can Call Me Al"*   This song was used in the movie trailer for the 1989 comedy film *Parenthood*, starring Steve Martin, and in the twenty-second episode of the fifth season of the American version of *The Office*, entitled "Heavy Competition." Andy Bernard presents Jim and Pam with a recording of his college a cappella group singing "You Can Call Me Al" as a possible processional for their wedding. The British indie folk band Noah and the Whale covered the song as a B side in 2008. "You Can Call Me Al" was the last Top 10 *Billboard* single Paul has had.

195   *"We all live out in"*   Laura Jackson, 187.

196   *"I'm not a jukebox"*   Chris Charlesworth, interview with author, May 2009.

Chapter 16 Saintly Rhythms

201 *musical styles on* The Rhythm of the Saints   John McCalley, *Rolling Stone*, November 15, 1990.

205 *"When they said okay"*   Interview with author. The subject, who was directly involved with the planning of the show, asked for anonymity.

Chapter 17 New Bohemian

210 *"He made me mess the song up"*   Edie Brickell, quoted in Wikipedia. No further source given.

211 *Willie Nelson's . . . sixtieth birthday*   This show was produced as a TV special. Paul also sang "Graceland" and "American Tune" with Willie. The show also featured Bob Dylan. Both Paul-and-Willie duets were included on Nelson's 1993 *Across the Borderline*, with the recordings remixed under the supervision of Roy Halee.

212 *"during those years"*   Paul Simon, from a radio interview with Don Imus, *Imus in the Morning*, November 17, 1997.

214 *"I began thinking"*   Paul Simon, published notes for *The Capeman*, which appeared in slightly different form as part of the CD package and theater program in 1998.

Chapter 18 The Singing Capeman

218 *"Like many New Yorkers"*   Paul Simon, published notes for *The Capeman*, which appeared in slightly different form as part of the CD package and theater program in 1998.

220 *"Theater music never"*   Paul, quoted in *Entertainment Weekly*, December 12, 1997.

221 *"It was like [they feared]"*   Susana Tubert, quoted by William Grimes in the *New York Times*, "The Capeman Cometh Slowly," January 31, 1997.

221 *"The insecurity level"*   Ibid.

222 *"all the decisions"*   Paul Simon, on *Imus in the Morning*, November 7, 1997.

222 *"The first person"*   Ibid.

224 *"forsworn the dense"*   Stephen Holden, *New York Times*, November 28, 1997.

224 *"terrifically satisfying."*   Anthony DeCurtis, *Rolling Stone*, November 14, 1997.

225 *"It's an American story"*   Guy Garcia, "It's on Broadway, But Will It Cross Over?" *New York Times*, November 30, 1997.

225 *"After announcing"*   Rick Lyman, *"Capeman* Team Says Delay Doesn't Spell Trouble," *New York Times*, December 18, 1997.

226 *"The show's director and choreographer"*   From a press conference Klores gave, and an interview and additional comments made to the *New York Times* at that conference.

228 *three Tony Award nominations*   In the year *Capeman* was eligible, Best Original Score Written for the Theatre was won by *Ragtime*, music by Stephen Flaherty, lyrics by Lynn Ahrens. The other nominees besides *The Capeman* were *Side Show*, music by Henry Krieger, lyrics by Bill Russell, and *The Lion King*, music and lyrics by Elton John, Tim Rice, Lebo M, Mark Mancina, Jay Rifkin, Julie Taymor, and Hans Zimmer. Best Orchestrations was won by William David Brohn for *Ragtime*. The other nominees were Robert Elhai, David Metzger,

and Bruce Fowler for *The Lion King*, and Michael Gibson for *Cabaret*. Best Scenic Design was won by Richard Hudson for *The Lion King*. The other nominees were Eugene Lee for *Ragtime* and the Quay Brothers for *The Chairs*.

Chapter 19   Ladies and Gentlemen, Simon and Garfunkel

232   Where have you gone, Joe DiMaggio   Paul's song was not the only one that had mentioned DiMaggio, nor the first to annoy him. Les Brown and his Band of Renown had a big hit (number twelve), "Joltin' Joe DiMaggio," released in 1941 to commemorate the fifty-six-game hitting streak, and he was celebrated by, of all people, Woody Guthrie in "DiMaggio's Done It Again," written about a dramatic Yankee victory over the Red Sox in 1949 and later covered by Wilco. In the Rodgers and Hammerstein score for *South Pacific*, "Bloody Mary" is described in the song of the same name as having skin "tender as DiMaggio's glove." John Fogarty also mentioned DiMaggio in "Centerfield." Other mentions are found in Jennifer Lopez's "I'm Gonna Be All Right," Madonna's "Vogue," Tori Amos's "Father Lucifer," Sleeper's "Romeo Me," the Mike Plume Band's "DiMaggio," Billy Joel's "We Didn't Start the Fire," Bon Jovi's "Captain Crash and the Beauty Queen from Mars," Tom Waits's "A Sight for Sore Eyes," and Diesel Boy's "She's My Marilyn Monroe."

233   *"Lots of things"*   Paul's and Dylan's quotes are from *USA Today*, June 5, 1999, in an article announcing the tour.

235   *"It was a time"*   Paul Simon's and Marc Anthony's comments at the Rock and Roll Hall of Fame induction ceremonies, March 19, 2001.

239   *"Why not"*   NPR, Weekend Edition, December 4, 2004.

239   *"The reason we came back"*   Ibid.

239   *"Once you go away"*   Paul Simon, quoted by Wikipedia.

240   *"Simon doesn't achieve"*   *All Music Guide*. Review by Stephen Thomas Erlewine, November 2006.

240   *"Working with Brian Eno"*   Paul Simon. Source unclear, possibly *New Music Express*.

240   *"Despite the album's"*   Christian Hoard, *Rolling Stone*, May 2, 2006.

242   *"A lot of the sounds and rhythms"*   Paul Simon, Barnes and Noble interview, November 13, 2008.

BIBLIOGRAPHY

Charlesworth, Chris. *The Complete Guide to the Music of Paul Simon and Simon & Garfunkel*. London: Omnibus, 1997.

Christgau, Robert. *Any Old Way You Choose It*. Baltimore: Penguin Books, 1973.

Clarke, Donald, ed. *The Penguin Encyclopedia of Popular Music*. London: Penguin, 1990.

Dannen, Fredric. *Hit Men: Power Brokers and Fast Money inside the Music Business*. New York: Random House, 1990.

Davis, Clive. *Inside the Record Business*. New York: Morrow, 1975.

DeCurtis, Anthony. *In Other Words: Artists Talk about Life and Work*. Milwaukee: Hal Leonard Corporation, 2005

Draper, Robert. *Rolling Stone Magazine: The Uncensored History*. New York: Doubleday, 1990.

Dylan, Bob. *Chronicles, Volume One*. New York: Simon and Schuster, 2004.

Eliot, Marc. *Death of a Rebel*. New York: Anchor Press, 1978.

Fornatale, Pete. *Simon & Garfunkel's* Bookends. New York: Rodale, 2007.

Fox, Ted. *In the Groove: The People behind the Music*. New York: St. Martin's Press, 1986.

Goodman, Fred. *The Mansion on the Hill: Dylan, Young, Geffen, Springsteen, and the Head-on Collision of Rock and Commerce*. New York: Times Books (Random House), 1997.

Guralnick, Peter. *Last Train to Memphis: The Rise of Elvis Presley*. New York: Little, Brown, 1994.

Harris, Mark. *Pictures at a Revolution: Five Movies and the Birth of Hollywood*. New York: Penguin Press, 2008.

Heylin, Clinton. *Bob Dylan: Behind the Shades*. New York: Summit Books, Simon and Schuster, 1991.

Humphries, Patrick. *The Boy in the Bubble: Biography of Paul Simon*. London: Sidgwick and Jackson, 1988.

Jackson, Laura. *Paul Simon: The Definitive Biography*. New York: Kensington Press, 2002.

Kingston, Victoria. *Simon and Garfunkel: The Definitive Biography*. London: Sidgwick and Jackson, 1996.

Kooper, Al, and Ben Edmonds. *Backstage Passes: Rock 'n' Roll Life in the Sixties.* New York: Stein and Day, 1977.

Marre, Jeremy, Director; De Grunwald, Nick, Jong, Bous de, Executive Producers; Eagle Rock Entertainment, "Paul Simon, *Graceland*—Recounting the journey of a legendary music recording." Rhino, Chatsworth, CA, 1999.

Marsh, Dave, and John Swenson, eds. *The Rolling Stone Record Guide.* New York: Random House/Rollin Stone Press Book, 1971.

Marsh, Dave, and John Swenson, eds. *The Rolling Stone Record Guide.* New York: Random House, 1979.

Morella, Joseph, and Patricia Barey. *Simon and Garfunkel: Old Friends.* New York: Birch Lane Press, 1991.

Phillips, John. *Papa John.* New York: Doubleday and Co., 1986.

Pollock, Bruce. *Hipper Than Our Kids: A Rock and Roll Journal of the Baby Boom Generation.* New York: Schirmer Trade Books, an imprint of Macmillan, 1993.

Prial, Dunstan. *The Producer: John Hammond and the Soul of American Music.* New York: Farrar, Straus and Giroux, 2006.

Rolling Stone, eds. *The Rolling Stone Interviews.* New York: St. Martin's Press/Rolling Stone Press, 1981.

Rolling Stone, eds. *The* Rolling Stone *Record Review, Volume II.* New York: Simon and Schuster (Pocket Books Edition), 1974.

Rodgers, Jeffrey Pepper. *Rock Troubadours: Conversations on the Art and Craft of Songwriting with Jerry Garcia, Ani DiFranco, Dave Matthews, Joni Mitchell, Paul Simon, and More.* San Anselmo, CA.: String Letter Publishing, 2000.

Rose, Frank. *The Agency: William Morris and the Hidden History of Show Business.* New York: HarperBusiness, a division of HarperCollins, 1995.

Schipper, Henry. *Broken Record: The Inside Story of the Grammy Awards.* New York: Carol Publishing, 1992.

Shales, Tom, and James Andrew Miller. *Live from New York: An Uncensored History of Saturday Night Live.* New York: Little, Brown and Company, 2002.

Shelton, Robert. *No Direction Home: The Life and Music of Bob Dylan.* New York: Beechtree Books, Morrow, 1986.

Simon, Paul. *The Concise Paul Simon Complete.* London: Anchor Brenden Ltd., 1981.

Smith, Joe. *Off the Record: An Oral History of Popular Music.* New York: Warner Books, 1988.

Stokes, Geoffrey, Ken Tucker, and Ed Ward. *Rock of Ages: The* Rolling Stone *History of Rock and Roll.* New York: Summit Books, 1986.

Van Ronk, Dave, and Elijah Wald. *The Mayor of MacDougal Street: A Memoir.* Cambridge, MA.: Da Capo Press, 2005.

Weller, Sheila. *Girls Like Us: Carole King, Joni Mitchell, Carly Simon—and the Journey of a Generation.* New York: Atria (Simon and Schuster), 2008.

Whitburn, Joel. *The* Billboard *Book of USA Top 40 Hits.* New York: Guinness (St. Martin's Press), 1985.

Whitcomb, Ian. *Rock Odyssey: A Chronicle of the Sixties.* New York: Doubleday Dolphin, 1983.

Wolliver, Robbie. *Bringing It All Back Home.* New York: Pantheon Books, 1986.

PHOTO CREDITS

INDEX